From a Honeymoon in Patmos

A work of hearts

Copyright 2018 / 2010   Michael L. Donaldson
   No part of this publication may be reproduced or transmitted in any form: by any means electronic or mechanical; including photocopy, recording, or any information storage and retrieval system, without permission in writing from both the copyright owner and the publisher. All scriptures and quotations used by permission. Mail requests for permission to make copies of any part of this to; Permissions Department, White Marlin Media, P.O. Box 356 Joelton, Tn. 37080. White Marlin Media is a division of Ashara Inc.

ISBN: 978-0979923029

- White Marlin Media -
- Exploring the ocean of your imagination -

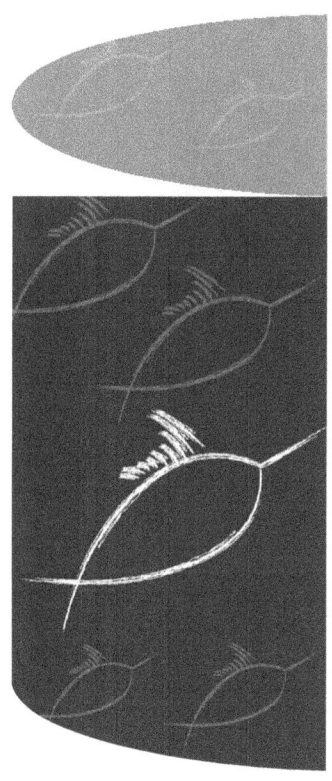

Cover design, Michael Donaldson
Salvatore Vuono, John Edlefson, http://www.freedigitalphotos.net provide some.

Used by permission

Dedicated

to

Johora Donaldson

Every fight has a start and an end. It took many years to realize that the fight did not start with you, the fight ended with you. God ordained marriage to be the answer to all our questions and sufficient for all our needs. When I asked God about Johora He said, "I did not call her to ministry I called you to ministry; I gave her to you as a Band-Aid. To put you back together when others use you." With that in mind, I guess, I am stuck on Johora, because Johora stuck on me.

Table of Contents

From the author's desk……………………………………………………………………..…12
About the Adam and Eve edition…………………………………………………………….13

Week 1……………………………………………………………………………..……….16
1.0 - About spiritual war……………………………………………………………………..17
    1.1 - About spiritual warfare…………………………………………………………….17
        1.2 - The wisdom of spiritual warfare……………………………………………….18
        1.3 - How humans entered spiritual warfare………………………………………..18
        1.4 - God's will articulated………………………………………………………….19
        1.5 - Satanic control…………………………………………………………………19
        1.6 - Mankind's war…………………………………………………………………19
        1.7 - Satan and spiritual warfare…………………………………………………….20
        1.8 - The cost of spiritual battle…………………………………………………….22
        1.9 - How mankind wages spiritual war…………………………………………….23
        1.10 - Why mankind uses spiritual weapons……………………………………….24
        1.11 - Spiritual warfare concepts……………………………………………………24
        1.12 - Spiritual warfare safeguards…………………………………………………28
2.0 - The flesh, spiritual warfare and marriage……………………………………………….31
    2.1 - The freedom of the flesh…………………………………………………………..31
    2.2 - Marriage and the flesh…………………………………………………………….32
    2.3 - The discipline of married flesh…………………………………………………….33
3.0 - About marriage…………………………………………………………………………35
    3.1 - The first marriage in history……………………………………………………….35
    3.2 - About Adam and Eve……………………………………………………………..36
    3.3 - The best made marriage in history………………………………………………..39
    3.4 - The temple as a marital model……………………………………………………40
    3.5 - The wedding………………………………………………………………………41
4.0 - The mysterious honeymoon……………………………………………………………44
    4.1 - The undefiled wedding bed………………………………………………………..44
    4.2 - The saddest honeymoon…………………………………………………………..49
    4.3 - The most mysterious of all marriage mysteries…………………………………..49
    4.4 - The Shulamite mystery……………………………………………………………51
5.0 - Marriage needs fortification……………………………………………………………53
    5.1 - Marriage fortifying concepts………………………………………………………53
    5.2 - Satan's attack on marriage…………………………………………………………54
    5.3 - How Satan wages spiritual war against marriage? …………………………………54
    5.4 - Same-sex marriage…………………………………………………………………58
6.0 - Week I - Work Area……………………………………………………………………61

Table of Contents

Week 2 64

7.0 - Building a marriage into a fortress..65
    7.1 - The blessed commandment..65
    7.2 - The fruitful marriage...66
    7.3 - Six purposes of marriage...67
8.0 - Marriage and the spiritual warrior...69
    8.1 - The discipline of marriage..69
    8.2 - A list of marital traits...70
    8.3 - The mind, marriage, and spiritual warfare............................71
    8.4 - The warrior's heart in marriage..72
    8.5 - Phases of the married warrior..74
    8.6 - Marriage and the spiritual warrior..75
    8.7 - The Sampson Principle as it applies to marriage..................75
    8.8 - Marriage and the traits of the spiritual warrior.....................75
    8.9 - Marriage and the heart of the spiritual warrior.....................77
9.0 - Fight right..81
    9.1 - Peace talks- For beginners...82
    9.2 - We fight with prayer..84
    9.3 - The mysterious power of prayer..85
    9.4 - Hitting is quitting..89
10.0 - Establishing spiritual warriors through marriage...........................90
    10.1 - A guide for establishing married spiritual warriors............91
11.0 - Marriage and the use of moats..95
12.0 - Week 2 - Work Area...97

Week 3 100

13.0 - Marriage and the use of walls..101
14.0 - Marriage and the use of supplies & stores....................................103
15.0 - Marriage and the use of barracks...107
    15.1 - Moral influence...108
16.0 - Marital discipline...109
    16.3 - The appropriate use of 'silent treatment'...........................110
    16.4 - Marital discipline..111
17.0 - The marital armory..113
    17.1 - Sex Toys...114
18.0 - Marriage and the use of sanitation...116
19.0 - Marriage and the use of God's armor...119
    19.1 - Armor basics..120
    19.2 - The proper way to put on armor.......................................121
20.0 - Week 3 - Work Area..123

Table of Contents

Week 4..126
   21.0 - Marriage and the loin protector of truth...127
      21.1 - Training our children..128
   22.0 - Marriage and the breastplate of righteousness...129
      22.1 - The three fingers of temptation...129
   23.0 - Marriage and the boots of the gospel of peace 131
   24.0 - Marriage and the shield of faith..135
   25.0 - Marriage and the helmet of salvation...137
      25.1 - God's two voices..138
   26.0 - Week 4 - Work Area...139

Week 5..142
   27.0 - Marriage and the sword of the Spirit..143
   28.0 - Prayer and marriage..145
   29.0 - Alertness in marriage..147
   30.0 - Marital armor...149
      30.1 - How does marital armor work? 149
   31.0 - Subjection to the husband as a piece of marital armor............................151
   32.0 - Subjection to the Lord as a piece of marital armor..................................153
   33.0 - Week 5 - Work Area...154

Week 6..156
   34.0 - Sanctification as a piece of marital armor..157
   35.0 - A Husband's love as a piece of marital armor..159
   36.0 - A husband's sacrifice as a piece of marital armor....................................161
   37.0 - A husband's self-love as a piece of marital armor....................................163
   38.0 - Unity as a piece of marital armor..165
   39.0 - Forgiveness as a piece of marital armor...167
   40.0 - Week 6 - Work Area...169

Week 7..172
   41.0 - Maturity as a piece of marital armor..173
   42.0 - Revelation as a piece of marital armor...175
   43.0 - Reverence as a piece of marital armor...177
   44.0 - Prayer as a piece of marital armor..179
   45.0 - Marriage as a weapon..182
   46.0 - Week 7 - Work Area...185

Week 8..187
   47.0 - The eyes as weapons...188

Table of Contents

    47.1 - The eyes as weapons...188
  48.0 - The flesh as a marital weapon...190
    48.2 - The way flesh works as a weapon..190
49.0 - Marital bed as a weapon..194
    49.2 - How sex work as a weapon...194
    49.3 - Man cannot serve two masters..197
    49.4 - Sex in the balanced marriage...198
    49.5 - But, I am not a missionary!..199
50.0 - Thoughts as weapons..202
    50.2 - How thoughts..202
  51.0 - The heart as a weapon..204
    51.2 - The heart as a weapon..204
52.0 -The tongue as a weapon...206
    52.2 - The tongue as a weapon..206
53.0 Week 8 - Work Area..208

Week 9..211

  54.0 - Un-forgiveness as a weapon against marriage..................................212
    55.2 - Un-forgiveness as a weapon...212
55.0 - The mystery of the lonely union...214
    55.1 - Marital loneliness vs. spiritual isolation...214
56.0 - Common problems in marriage...216
    56.1 - How long do we hold the fake smile?..216
    56.2 - Bait and switch..216
    56.3 - Peek-a-boo...217
    56.4 - MILFs (Mates I'd like to fight)...218
    56.5 - A Mephibosheth styled marriage..218
57.0 - The mystery the marriage's ultimate foe..220
    57.1 - 2-tiered mystery of why marriages fail..220
58.0 - Week 9 - Work Area..225

Week 10..228

59.0 - The weapons of the enemy against marriage......................................229
    59.1 - Ungodly spiritual influences...229
    59.2 - How spirits gain entrance..234
    59.3 - The mark of the beast...236
    59.4 - The mark on the right hand..237
60.0 - Civil war as a weapon against marriage..244
    60.2 - How civil war is used..244
    60.3 - Sexless marriages and divorce..245
    60.4 - What to do when they cheat?..248
    60.5 - Why divorce is bad..249

Table of Contents

    60.6 - Divorce tears apart relationships..252
    60.7 - Rope-a-dope...254
61.0 - The eyes as a weapon against marriage...255
    61.2 - How the eyes work against marriage...255
62.0 - The flesh as a weapon against marriage...257
    62.2 - A dirty little secret..261
    62.3 - How the flesh works against marriage..261
63.0 - Fornication as a weapon against marriage..261
    63.2 - How fornication works against marriage...261
    63.3 - Redefining the definition of cheating...264
    63.4 - Cheat sheets..265
    63.5 - Adam's cheat sheet...265
    63.6 - Eden's cheat sheet..266
    63.7 - Eve's cheat sheet..266
    63.8 - What we learn from unhappiness..268
64.0 Week 10 - Work Area..269

Week 11..273
65.0 - Lust as a weapon against marriage...274
    65.2 - How lust works against marriage..274
    65.3 - Design flaw - incest and molestation...276
66.0 - The thoughts as a weapon against marriage...278
    66.2 - How thoughts work against marriage...278
67.0 - The heart as a weapon against marriage...280
    67.2 - How the heart works against..280
68.0 - The tongue as a weapon against marriage..282
       68.2 - How the tongue works against weapon..282
69.0 - Un-forgiveness as a weapon against marriage..284
    69.2 - How un-forgiveness works against marriage...284
70.0 - Anger as a weapon against marriage..286
    70.2 - How anger works against marriage...286
71.0 - Jealousy as a weapon against marriage..288
    71.2 - How jealousy works against marriage...288
72.0 Week 11 - Work Area..290

Week 12..293
73.0 - Tactical marriage..294
    73.1 - Tactic one: Defense..294
    73.2 - Tactic two: Counter-attack...295
    73.3 - Tactic three: Attack..295
    73.4 - Types of attacks...296
    73.5 - Tactic four: Withdrawal..297

Table of Contents

    73.6 - Tactic five - Surrender..297
74.0 - Evangelism, marriage, & demoniacs...298
    74.1 - Demonic tactics and marriage..298
    74.2 - Deploying married evangelists..299
    74.3 - Spiritual casualties and marriage..300
    74.4 - Spiritual first aid and marriage..301
    74.5 - Children and Evangelism..303
   75.0 - Marriage: A life unto death..304
        76.0 - Tai Sabaki - Oneness of movement...308
    76.1 - The Art of Christ...308
    76.2 - The Art of Christ revealed..308
    76.3 - The Art of Christ revealed in warfare..309
    76.4 - The Art of Christ revealed in marriage..310
77.0 - Eden Work Area...312
    77.1 - 8 ways to revive your marriage and maintain the love....................................313
    77.2 - 20 ways to make your marriage stronger..313
    77.3 - About Adam..314
    77.4 - About Eve...314
    77.5 - About Us...316

78.0 - Glossary of marriage mysteries...324

79.0 - Disciple-makers basics..329

80.0 Facilitators section...335
    80.1- Facilitators format..335
    80.2 - Facilitator's Bible verses about love and marriage..335

81.0 Bibliography 344

From the Author's Desk

"It is not a lack of love, but a lack of friendship that makes unhappy marriages."
- Friedrich Nietzsche -

The Donaldson's founded of Ashara Ministries[2] Charter Family. The motto of Ashara is, *"Building people not churches."* Under that mission, Ashara has developed numerous programs to teach and reach lost sheep.

Michael Donaldson has a Certificate of Theology from Falwell University, a Master of Science in Public Administration: Policy, and Planning from Cumberland University, where inducted into Pi Gamma Mu International Honor Society in Social Science and a B.S. in Political Science. Their list of published works consists of;

- From a Fishing Trip in Patmos: The Handbook
- From a Fishing trip in Patmos: Disciple-maker's Edition
- The Lights in Patmos
- From a Fortress in Patmos
- From a Honeymoon in Patmos
- Black coffee
- The Butterfly Veil
- From a War in Patmos
- Becoming a More Effective Teacher: Teaching Master's Edition
- Becoming a More Effective Teacher

According to the authors, they never knew how important marriage is to the Christian faith walk and God's kingdom. It was not marriage that brought this to light, nor the years of marital council given to soldiers and Law Enforcement, instead it was the research put into this resource that opened a new appreciation for marriage, family, and spiritual warfare.

Years of marriage and teaching, providing marital counseling, studying, meditation and conversation required bringing this work to life, and the understanding of Satan's insidious plan makes this resource the single most important work yield by the Donaldson Ministry Team.

The ultimate mystery we hope you walk away from this resource understanding is not that marriage is the ultimate battlefield; it is the ultimate weapon.

About the Adam and Eve Edition

"And He saith unto me, '**WRITE, BLESSED [ARE] THEY WHICH ARE CALLED UNTO THE MARRIAGE SUPPER OF THE LAMB.**' And He saith unto me, '**THESE ARE THE TRUE SAYINGS OF GOD**'" - (Revelations 19:9).

This book may not be for the parochial Christian, because of the undefiled wedding bed content. From a Honeymoon in Patmos is the fourth installment in the Patmos Wilderness Series. From a Honeymoon in Patmos breaks down components of armament and warfare from a marital perspective. Reading this book would be more useful and much easier to understand if you read the other three components first [3].

God gave us ministries and gifts for the church. The church exists to serve God and resist Satan. God gave us ministries and gifts for marriage. Marriage exists to serve God and resist Satan. It makes sense that the parallel between marriage and the church continues into spiritual warfare.

The earth is Christ's mother, so God will not let Satan have her [4]. However, the bride of Christ, the wedding of Christ, and the children of Christ are constantly, completely, and thoroughly under attack. God foresaw and understood the impending war against the church, so He equipped men with women with other armaments, so they could withstand attacks. Although many think Eve created our problems, they are wrong. The addition of woman gave man the one thing he did not have before, the ability to righteously satisfy his flesh.

God intended for Adam to control his flesh, but Adam failed. God arranged for Adam to satisfy his flesh righteously, but Adam satisfied his flesh incorrectly. God's model works by CONTROLLING our flesh through Godly means. If we want kids, sexual intimacy, companionship, and a life-long bunkmate God says obtain these things through marriage.

Within the marriage paradigm, we do not take decrepit flesh into the armor. Think of armor as a spaceship. If we blast off into space, with the flu, all the germs go with us and we remain trapped in the craft with them. However, if we put two healthy people into a craft they can encourage, entertain, and indulge in each other without the disease spreading. Blessed marital indulgences (fleshly and spiritual) are the way in which marriage works its mystery against Satan. Satan can see the two people, sometimes hear them but he cannot reach them in their spacecraft. Between the armor of God and the fleshly benefits of marriage, there is no room in a balanced marriage for Satan to infuse germs.

This book is about marriage, it discusses sexuality. There are a few points to clear up about term usage in this book. References to incidents as examples, made use of by permission, agreement, and understanding of my wife -- bless her heart and soul. Block text represents words spoken by the Godhead, all scriptures King James Version unless otherwise stated.

1. *Marriage* - is a holy union between one man and one woman.
2. *Fornication* - the term *fornication* in this book refers to any kind of sex outside of marriage. Any other term used for sexuality refer to God's plan for His people.
3. *Salvation* - the term *Salvation* in this book refers matters of the soul exclusively.
4. *Deliverance* - The term *Deliverance* in this book refers to matters of the flesh exclusively.

5. *Righteousness* - The term *Righteousness* in this book refers to a lifestyle of Godly behavior, and decisions.
6. *The Godhead: The Trinity explained* - I once asked God for an easy way to explain His Holy nature. To which He responded:
    - God the Father is the ocean
    - God's Holy Spirit is the salt in the ocean
    - The Son is a glass of salt water

The ocean is deep and vast, its depth and marvels are without end. There would be no life on this planet without oceans. The oceans could not support the life they do without salt. In every drop of ocean, there are equal amounts of salt. A glass of salt water has the properties and salinity of the ocean. The only limitation to the cup of salt water is that it is enclosed, trapped inside the glass. Christians speak of *God in three persons,* but we separate the Godhead.

In Matthew 28 Jesus tells us to baptize in the name of the Father, the Son, and God's Holy Spirit. This we do because each has an area of responsibility.
   a. *The Father* - Is responsible for the universal balance and keeping Satan's kingdom under control.
   b. *God's Holy Spirit* - Operates in the earth realm under the permission of redeemed human authority.
   c. *The Son* - Redeemed the earth realm and restored God the Father's relationship ability to help humans.

Each portion of the Godhead has a purpose and to explain the purposes further we look at King David as an example of the Father and Son. In the court of the king, no one but an equal or a designee may approach the king. Many people wished to speak to King David, but they had to settle for a court appointee. If the appointee (the equivalent of a priest in the temple) cannot address the issue the prince, or heir-apparent contend with the issue. If the issues are of dire importance, the king addresses it personally and makes law. It is not that the king's underlings lack wisdom; they have little to no authority. The king's court operates under and within the power of the king. When power is required, the king acts personally. For this reason, Jesus the prince instructs believers to beseech the Father for help and power. Remember the prince acts in the power of the king, Jesus tells us this repeatedly that He and the Father are one and that He does nothing without permission of the Father.

This information may confuse some people that inadvertently developed the habit of praying to Jesus or Mary. While this is incorrect, it is not necessarily fatal. However, we must ascertain the truth or continue to fail in our darkness. We do not pray to Jesus or anyone else in the universe. We do not pray through Jesus or any other person in the universe. There is a High court that we must address the Holy Spirit is not running interference He is the translator. We do NOT live in the spirit; therefore, we do not speak the tongue of angels. Even those of us who pray in tongue still need and interpreter. God's thoughts are not our thoughts, and our best intentions the Bible calls *filthy rags*[5].

Consequently, we should pray to the ONLY One in the universe that can and does answer prayers. Look to this out with scripture from Matthew 6, Jesus tells us to pray to THE FATHER WHO ART IN HEAVEN. The reason Jesus tells us to pray to the Father is that HE IS THE POWER AND THE GLORY. Christians must adhere to the tenants of our faith. If we are followers of Christ, then we must follow all His tenants. The most important of Christ tenants is that we understand that The Father, the same Father that so loved the world that He gave His Son, always IS the power.

While you may not agree with the subject matter of some of the issues covered in this resource, the topics came up through audiences poling, seminars forums and or counseling sessions.

Week I
Spiritual Warfare and Marriage

"*For thy Maker [is] thine husband; the Lord of hosts [is] His name; and thy Redeemer the Holy One of Israel; The God of the whole earth shall He be called. For the Lord hath called thee as a woman forsaken and grieved in spirit, and a wife of youth, when thou wast refused, saith thy God.*" - (Isaiah 54:5-6).

1.0 - About spiritual war
2.0 - The flesh, spiritual warfare, and marriage
3.0 - About marriage
4.0 - The mysterious honeymoon
5.0 - Marriage needs fortification
6.0 - Week I - Work Area

1.0
Spiritual Warfare and Marriage

1.1 About spiritual war

"And there was war in heaven: Michael and his angels fought against the dragon; and the dragon fought and his angels." - (Revelations 12:17).

There is nothing as great as spiritual war. There is nothing as terrible as spiritual war. The cost to humanity from spiritual warfare is incalculable by human standards. Although man has no input in spiritual war, he is a victim and a pawn in spiritual warfare. A basic rule is that only spiritual beings can engage in spiritual warfare. Although humans do not engage in spiritual warfare between heavenly beings, there is constant interaction and residual effect of these wars in the human world and in human lives. Let us understand the concept clearly; the phrase Spiritual Warfare is not so much a statement of a direct attack against humans-a more accurate phrase would be spiritual war zone. Although you may not constantly be under assault believers, we live in a heavenly war zone.

In the Old Testament, angels constantly maintained the balance of power in the earth realm. Angels could not reclaim the earth realm, because of God's promise that men dominate the earth. The war between heaven and earth did not arise because of humans; it arose because the war in heaven spilled over into this world. God ordained man to glorify Him and to bring honor and joy to him.

God cast Lucifer and his followers from heaven. The book of Isaiah records that Lucifer fell to earth. Once settled in the earth, Lucifer took hold of everything he could. The first thing Satan seized was that which was unclaimed; the air. Satan then beguiled humankind and was able to gain control over the earth.

Lucifer's desire to be God resulted in his fall. When Satan regained his footing here on earth, he immediately sought to set up a kingdom for himself in the Kingdom of God. The war for humanity is not a war to help humanity but a competition for the worship or subjection of souls. Unlike WWII when the allies went to the aid of Europe against an invader, God is not saving humanity from an invader; God is saving us for Himself.

The rationale behind the fighting the Vietnam War was to aid the Vietnamese retain their right to *choose*. In like manner, God fights for our right to *choose*. God allows humans to *choose* their eternal resting place. If humans *chose* to go to hell that is their *choice*, heaven is also a *choice*. The war waged in the earth realm is not for the human soul, it is for the human's right to *choose*. God loves us and desires salvation for all humans. Because God loves us, He enables us to live any life we *choose*. When God tallies the results of our lives, His judgment is still just.

___
___
___
___
___
___
___

1.2 The wisdom of spiritual warfare

Though war is terrible, it is necessary to maintain God's will. In the Old Testament God had many of His enemies vanquished. In modern times, Gods still vanquishes His enemies, but He allows the Holy Spirit to accomplish the work. Old Testament spiritual warfare was limited because God could not fully engage. After Christ liberated the earth, the Holy Spirit moved, and with the help of humans, aids in the recovery of the earth.

The reasons Christians are such poor spiritual warriors, is because we fight the wrong foe. The flesh is not Satan's enemy salvation is Satan's enemy. Our war is not for Salvation, or redemption it is *staying righteous*. Salvation is a gift freely given which means the war is not for salvation. Jesus crushed the head of Satan's kingdom and overthrew the illegitimate king, redeeming man's dominion over the earth realm.

1.3 How humans entered spiritual warfare

If Jesus redeemed the earth and crushed Satan's kingdom, why is there still a war?

1.3.1 There is still a war because Satan is not bound.
1.3.2 There is still a war because he still converts followers to his revolution against God.
1.3.3 There is still a war because the human creature is evil and strives against God continually. There are no scriptures I am aware of where God states that man, wages war against Satan. Consequently, it appears that humans wage war against God's will, and Satan's control.

There are no scriptures I am aware of where God states that man, wages war against Satan. Consequently, it appears that humans wage war against God's will, and Satan's control. Therefore,

1.3.4 God gave man dominion over the earth.
1.3.5 Satan rules the air (Ephesians 2:2).
1.3.6 Satan dwelt in the earth.
1.3.7 Man ruled the earth.
1.3.8 Satan wanted to rule somewhere.
1.3.9 Satan deceived woman and man and stole man's throne.
1.3.10 Jesus redeemed the throne
1.3.11 Jesus returned control over the earth to mankind.

1.3.12 Satan seeks to regain control over the earth realm by a human revolution against God in order that Satan wins; he needs numbers, more numbers than God.
1.3.13 Satan wages war against the power system God set in place, Married Christians.

1.4 God's will articulated

It is the articulated will of God that man live in peace, humility, service, righteousness, faith, joy, health, and that man's soul prospers. To this end, God's will is that we rejoin His spirit and worship Him from His bosom. **"The Lord is not slack concerning His promise, as some men count slackness, but His long suffering towards us, not willing that any should perish but that all should come to repentance**" - (2 Peter 3:9).

1.5 Satanic control

It is the stated desire of Satan that man live in his darkness, "...**The bramble said to the trees, 'If in truth you anoint me king over you, then come and take refuge in my shade; and if not, let fire come out of the bramble, and devour the cedars of Lebanon'** - Judges 9:15". In the chapter Stones of Fire[6], scripture showed us that God removed the *fire* (Glory) from Lucifer. Therefore, the 'fire' Satan refers to is his rage. This is another difference between God and Satan, both have an angry side God is wrathful--Satan hates.

1.6 Mankind's war

The desire of man is to live a sin-filled, self-serving, narcissistic life, devoid of the love and rules of God. Men want the pleasures Satan offers, but we want them to be free of consequences. Satan requires servitude, and worship his reward is our death. God requires servitude and worship, but the reward He gives is life. Consequently, mankind does not war against sin we fight to remove the sting from sin. There is only one way to remove the sting of sin, *righteousness*. This is where spiritual warfare begins; in our *choice* not to sin.

1.7 Satan and spiritual warfare

Hitler waged one of the most brilliant wars in modern history. The fact that it was an immoral war is of no consequence to this discussion. Not only are we not discussing the morality of war, almost all war is immoral. No matter what we make of war and what we determine the rationale for the war unless declared by God it is immoral. Some contend that stopping genocide is a valuable goal. How do you stop genocide except killing the side committing the atrocities? However, is that not genocide?

Some ask about a war for independence. Is it moral to fight for 'independence' only to use that independence to enslave and murder other people? No matter how we slice it warfare is immoral. It is to this penchant for immorality, violence, and indifference, Satan devotes his wiles. A creature that preys on its own young, the helpless, and the fallen calling it a better way is perfect fodder for Satan. The scriptures say that we sacrifice our children to idols. The idolatry we practice costs humanity its souls and its future. In Luke 8:44, Jesus tells us it is because we are like our father the devil that we have his traits.

According to Ezekiel 28:25, evil existed in Lucifer before violence. The human equivalent is Adam and Eve. In this couple, we see that evil existed in humankind prior to violence. The violence in this couple manifested itself through Cain their son.

After Lucifer filled himself with evil, he became murderous and violent, as his children also have become. The way Lucifer wages war is thorough his children, his fruit, his followers. What or who are Lucifer's followers or children? There are only two types of people according to the Son of Man;

1.7.1 People who are with Christ (Matthew 12:30)
1.7.2 People who are against Christ (Matthew 12:30)

There are billions of human creatures on the planet, 25% percent of these people claim to be for Christ. Of this 25% they fall into three categories;

1.7.3 Laborers
1.7.4 Marginal workers
1.7.5 Lukewarm followers

The 50% of the earth that does not profess Christ is against Him. The billions of people on the earth that are against Christ are fodder for satanic warfare, and satanic missions. Despite rhetoric, God does not damn these people they are lost. The war against Satan is against His methods, actions, desires, and plans. THE CHRISTIAN WAR IS NOT AGAINST ANY PEOPLE, IT IS AGAINST THE PLAN TO OVERTHROWN GOD'S KINGDOM.

Like his offspring Hitler, Satan has the ultimate strategy--to take over the world. Like Hitler, Satan also is neither a general nor a tactician. Satan understands some of the basics of war;

1.7.6 Divide and conquer
1.7.7 Victory by attrition

        1.7.8   The use of weapons of mass destruction
        1.7.9   The use of human fodder
        1.7.10 Humans are less costly to replace than machines

Satan has only one weapon against the human creature: The human heart. It was through the human heart that sin entered the world and by the human heart overcame sin. The sin in the hearts of men is the last frontier for spiritual warfare. There is nothing in the universe not subject to the will of God except the human heart.

No human is naturally immune to temptation. In the same manner, we instruct children not to steal, lie, or cheat believers must learn to overcome temptation. The Godly lesson is that **subjected flesh is not immune from temptation it resists temptation.** What Jesus showed us in the wilderness is that a man committed to the will of God and denies his flesh can accomplish the will of God in the earth realm.

Satan cannot subvert nature, but humans can. In order to destroy nature Satan uses the greed in men's hearts to destroy creation and creatures of God. In this same manner, Satan uses the sin-filled hearts of men to subvert God's will and to wage war against believers. The issues of life listed in Matthew 15:13 assure us of the wickedness of the human heart. The Bible lists no humane traits listed for the human heart. If there is nothing good in the human heart, the actions of the normal human heart cannot be good[7].

A man once asked me what God does when good people do evil things? I replied that good people do not do evil things. When the Bible describes people as meek, gentle, or peacemakers, it is not referring to isolated behavior. The Bible refers to a lifestyle of this behavior. Therefore, in order for a person to be *good* by Godly standards they cannot or do not do evil things. This is why Jesus says, "**No one is good but the Father Who art in Heaven.**"

According to Luke 4:8, men gave Satan all his power. The evil found in the wicked hearts of humans belongs to the enemies' kingdom. To confirm this, Jesus says that we that are not with Him are against Him. The sooner believers learn to fight for God's plan and stop trying to crucify people, the more successful our efforts. There is a difference between being anti-something and pro-something. In the American Civil Rights movement, many whites were pro-white not anti-black. The difference is that they were happy living separate from Blacks. Those that were anti-black hurt them, stoned them, lynched them, burnt their churches etc.

God has called His army to be pro-God not anti-sinner. God's people are anti-sin, not anti-people. Jesus did not condone the practice of judging people. Romans 1:32, Hebrews 10:26, and 2 Peter 2:20-22, say that those in Christ who walk away from salvation face judgment. The lost are NEVER spoken of as worthy of death.

Many battles waged by Christians fail. Just as the Maginot Line France built in WWII faced the wrong way, Christians point their war and defenses in the wrong direction. **WE CANNOT WIN A WAR FOR GOD THAT HE DID NOT ORDAIN**. This being the case the war cry of all Godly soldiers must be DEATH TO OUR SIN! If we really want to be warriors for Christ, we must; conquer self, defeat our own wicked hearts, and stand righteous in His sight. It is to this war cry that we must rally. The greatest victory in a believer's life is to be pure when He returns. It is by the strength of our choice to live righteous that we aid the Lion in defeating the dragon. In the final count, when God's people stand Satan will see that God's love prevailed.

_____

_____

1.8 The cost of spiritual battle

How do we count the cost of a spiritual battle? In the same manner as we calculate any war; gains versus loses. For many on the battlefield, the cost of spiritual warfare is not always evident. I assure you that spiritual war takes its toll.

There are many similarities between conventional warfare and spiritual warfare. One of the main similarities is that the causality and death tolls are high. What most do not realize is that human death tolls exclusively belong to spiritual warfare. There is little that goes on outside of nature (natural order includes storms, disasters, flood etc.), which is not a result of spiritual warfare. The spiritual war that wages in the heavens plays out here on earth through the flesh of human creatures. Murder, rape, greed, lust, envy, genocide, Nuclear-Biological-Chemical warfare are all products of satanic influence

Spiritual warfare takes its toll on the souls of men. Damaged souls hold the evidence of ongoing battles. I cannot count the wars that I have seen fought and lost. Spiritual battles rage in the hearts of men every day. Spiritual wars ruin homes, families, and marriages. Spiritual coup d'états ruin churches and spiritual relationships. We blame many things for these losses, but the truth is it is all spiritual warfare and at the heart of spiritual warfare lays sin.

How does one go from a televangelist to a rapist? It does not happen overnight and the reason it happens is sin. No, Satan does not cause sin he benefits from it. Yes, Satan entered Peter and he entered Judas: but only one of them betrayed Christ. Why, what was the difference? One was a thief in his heart and the other was not. Therefore, we see two men, both entered by Satan, but they did not do the same thing. This too is spiritual warfare, Satan uses whom he can, when and how he can; but so does God.

I am not masterful at explaining sin, but I assure you that mastery at explaining sin lies in the scriptures. I do not presume to explain the nature of sin other than to say that it manifests itself in the flesh in one of 10 ways. I know this because there are only 10 commandments; through these 10 commandments, God governs all human behavior.

In the story of Sodom and Gomorrah, tradition blames homosexuals for the demise of the city. Scripture clearly states the wickedness of the people waxed great in the sight of God and resulted in judgment. Sexuality is cadres of favorite sins. Perhaps it is because it is one of the greatest physical pleasures or perhaps sex like drugs has an exaggerated effect. Bonding with another person heightens the already effervescent feeling. I do not know, but look through the Bible from Genesis to the church at Corinth and for every problem, sex is not too far behind.

As early as Genesis 6, the fallen angels learned to use sexuality against the human creature. The Bible speaks against binding with whores, and adulterers, because we become one with them. This too is spiritual warfare. The subtlety is that innocent/righteous' men do not bind to a whore. Jesus points this out by simply drawing a line in the sand. Hypocrisy and bigotry are also parts of spiritual warfare because while we stone the woman and she falls to the ground bleeding how many of our business cards, telephone numbers, and dollar bills fall from her bra?

The cost of spiritual warfare is the lying that turns man against their sexual partners, wives against husbands, kids against their parents and believers against God. Flaws in current spiritual warfare tactics make God, ask from the clouds, why we persecute Him? How little we know about the true nature of spiritual warfare. Like Saul of Tarsus, we do not even know that we wage war against and persecute God, by attacking the innocent, cajoling the lost, and manipulating the righteous. This is the cost of spiritual warfare; it leaves casualties everywhere[8].

1.9 How mankind wages spiritual war

Mankind engages in spiritual warfare for selfish gain. Satan rewards his soldiers in this life. Many believe falsely that spiritual warfare is a *choice* and pretend that if they never enter the war they do not have to fight. There are no conscientious objectors in spiritual warfare, we fight, or we lose by default. Even God does not defend the lazy; He is the Champion of the lost and defeated.

1.10 Why mankind uses spiritual weapons

Spiritual warfare also developed through the span of time. A major development in spiritual warfare is spiritual weaponry. The two greatest weapons in spiritual warfare are love and the hate. Despite the misunderstanding of Ephesians and the armor of God, the entire concept works only if we love the things God loves and love the way God loves. The way the warrior accomplishes this type of love is through the Holy Spirit. Most spiritual leaders are cowards and they only want to try to scare Satan into leaving them alone. Satan does not fear men or their armor because Satan knows that without love, faith, and the Holy Spirit the weapons are just religious icons, useless against him.

Spiritual Warfare is the costliest type of warfare because the battle affects the hereafter. Although conventional, biological and nuclear wars destroy the flesh war are encouraged to not fear them, fear only He that can destroy the body and the soul. Although Satan cannot destroy our soul, he can encourage us to throw it away or destroy it ourselves. This book is important because like any good instruction manual it offsets the damage ignorance and inexperience cause. Although weapons make fighting more effectual, the best method for fighting spiritual warfare is never leave God's shadow.

1.11 Spiritual warfare concepts

One of the greatest causes of confusion in scripture reading is contextual errors. Word usage throughout the Bible varies from literal, to metaphor, to onomatopoeia. As a result, the reader often does not know when to transition. I pray we take the time to learn this skill by practicing in this book with a limited number of words. Before we begin any undertaking, we must understand the rudimentary principles applicable to that faith. Without understand the rudimentary principles, there can be no commonality, communication, or for that matter preparation. To that end, we will use the following basic definitions[9]. For the duration of this work, these are the only definitions used. This ensures that we communicate equivalently.

> 1.11.1 *Spiritual - refers to the fact that the interactions occur in the spirit realm amongst spirit beings or powers.* Believers must stop believing in ghosts, goblins, haunted houses, séances, and fortune telling. If we genuinely believe the Bible to be the guide for truth, it must also be the guide for possibilities. In the entirety of the Bible, there is no evidence of haunting, or haunted houses. Demons DO NOT POSSESS inanimate objects. Ghost-busters is a movie; there has never been a biblical example of demonic inhabitation of inanimate or dead things. Demons have no interest in ruling the dead, demons just happen to inhabit the underworld. If

demons wanted to rule the underworld, they would stay there. What demons want to rule is the living, so that they can alter the will of God. How does inhabiting a rock hamper the will for God? God has no will for rocks or animals, so demons do not spend a great deal of time dealing with rocks & animals[10].

1.11.2 ***War - is a violent, costly battle or struggle between uncompromising parties.*** What fellowship has light with darkness Paul once asked? There can be nothing but enmity between demons and humans. Demons have no good will towards anyone, not even each other. Satan never promised anything but darkness and death to his followers. The war between demons, angels, and humans continues whether we participate or not.

    Anyone on the opposing team benefits or loses, as do the soldiers. In the American war for independence, those that did not fight still won independence. In the American Indian wars, the natives who did not fight received the same treatment, the same reservations, the same small pox infected blankets, and the same rancid meat. This is war! War does not to do anything but destroy. The only morality in war occurs at the onset. The decision to kill or not to kill is the moral dilemma. Once we make the determination to kill, it no longer matters which method we used.

1.11.3 ***Spiritual Warfare - is a violent, costly battle or struggle between uncompromising spiritual entities.*** As we now see, there is no way for God and Satan to coexist peacefully. Although a Christian may have traits of both spirits the one thing I guarantee is that, anyone with traits of both spirits has NO PEACE. This is the result of spiritual warfare a life altering, heart wrenching battle between spirits and a mound of sinful flesh. There is no peace in the conflict and no cease-fire, the only way to win is to choose a side and stay there. It is not the attacks of Satan that cause misery. The misery arises when we allow Satan to attack God's dominion -- God defends His territory zealously. The misery arises because WE ARE THE BATTLEFIELD. Just like the Germans moved from country to country during the world wars this battle rages on different frontiers: home, heart, marriage, mind etc.

1.11.4 ***Armor - Is a defensive covering, as a safeguard, or protection*** - armor serves to protect the wearer, but it is just as effective as a weapon, especially against the unprotected.

1.11.5 ***Spiritual Armor - is a safeguard or protection for our spirit*** - armor serves to protect the believer, but it is just as effective as a weapon, especially defending the weak and captive.

1.11.6 ***Weapon - is an instrument or member (body part) used to attack, disarm, or persuade*** - we use weapons to protect ourselves during attacks as well as to cause maximum damage to our opponent.

1.11.7 ***Spiritual Weapon - is an instrument or member (body part) used to attack, disarm, or persuade spiritually.*** God no longer ordained for His people to wage all-out war against anyone. Even in the Old Testament when God declared war, it was against His enemies, not the enemies of His people. God reserves the right to judge[11] who is worthy of death. God also reserves the right to wage war when, how and against whom He pleases. Unbelievers are not God's enemy, although they are potential weapons against God's people. Only the debase haters of God are God's enemy[12]. For them He has a set time to judge them.

1.11.8 **Authority - is the power to command, exact obedience, or inform.** Authority is a difficult position to maintain, because it requires integrity. As we know, humans do not have an innate desire to be good, so goodness is learned. Many say people are born leaders, but history disagrees. History does not show strong leaders but a gamut of weak people. History credits Emilano Zapata for saying, "*A strong people do not need a strong leader.*" God's kingdom has a powerful leader; we can therefore conclude that Christians are not as strong a people as we pretend.

1.11.9 **Spiritual Authority - is the power to command, exact obedience, or inform spiritually.** Spiritual authority only comes from God. Although God establishes leaders to accomplish His will, **only God commands**. Those above us manage. As with any manager, leaders are frequently wrong. The book of James says that **the righteous do not resist**, but the righteous also do not think as soldiers.

Non-resistance does not mean to surrender; it means to find another way to accomplish the task. There is no calling to lie down and die except to sin. Jesus' death did not further the cause of righteousness it restored the effect. We will not find a command from God to any of His flock to lie down and die before men.

Do not confuse what Jesus did with martyrdom. Jesus did not die for a cause; He is the cause of redemption and Salvation. The war is between two kingdoms Jesus' actions checkmated Satan. The Bible says that Satan does not know all, for if he did he would not have killed the Christ[13]. What the world thought was killing a man liberated a Spirit and raised a King. The flesh for Jesus was a tomb of death. When He hung on the cross, He told the thief that as soon as He was free of the carcass He would be in paradise. Remember we decided based on scripture that paradise is the presence of God. Therefore, what Jesus told the man was that as soon as they were free of the flesh they would be closer to God.

God's *Spirit of authority* works only to serve God's will and kingdom. The call and gifts are without repentance God says, but He monitors them intensely. He forewarns that it is better to drown that to hurt one of the sheep[14]. It is of no surprise that judgment starts at the church. How can a just God punish the soldiers of the enemy for crimes while overlooking the transgressions of His soldiers? Human leaders may overlook the crimes of their friends, but God does not. **God is a warrior king He has needs no friends**.

1.11.10 *Army - a large, organized body of soldiers for waging war.* Men use armies to further their own selfish, fear filled desires. Rarely in history have armies been used for the good of humankind.

1.11.11 *Spiritual Army - a large, organized body of disciples for waging spiritual war.* Like secular leaders, spiritual leaders amass large disciples unto themselves. The purpose of raising an army is to defend, and wage war. An army that never leaves the temple makes of itself a target. The attacker has no choice but to destroy a defending army, whether they fight or not. Destruction is the safest way to deal with an army, lest it rise again within our borders and creates a civil war. Leaders therefore leaders that raise huge temples full of passive, untrained, cowardly soldiers create victims.

1.11.12 *Siege - the encirclement of a fortified place by an enemy intending to take it, persistent attempt to gain control.* Siege is one of the most effective forms of warfare ever created. Although the siege is expensive in terms of logistics, it yields the greatest reward in terms of property and casualties. During a siege, the best and largest numbers of enemy troops become captive in their own fortress. It is just a matter of time until their water or food runs out, or disease causes them the leave. The other benefit to the siege is we immediately take control of the enemy's greatest defenses and resolve upon victory.

1.11.13 *Spiritual Siege - the encirclement of a spiritual stronghold or place set aside by an enemy intending to take it.* This is the least effective spiritual weapon for believers, but the most often used by Satan. For believers the idleness of the siege has negative results. While in close quarters with other saints, the vileness of our hearts comes to life. Satan on the other hand uses siege masterfully. I call this technique-*playing possum*. Satan knows that it is just a matter of time before a saint falls to the contents of their heart.

1.11.14 *Attrition - a wearing away by as by friction, a normal loss of persons.* This is an integral part of the siege, whether active or implied. America's use of this tactic won the cold war against the Union of Soviet Socialist Republic (USSR).

1.11.15 *Spiritual Attrition - a wearing down or falling away caused by spiritual trials, spiritual hardship, and spiritual warfare.* In the end times, the Bible warns us that Satan will wear down the saints. Attrition, falling away, and apostasy creates many chinks in the armor of God's people. Christ told us that it is not within Satan's ability to snatch us away. Christians walk or fall away from the body of Christ. When we fall from His army, we automatically become a spy for the enemy. Through our behavior, Satan sees the heart of the temple to which we belong. This is why it is important to capture deserters; interviewing them yields temple secrets.

1.11.16 *Attack - to use force, to order, to harm, to make an assault, to speak or write against.* Attack is always an aggressive action against an enemy.

1.11.17 *Spiritual Attack - to use spiritual force to harm, to judge, make a spiritual assault, or speak against.* Attack is always an aggressive action, but it does not have to be violent. **'Since the death of John the Baptist the kingdom of heaven suffers violence'** the scripture says, and He did. What people do not realize is that Satan was actually counter attacking. Satan was under attack the moment Mary conceived Christ. This is why Satan hunted Christ so adamantly. The attacks Christ ordained when He ordered us to go forth and teach are no different than the Mongolians *go forth and conquer*. The difference is in the method, the Mongols killed, and Christ died for our sins. The way in which we attack is through spreading the Art of Christ into the world and letting Him do the actual fighting.

1.11.18 *Defense - to guard from attack; protect, to support or justify.* Defense is the manner in which we repel or protect ourselves from an attacking enemy. Whether the army uses words, actions, or weapons, defense is only necessary when danger is imminent.

1.11.19 *Spiritual Defense - to guard from spiritual attack, protect, to support or justify.* Spiritual defense is a super-natural manner in which we repel or protect ourselves from attack. Defense in the physical relies on training and fleshly wiles; spiritual defense relies ENTIRELY on our relationship with God.

Although these concepts comprise the basics of spiritual warfare, some of the more advanced concepts do not appear in this book. The reason the concepts do not appear here is that the most advanced concepts surround the effects warfare has on us.

1.12 Spiritual warfare safeguards

The following spiritual warfare safeguards (Marriage mysteries) come from biblical principles.

1.12.1 Do not begin a conflict against Satan alone
1.12.2 Do not begin conflict without proper prayer and fasting
1.12.3 Do not stay exposed to temptation longer than necessary to deliver the message
1.12.4 Know within what territory you fight
1.12.5 Know for what territory you fight
1.12.6 Know against what level of demon you war
1.12.7 Understand your relationship to God and His will
1.12.8 Keep your personal ambitions out of God's war

Everything written about in the Patmos series comes from the Bible, or the God of the Bible. Since opinion does not contain the ability to save lives, bring about righteousness, or change lives I keep opinion to myself regarding God's word. However, I do feel qualified to point out the above listed safeguards; gleaned from the Bible regarding Spiritual warfare. These safeguards exist to offset the damage we occur during spiritual warfare. There will always be some damage; otherwise, the Bible would not have forewarned us against swords formed against us. The thing God does promise is that NO WEAPON FORMED AGAINST US SHALL PROSPER. God promises that men will be hate you and will attack, but it is only because you chose to walk in His light. If you opt to walk in the shade, then you will have a different type of interaction with Satan. Like the rulers of the Third Reich, your journey will bring you temporary position and power, but inevitably, you earn death.

In the book, From a Fortress in Patmos, we discussed many spiritual warfare topics let us remember together. Jesus redeemed the earth and crushed Satan's kingdom but there is still a war?

There is still a war because Satan is not bound, and he still converts followers to his revolution against God. There is still a war because the human creature is evil and strives against God continually[15]. There are no scriptures I am aware of wherein God states that man started war against Satan, Satan fights man. Consequently, it appears that humans wage war against both God's will, and Satan's control.

According to scriptures, the war for the CHOICE of men continues until God puts an end to it. Nothing Satan or humans do changes God's plan. What God and Satan vie for is choice; God's plan is set. Spiritual warfare is not for material wealth, although kingdom building may entail material gain. Men promise wealth and pomp if we succeed at spiritual warfare, this is a lie. The cup of victory set forth for God's people walks us into;

1. The valley of the shadow of death
2. A table beset with our enemies
3. The lion's den
4. A fiery furnace
5. A hill of skulls
6. A cross with nails
7. Even unto death

Solomon stays heralded as the wisest man in history. To the cup from which we drink he writes, with much wisdom comes sorrow. This principle applies to spiritual matters as well. There is no way to be a part of the heart of God and not feel the way He does. Sorrow is a part of love, and no one loves like God. Despite the immense sorrow humanity causes God, He loves us still.

As a part of the journey to eternal life, we meet many other spiritual beings while trying to tie into God. If we search the heavens with our souls to find God, we will meet God's enemy. Spiritual warfare only happens in the lives of spiritual people. Satan does not vie for the spiritually dead; he gets them all by default. If we never tie into God, we end up with in the *shade;* the place ruled by the prince of darkness.

    Christians who marry find that the battle for choice and over the flesh is not over; a new frontier simply begins. Once we only fought to subdue the flesh, we knew, once married we fight to change into one flesh and then subdues the new flesh that emerges from within marriage. It is difficult to subdue our own flesh, trying to hold on to that balance while our flesh wrestles what the issue of our spouse simultaneously often is too fierce a battle for many to maintain.

    It is because we do not understand that marriage is the cure for the diseases of the flesh that we run away. Like we whence and shrink from alcohol as it stings the open cut we flee the sting of marriage. However, like alcohol, that sting is healing and salvation at work. The cut and the sting are painful, but the uncured infection is much worst. Marriage is harsh, but the result of not subduing our flesh, which is also HELL; is much worse. Stay married, even a troubled marriage is better than hell. Do not be fooled, the wealth of sadness we find in troubled marriages fails in comparison to what waits on the other side for the casualties of spiritual warfare.

2.0
The Flesh, Spiritual Warfare and Marriage

In every marriage, there is room for both change and growth. When we look at the difference between perfection and righteousness we find that being *perfected,"* means that absence of sinful desires in our hearts (Matthew 5:8). We therefore understand that *righteousness* is the choice not to act on sinful desires. I hope that the Lord never sees fit to take away my ability to appreciate beautiful women, as that would adversely affect my relationship with my wife. In time my daughter will also grow into a beautiful woman, I would like to be able to appreciate her blossoming into a butterfly as well.

The word *spirit* appears in the Bible #456 times and flesh appears #369 times. The battle rages on between the two and it does not stop just because we marry. What we find however in marriage is a place devised by God where the spirit and the flesh do not have to war. **"Let us be glad and rejoice and give honor to Him: for the marriage of the Lamb is come, and His wife hath made herself ready. And to her was granted that she should be arrayed in fine linen, clean and white: for the fine linen is the righteousness of saints** - Revelations 19:7-8."

Revelations confirms for us that through marriage, through the *fine linen* ordained by God the saints can achieve and maintain righteousness.

___
___
___
___
___

2.1 The freedom of the flesh

The flesh is free to do as it pleases, but it has nothing good in it the bible says, **"Man, that is born of a woman, is of few days, and full of trouble. He comes forth like a flower, and continueth not. He also flees like a shadow and does not continue. And doth open thine eyes on such a one, and bring me into judgment with you? Who can bring a clean thing out of an unclean? Not one"** - (Job 14:1- 4). The flesh is free to choose, but it never chooses righteousness. In every given opportunity, the flesh chooses what is pleasing to the eyes and desirable. Our fleshly nature creates an abyss between men and God. The flesh cannot stop being flesh enough to please God. In order that Jesus completed His task, His flesh had to die. Although the parable states wheat must die to give life, the spiritual application for humans is that our flesh must die so we can receive Life.

Another marriage mystery, just as we cannot enter heaven without change, we cannot have a successful marriage without change. The flesh is a greedy animal, an animal that thrives on life. The flesh does not relinquish control easily, but the flesh must die that we may live.

Sexual freedom is the ultimate expression of pleasure and freedom. Believers do not understand the parallel depth and pleasure available in the presence of God. If believers understood the pleasure available in the presence of God, they would stay in the presence of God. In infidelity, we see the reason many Christians fail at their relationship with God is that greed makes it difficult to stay faithful.

2.2 **Marriage and the flesh**

People appreciate sex for the good feeling. What we miss is that sex is supposed to over shadow the darkness of what we were and inspire us to grow into what God wants. In other words, sex is the flavoring in our *medicine*--lest we decide not to become one flesh with our spouse. The *medicine* God has for us; the bitter cup from which we must drink is a part of our growth. Jesus drank vinegar to understand the bitterness of this life. Jesus was not the first to experience the bitterness of this life; the Hebrews did at the Golden Calf. The Hebrews had to grind the calf into dust and drink it. God uses the bitterness of this life, so we can differentiate between His taste and the flavor of Satan. Although Satan offers the pleasure of the flesh, God offers the pleasures of the flesh and eternal life.

Married people can have all the sex they want and still get to heaven. The favorite sin is fornication; it is the thing most likely to keep people out of heaven. Through marriage, we can have our cake and eat it too, yet people refrain from marriage or disdain fidelity in marriage. Fidelity REQUIRES DISCIPLINE. Righteousness is a choice; it has absolutely nothing to do with feeling. Either we do what God requires or we suffer the consequences.

Growing pains in marriage are a natural part of the process. Something is dying so that a new life can begin. Through the undefiled bed, God allows us to overshadow growing pains with pleasure. The troubles of life and eternal life do not go away if we have adulterous relationships. On the contrary, adultery only makes things worse. Adultery may make us feel better, like crack or any other drug but the result is the same--destruction and eventually death. Are there bad marriages? No, not bad marriages there are marriages that have trouble because of people who are unwilling to change. Everybody wants the fun, vacation, and Christmas promised in the family photos, but that life is expensive. Christians want the life at the banquet and around the throne, but it too costs. The price of our marriage and life is our flesh: hence circumcision.

2.3 **The discipline of married flesh**

God designed marriage to be the easiest discipline in the Christian arsenal. This discipline is not only easy to attain it is easy to maintain; all we have to do is give in to our spouse. Repeatedly the Bible warns us not to *'give in'* to distractions of the flesh. Conversely, the same Bible instructs us to give ourselves to our spouses in marriage. **"Let the husband render unto the wife due benevolence: and likewise, the wife unto the husband. The wife hath not power of her own body, but the husband: and likewise, also the husband hath not power of his own body, but the wife**[16]. We are to give ourselves to our spouses with body and soul, our spirit however belongs to God. For these reasons, the undefiled bed is the easiest way to discipline the flesh. In Paul's way, we have to crucify our flesh. In God's way, all we must do is redirect our passion, lust, desire, and sexuality into our spouses.

3.0
About Marriage

"**And when the dragon saw that he was cast unto the earth, he persecuted the woman which brought forth the man [child]. And to the woman were given two wings of a great eagle, that she might fly into the wilderness, into her place, where she is nourished for a time, and times, and half a time, from the *face of the serpent*. And the serpent cast out of his mouth water as a flood after the woman, that he might cause her to be carried away of the flood. And the earth helped the woman, and the earth opened her mouth, and swallowed up the flood which the dragon cast out of his mouth. And the dragon was wroth with the woman and went to make war with the remnant of her seed, which keep the commandments of God, and have the testimony of Jesus Christ**" - (Revelations 12:13-17).

3.1 The first marriage in history

The first marriage in history appears in the book of Genesis "**Therefore shall a man leave his father and his mother and shall cleave unto his wife: and they shall be one flesh. Therefore, shall a man leave his father and his mother, and shall cleave unto his wife: and they shall be one flesh**" - (Genesis 2:23-24). The first marriage took six days to build and consisted of two bodies and three spirits.

In every marriage, God ordained checks and balances. Humans live in the flesh. In the human body, there are two functioning halves left and right. The flesh is unbalanced, so God cut it in half and uses each half to balance the other half. There are many duplicate body parts, but the most important parts are singular: one heart and one brain. The mystery of this arrangement is that we MUST bring our duality under unified command in order for it to function properly. Bad health practices adversely affect both the heart and the brain, just as bad marital practices adversely affect the marriage. Many of the sub-components of marriage spin out of control destroying the wife (heart) and the man (the brain). Ignoring media lies; the man is the brain of the marriage because he is the head. These tasks do not make the woman less or the man more important, what good is a heart without a brain?

In the garden, it was not good for man to be alone. The resolution to the problem of the flesh was not another man; God did not clone Adam; He made suitable woman. The resolution to flesh's loneliness was a creature of like kind but different parts. In the marital apportionment, God created balance. God took the man's flesh and made another fleshly creature, suitable for the man.

We learn in Genesis, that God made another creature of equal desire to balance Adam. In love, we learn appreciation, care, and discipline. The two humans becoming one must infer a different state then the *oneness* Adam and Eve formerly enjoyed. One in the will of God's implies that their flesh is under subjection. The relationship between men and God consist of sanctifying the flesh through discipline.

According to scripture, man does not have the necessary controls to be Godly. God did the next best thing; He made Adam learn to appreciate what he had. In giving the man something that needed care, tenderness, and protection God set man's path to love. Instead of forcing man to fail and watch us pretend to have control, God made it, so we did not need controls. God made it clear that He understood the needs of the flesh understanding that the flesh needs flesh--not spirit. In order to control our flesh God ordains prayer and fasting. Prayer allows God's controls to take over our spirit and thus control the movements of our flesh. While prayer can assuage fear and distress, prayer does not abate loneliness and sexual desire, only flesh does that. It is to this paradigm that God created the marriage solution. The purpose of the first marriage was to subject flesh in the righteousness of God.

There are many mysteries hidden within the folds of the Bible. Within the scriptures pertaining to Adam and Eve we find even more spiritual mysteries applicable to this war.

_____
_____
_____
_____

3.2 About Adam and Eve

"**And the LORD GOD formed man of the dust of the ground and breathed into his nostrils the breath of life; and man became a living soul. And the Lord God planted a garden eastward in Eden; and there he put the man whom he had formed. And out of the ground made the Lord God to grow every tree that is pleasant to the sight, and good for food; the tree of life also in the midst of the garden, and the tree of knowledge of good and evil. And a river went out of Eden to water the garden; and from thence it was parted and became into four heads. And the Lord God took the man and put him into the garden of Eden to dress it and to keep it. And the Lord God commanded the man, saying, of every tree of the garden thou mayest freely eat: But of the tree of the knowledge of good and evil, thou shalt not eat of it: for in the day that thou eatest thereof thou shalt surely die. And the Lord God said, 'It is not good that the man should be alone; I will make him an help meet for him'. And out of the ground the Lord God formed every beast of the field, and every fowl of the air; and brought them unto Adam to see what he would call them: and whatsoever Adam called every living creature, that was the name thereof. And Adam gave names to all cattle, and to the fowl of the air, and to every beast of the field; but for Adam there was not found an help meet for him. And the Lord God caused a deep sleep to fall upon Adam, and he slept: and he took one of his ribs and closed up the flesh instead thereof; And the rib, which the Lord God had taken from man, made he a woman, and brought her unto the man. And Adam said, this is now bone of my bones, and flesh of my flesh: she shall be called Woman, because she was taken out of Man. Therefore, shall a man leave his father and his mother, and shall cleave unto his wife: and they shall be one flesh. And they were both naked, the man and his wife, and were not ashamed** - (Genesis 2:7-3:24)."

- 3.2.1 **God formed Adam of the dust** - God personally formed Adam of the dust of the earth. Adam and the earth were of the same material they were not like those in heaven. Adam and the earth were one they were married. According to Etymologists, the name or word Adam means 'the red earth,' 'red,' or 'mankind.' Adam therefore was not on the earth; he was of the earth. His name indicates that he was married (one flesh) with the earth. Therefore Adam's dominion of the earth, included dominion over all the other things of the earth.

- 3.2.3 **God breathed into Adam's nostrils** - In order to separate Adam from the earth, God breathed His spirit into the man's body, and that point Adam became a Living soul. Up to that point he was just earthly he was fleshly he was not a spiritual man and he had no spiritual relationship with God.

3.2.4 **God placed Adam in the garden** - Once Adam and God had a relationship God set aside a special place that we later called the *Holy of Holies* God to meet with His spiritual creatures.

3.2.5 **God told Adam to dress and keep the garden** - After blessing this union between the man and the garden, God told him dress it and keep it God made Adam the first husband in history.

3.2.6 **...tree that is pleasant to the sight** - The trees God planted were pleasant to the sight both flesh and spirit.

3.2.7 **... the Lord God commanded the man** - God gave the instructions pertaining to eating of the trees personally, unlike with Eve.

3.2.8 **...and the Lord God said, 'It is not good that the man should be alone'** - God determined that is was not good for man to be alone - God looked into the garden and so that the man was alone and He said that it was not good the Bible never explains why He said it was not good but he determined that it was not good for the man to be alone.

3.2.9 **...the Lord God formed every beast** - In order to fix the man's being alone God resolved to make other beasts like him also of the dirt also of the earth but even after seeing that God determine that the man was still not complete, and he needed something different to make him no longer alone.

3.2.10 **...I will make him an help meet for him** - God decided upon the solution for man's lonesomeness and made for the man from Adam's rib, which was from the earth God made yet another creature the Bible never said however that he breathed into eve's nostrils.

3.2.11 **...the Lord God had taken from man, made he a woman** - God decided what the man needed to be complete, the Bible says did

Adam and Eve were to become one flesh this was doable because Eve was made from Adam and Adam was made from the earth so they will all one flesh but Adam had something that Eve did not that this is where marriage comes in this is the mystery of marriage as Christ died for the church.

Chavvah and *Heua* are words used in the bible for Eve. Etymologist tell us the name or word means, 'life' or 'living' and the Bible says she was called thusly because she was the mother of all things.

Eve was not the mother of all things because she gave birth to them; she was the mother of all things because she was married to Adam, the father of all things. All livings things God made from '*Adam*' the red earth, not the man, but the earth. All living things according to Genesis Gad made to live and subsist on other living things. Eve, came from the red earth (Adam) as well, she therefore was *married* and one flesh with Adam.

God saw a thing in man that He decided to reconcile, before it created a problem. God saw that the husbandry between He and the man, was not enough. God saw that although the man could have a relationship with God, his flesh would always be an issue between them. Adam had a wife, the Earth and they were one flesh, but Adam could not adhere to Genesis 1:11 wherein God decreed, "**And God said, 'Let the earth bring forth grass, the herb yielding seed, and the fruit tree yielding fruit after his kind, whose seed is in itself, upon the earth': and it was so**". ADAM COULD NOT REPRODUCE HIMSELF; HIS SEED WOULD NOT PRODUCE WITH THE EARTH ANOTHER HUMAN. God therefore gave Adam a suitable mate, with whom his seed could yield fruit after its kind, whose seed was within itself.

This is why homosexuality and bestiality are abominations, because they violate this decree and the intertwining of the seed in these abominable relationships, cannot comply with this decree.

3.2.12 ...the Lord God brought her unto the man - God will the woman until the man and gave Eve to Adam. Adam recognized that Eve was like him and came from him and could bond with him, but he did not understand at the time if he needed to give Eve the piece that she needed to bind with him completely Adam did not understand that marriage was not just about flesh that is where it starts. God brought Eve to him, so that Eve would join with Adam and become one flesh, controlled by God's Holy Spirit. The bible never says that Eve became a living soul based upon an action of God.

We know the rest of the story, but all is not as it seems. The woman when approached by Satan responded with words that came from her husband there is no indication that God spoke to her and gave her the law face to face as he did Moses and Adam. Eve said whatever she said based on what she understood and then she did which she understood she was supposed to do. Eve took that which she found to be pleasant to her flesh back to he who had Dominion over the flesh. Adam failed in his duties to use his relationship with God to be a better husband this thing marriage is a mystery. This book is about the mystery of the marriage and the mystery of the church and the question remains to this day, why men are still not using their relationship with God to make marriages better.

3.3 The best made marriage in history

Let us look to John 15:1-5 pertaining to Godly marriage and see what makes it unique[17].
"I AM THE TRUE VINE, AND MY FATHER IS THE HUSBANDMAN - Husbandman or gardener is the tender of a marriage. God told Adam to take care of (husband) the garden. Thus, Jesus says to us the He is the suitable help-meet for this marriage[18]. In Genesis, the Bible says this about the fleshly creature and the marriage institution, **"And Adam said, 'This [is] now bone of my bones, and flesh of my flesh: she shall be called Woman[19], because she was taken out of *Man.*' Therefore, shall a man leave his father and his mother, and shall cleave unto his wife: and they shall be one flesh. And they were both naked, the man and his wife, and were not ashamed"** - (Genesis 2:23-25). Although Jesus came from Mary He is still the bone of God's bone, for He came from God.

3.4 The temple as a marital model

The 'greatest' of all commandments comes from Deuteronomy 6:5 where in the Bible instructs us to, "… **love the Lord thy God with all thine heart, and with all thy soul, and with all thy might**." We also saw in the temple model[20] the sanctification God requires of the temple.

Typical wedding vows betroth people endearing them together to love each other with *their hearts, bodies, and souls until death do them part*. Now let us compare wedding vows to Exodus 20:3 and Deuteronomy 6:5.

I, (name), take you (name), to be My (wife/husband), to have and to hold from this day forward, for better or for worse, for richer, for poorer in sickness and in health, to love and to cherish; from this day forward until death do us part.	**"Thou shalt have no other Gods before me. And thou shalt love the Lord thy God with all thine heart, and with with all thy soul and thy might."**

In keeping with this comparison, is not Ephesians 5:25-28 not a mature application of 1 Corinthians 3:17?

Immaturity requires punishment
"**If any man defiles the temple temple of God, him shall God destroy; for the temple of God for it; That he of God is holy, which [temple] ye are.**"
- (1 Corinthians 3:17).

Maturity requires self- Discipline
"**Husbands, love your wives, even as Christ also, loved the church, and gave Himself that He might sanctify and cleanse it with the washing of water by then word, that He might present it to Himself a glorious church, not having spot, or wrinkle, or any such thing; but that it should be holy and without blemish. So, ought men to love their wives as their own**

bodies. He that loveth his wife loveth himself - (Ephesians 5:25-28).

Can we not see together that the love for the temple, and the love for marriage are the mystery…they are a love for the things of God? Can we not see together that the same sanctification God requires from the temple He requires from the sanctified marriage?

It is difficult to respect and honor marriage because we do not respect and honor God. To this, God commands us to (learn to) love Him with all our being. In this journey, in trying to love a God that we cannot see, we often fail. God therefore brought the temple construct[21] home and gave us spouses that we could see.

3.5 <u>The wedding</u>[22]

"The average wedding cost in the United States is $26,444. Couples typically spend between $19,833 and $33,055 but most couples spend less than $10,000. This does not include cost for a honeymoon." Having counseled marriages successfully and unsuccessfully for more than 10 years I make commentary on one major mistake women make. THE WEDDING CANNOT BE MORE IMPORTANT THAN THE MARRIAGE. I wager, that based on the average wedding cost, the combined gifts given to the husband do not equal the amount paid for that one day.

We place too much emphasis on the wedding day the problems with this flawed concept are numerous. We looked at the most articulated reasons the wedding day is important to women[23].

- 3.5.1 **Childhood dream** for most women to be swept of their feet and taken to their new castle to hide within.

- 3.5.2 **Emotional security** from most women is desirable. They feel loved, wanted and appreciated.

- 3.5.3 **Pressure from parents** - many young ladies find the constant familial guidance towards marriage a form of pressure; positive pressure. The pressure changes when a parent picks the suitor, but the idea of marriage is still sacred to most parents, as it provides them a sense of completion of the family tradition. The 'biological' clock is not the main concern, although it often seems like it. There is a drive in God's creatures to be fruitful and multiply, and marriage is the vehicle He ordained.

- 3.5.4 **Societal pressure** - the least important of the six, is keeping up with trends. However, social media and trends are fast out ranking Godly tradition and order.

- 3.5.5 **Declaration to the world** - Marriage, for a woman is merely not a commitment to a man but is the public declaration of love and acceptance. Marriage signifies to the world, that I have been chosen for my value to this man above all others.

- 3.5.6 **Maternal instinct** - Marriage brings decency and honor to maternity. Illegitimacy, though ascribed to the child is not the child's fault; it is the mother's fault. However, in marriage; all is honored before men, and God. Even in this world sinking into darkness, the word wife holds kids as part of its sanctity. Mother, by itself, does not imply marriage, regardless of the conventions of modernity; marriage is still sacred to most people. As fate would have it, even the enemies of decency regard marriage in high esteem and to them. While we see that the LGBT community pretends to not know the truth of God (Romans 1:21) even they seek to imitate His order. The children of pride do not do this to please Him, but because marriage as an institution is part of the salvation, process built into the model in the garden. Cain sinned, but he was still Adam and Eve's son. Charles Caleb Colton was correct; imitation is the sincerest form of flattery.

The prize at the wedding is neither the dress nor the diamond. The prize at the wedding is the pristine, pure, virgin given in marriage; unblemished and without spot. The question at many weddings is when does this person arrive?

We maintain the tradition of the diamond ring; we maintain the tradition of the white dress we have maintained the tradition of the father giving away the bride. The tradition that we did not maintain is the one that is the most important to the wedding it is giving away of a virgin to man for the first time on their wedding night; that tradition we no longer hold sacred.

If the most important of the wedding traditions is no longer sacred, how can we expect the marriage to be sacred, why should we expect the wedding to be sacred? What exactly is the purpose of celebrating a life together predicated on a lie. I believe this cavalier attitude towards decency is also a problem in marriage. People no longer hold the esteem when they enter marriage that they should for each other, and by default the marriage. This may seem hard but it is no harder the reality that people spend on average $26,000 on the wedding dress. Once the wedding is over the dress goes in the closet. The importance of the marriage is diminished because there was no true impetus on the marriage in the first place because they have already practiced all of the lifestyle with none of the vows.

The wedding then is merely an expression of a princess fantasy. For if the truth be told (traditionally speaking), no dowry is given for a bride who is not a virgin. Did not Joseph allow the wedding, yet put his bride away from the marriage as she had defiled the vows of sanctity?

How does the man comply with Ephesians 5, where we are required to present the wife without spot or blemish if when we married she had blemishes? We spend the majority of our spiritual lives trying to make her clean; a task that we cannot do. Salvation becomes even more important because we do not want to lie in the defiled bed, so we must put her under the Blood after we marry to fix the lifestyle from before she took the vows. The same is true for the man, except men are not the ones demanding the white dress and ceremony.

4.0
The Mysterious Honeymoon[24]

"And the vine said unto them, SHOULD I LEAVE MY WINE, WHICH CHEERETH GOD AND MAN, AND GO TO BE PROMOTED OVER THE TREES" - (Judges 9:13).

A honeymoon affords newlyweds long nights of talking, lovemaking, and tenderness, before the dawning of the Son. It is no accident that the event is named for the moon, which fabled to represent love, gentleness, and kindness. The sweet tenderness of the honeymoon comes before the change takes place and the reality of the light begins. Before the old flesh dies and the growing pains begin, God allows us to enjoy the darkness together.

In the marriage bed the same bed God joined, He created an unholy of holies, a place for our flesh to fully express itself. God does not meet us in our bedroom it is for our flesh. God ordained the *prayer closet* as a place for us to meet with Him. Once we control our flesh through undefiled-marital sex, we go to the closet and rejoice in a clear moment with God.

The honeymoon affords newlyweds to walk into the new life together. Remember, both spouses are growing and changing. The honeymoon enables them to do this together, to shed their old flesh simultaneously and safely, and grow into their new life. This is the Adam and Eve effect, what better way to learn about the power and the control of our flesh, than naked with our spouse.

Quintessential to marriage and parallel to righteousness is that the old person dies. Ephesians explains this concept to us in chapter 5. God makes us one flesh, so we will be willing to die to save our spouses. We learn to make this sacrifice because in our spouse we work out our salvation in fear and trembling. In our spouses, half of our being dies to live. In order that our prayers go unhindered, the Bible admonishes us to kill the rest of what holds us trapped in our premarital problems.

_____
_____
_____
_____
_____
_____
_____

4.1 The undefiled wedding bed

Historically, the 'honeymoon' for a month after a marriage event, wherein the bride's father would give the groom all the *mead* he wanted. Mead is a honey beer. While the Babylon calendar was a lunar calendar. The Babylonians started calling the month the "honey month" but we now call it the honeymoon.

Although the tradition may be named for beer, this is not the only thing formerly withheld, given in abundance as part of the marital celebration. Moses recommended, one a year honeymoon, wherein no war or business was to be assigned to the man. Although sex is not the focus of the honeymoon, it is the main benefit.

During courtship the man and woman talked, they dated, emailed, they wrote letters, laughed, walked, and ate dinner. The only thing the bride truly withholds until the wedding night, is her 'virtue'

One year of getting to know each other, was the time afforded men to enjoy her honey, produce at least one heir, and enjoy the wife of their youth. For the woman, it was a new life away from home, learning to care for her own home, develop her own place in the world, and become a mother. Therefore, we find see that sex is not the only honey from the festivities, all manner of sweetness comes from the blessed unify of the man and this woman.

This is what Adam and Eve did all day. Walk around naked and learn to be close to one another. Regardless of the activity of the day, the constant state of nudity, also kept the fleshly appetites as an undertone. No matter the argument; anger, hurt, disgust, or irritation, seeing their spouse naked, always having access to their partners 'honey' God designed to help make marriage less tumultuous. After all, did we not agree, by our lustfulness that we pend must of our lives controlled by our flesh. Therefore, should not marriage make for us a honey filled adventure through this life.

Undefiled is not just a reference to before marriage, it also implies that that marital bed, is a place of flesh, this is where the humans mesh. The rules in the bible about the goings on in the bible are far fleshlier than church admits. It is this parochial attitude that fostered the concepts such as Nunnery, Monastics, and therefore opened the door to centuries of sexual abuse and molestation in the church.

Not admitting the sexual nature of the human is a mistake, divorcing this nature from the creation of God is the second. The flesh has appetites. According to the internet, Porn sites get more traffic each month and stream more movies that Twitter, Netflix, and Amazon combined[25]. Where does this appetite go? Where do married people who do not have sex do with their appetites?

God did not ordain for His people to find alternate means of satisfying their appetites. It is not our appetites God disdains[26]; it is the solutions we devise to cater to our appetites that displease Him[27].

This is the Adam and Eve Edition, so let us hear what scripture has to say about the undefiled wedding bed.

    4.1.1 **Love is better than wine** - (Songs 1:12).

    4.1.2 **Because of thy savour of thy good ointments, thy name is as ointment poured forth therefore do the virgins love thee** - Describing the musky dew of the man (Songs 1:3).

    4.1.3 **A bundle of myrrh is my well beloved unto me, he shall all night betwixt my breasts** - Speaking of both sex and intimacy where he lays upon her (Songs 1:13).

    4.1.4 **Behold thou art fair, my beloved. Yea pleasant: also our bed is green** - Green is the color of growth, and to farmers green symbolizes wealth because it promises growth and food (Songs 1:16).

    4.1.5 **As the apple tree among the trees of the wood, so is my beloved among the sons. I sat down under his shadow with great delight. And his fruit was sweet to my taste** - A reference to the woman's finding pleasure in being beneath the strength of his body. And she is quite pleased with their passionate kisses and the taste of his body (Songs 2:3).

4.1.6 **He brought me to the banqueting house and his banner over me was love.** (Speaking of the new-found security stayed in the power of his might and ability to protect and provide for her (Songs 2:4).

4.1.7 **Stay me with raison cakes comfort me with apples for I am sick with love, His left hand is under my head, and His right hand doth embrace me** (Apples represent his fruitfulness and the treasure in his loins which he shares, and with his right hands (the hand of strength) describes the power of their making love in her mind (Songs 2:5-6).

4.1.8 **My beloved is mine and I am His, He feedeth among the lilies** - A reference to him satisfying his sexual appetites in her virginal field of the white flowers which represent her (Songs 2:16).

4.1.9 **Until the daybreak, and the shadows flee away, turn my and be thou like a roe, or a young hart upon the mountains of Bether** - (Her breast represent the mountains he bounds upon and grazes in. This is a sexual reference to breast, she does not mean bosom (Songs 2:17).

4.1.10 **Thy two breasts are like two young roes that are twins, which feed among the lilies** - Speaks to the beauty of her young breasts, and how sweet and clean she looks to him (Songs 4:5).

4.1.11 **Thy lips, O my spouse drop as the honeycomb, honey and milk are under thy tongue** - Deep kissing and sweet words (Songs 4:11).

4.1.12 **A garden enclosed is my sister... A fountain of gardens, a well of living waters and streams from Lebanon** - referring to the response of her body to his touch, and to the separation of herself from others to keep her pure - (Songs 4:12-15).

4.1.13 **Awake, O north wind; and come, thou south; blow upon my garden, that the spices thereof may flow out. Let my beloved come into his garden and eat his pleasant fruits** - Relying on arousal from his gentle breath, the husband is

_____
_____
_____
_____
_____
_____
_____
_____
_____
_____
_____
_____
_____
_____
_____
_____
_____
_____
_____
_____

relying on this technique to arouse her that he may delight in her flavor - (Songs 4:16).

4.1.14 **My beloved put his hand by the hole of the door, and my bowels were moved for him** - A coy way of describing touching and arousal and the way her husband's touch made her respond - (Songs 5:4).

4.1.15 **I would lead thee and bring thee into my mother's house who would instruct me, I would cause thee to drink of spiced wine of the juice of my pomegranate. His left hand should be under my head and his right hand shall embrace me** - A reference to the husband kissing her breast as they lay together (Songs 8:2-3).

4.1.16 **How beautiful you are and how pleasant, my love, with such delights! Your stature is like a palm tree; your breasts are clusters of fruit. I said, 'I will climb the palm tree and take hold of its fruit.' May your breasts be like clusters of grapes, and the fragrance of your breath like apricots** -A husband admiring his wife's body and bare breath. Speaking to her about making love to her and kissing her (Songs 7:4-8).

4.1.17 **I am come into my garden, my sister, my spouse: I have gathered my myrrh with my spice; I have eaten my honeycomb with my honey; I have drunk my wine with my milk: eat, O friends; drink, yea, drink abundantly, O beloved** - sounds like a breakfast basking in each other and enjoying food. The lovers express their delight in each other (Songs 5:1)

4.1.18 **I am my beloved's, and his desire is toward me. Come, my beloved, let us go forth into the field; let us lodge in the villages. Let us get up early to the vineyards; let us see if the vine flourish, whether the tender grape appear, and**

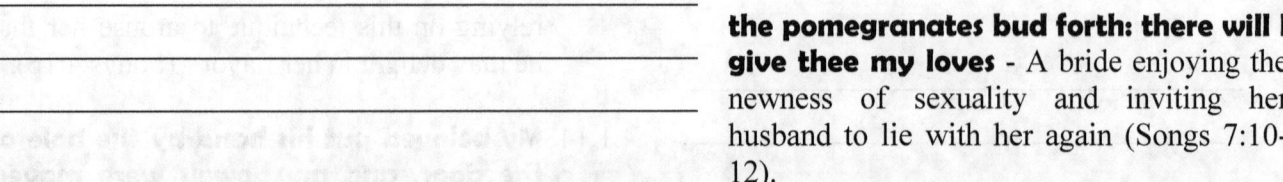
the pomegranates bud forth: there will I give thee my loves - A bride enjoying the newness of sexuality and inviting her husband to lie with her again (Songs 7:10-12).

Genesis 2:23-25 gives the first preview of the undefiled wedding bed. Wherein we see that, the man and the woman were naked and not ashamed. Adam and Eve did everything naked they had nothing to hide. Unlike today's society where we must cover ourselves, it was not until sin entered the world did Adam feel a need to cover himself. The bed did not defile Adam the converse is the case. Adam and Eve's sin gave them something to hide, the hid the evil in their hearts. In the instant Adam and Eve sinned, the flesh came to its fullest power, and they knew that what they thought and felt did not please God.

When Christ died for our sins, He re instituted the undefiled wedding bed. Now, no matter who we are, the fleshly appetites we share in a Godly marriage does not drive us away from God[28].

John 1:2-6 gives a spiritual application of God's Seeding principle. It explains what the purpose of bearing fruit is and shed light on the women's curse in Genesis. No matter what happens God made the plan within marriage to be fruitful. Without His input the species might have problems, more importantly, Jesus might have never come. The seeds required to bring about His lineage all were necessary to fulfil prophecy.

4.1.19 **EVERY BRANCH IN ME THAT BEARETH NOT FRUIT HE TAKETH AWAY** - Jesus accepts with pride the duty to share childbearing in this marriage. There are few things as intimate as parenting, and few things as difficult. Jesus understands that Godly marriages must bear fruit, and as the good wife, He obeys.

4.1.20 **EVERY [BRANCH] THAT BEARETH FRUIT, HE PURGETH IT THAT IT MAY BRING FORTH MORE FRUIT** - Here we see good parenting. The wife and the Husband agree upon both the direction and purpose of their children. The wife honorably submits her children to discipline and training to please God. This type of complete submission (one to another), results in generations of Godly children.

4.1.21 **NOW YE ARE CLEAN THROUGH THE WORD WHICH I HAVE SPOKEN UNTO YOU** - The Bible instructs us to sanctify and wash our wives by the water of the word. 5:26 is a clearer expression. What a wonderful husband, to wash his wife with loving kindness and feed her the Bread of life. What a wonderful husband that presents his wife without spot or blemish thorough love, kindness, and sacrifice. This would be more important in a culture where the pure virgin still held esteem. If men understood the benefits of purity, they would relish the task of keeping their prize pure.

4.1.22 **ABIDE IN ME, AND I IN YOU** - Again we see the bride allude to the importance of intimacy. Nothing makes marriage as strong a fulfilling as unity and intimacy. We cannot have intimacy without unity; they do not function well alone. Sex is _not_ intimacy, but it is a step in the right direction. Intimacy is a perpetual bond that continues without the presence of the persons. This is why the text likens the relationship with God to intimacy and _not_ sex, because it is perpetual closeness, without the interaction of the flesh.

4.1.23 **AS THE BRANCH CANNOT BEAR FRUIT OF ITSELF, EXCEPT IT ABIDE IN THE VINE; NO MORE CAN YE, EXCEPT YE ABIDE IN ME** - Without a suitable helper, Adam's life was *not good.* Here the good wife avails herself to her purpose and reminds her Husband that they cannot make children without Her. It appears that the strength in the woman does not emanate from withholding sexuality, but from the fullest expression of her sexuality.

4.1.24 **I AM THE VINE** - Just as Eve is the mother of all living things, all Living things spring from God[29]. Through God, life came back to the earth. He is the way, truth, and life, and like the virtuous woman, no one approaches, has dealings with or business with the Husband unless they first go through the bride. God so loved the world that He sired an only Son, which He gave to us via a mother. The purpose of marriage is to control the flesh--therefore God's Son had to be born of flesh, to be flesh, to control the flesh. Although Jesus' flesh drew strength from His Spirit, He conquered the flesh with His flesh.

4.1.25 **YE [ARE] THE BRANCHES: HE THAT ABIDETH IN ME, AND I IN HIM, THE SAME BRINGETH FORTH MUCH FRUIT: FOR WITHOUT ME YE CAN DO NOTHING** - Here the mother tells the children that the head of this body is the Father. She submits to Him with pride and honor for He tends to her garden completely; He is a good Husband. Then she wisely and confidently tells the children that the marriage union gives her power and authority over the children and all the Father makes. It is from this relationship that she provides for the children's needs: body and soul.

4.2 <u>The saddest honeymoon</u>

Jesus laid the mold. To accept the new life, He too became one flesh with His bride. As He lay in the tomb in virginal white robes with His bride, the two became one flesh[30]. After three days, Christ left the flesh and left His bride to stand before the Father. When He died, Christ presented His bride without spot and blemish. Like the good Husband, He love us, He does not hate His flesh but died to redeem it. What a sad honeymoon for Christ. Through His sadness, He ushered into our lives what the honeymoon brings to our flesh a sinless, righteous beginning from which to start a new lifestyle. Christ's honeymoon; the dark night in the bed with His bride, gave humans a new way to live in the flesh, without being under the power of the flesh.

4.3 The most mysterious of all marriage mysteries

A man once argued that it could not be Godly to marry just for sex. Why not? Was my response. If we are willing to go to hell for sex, it must be especially important[31]. I then explained that this passage is not a bidding to marry just because we want sex, it is a condemnation of immaturity. God; the good Father, knows that we cannot overcome the urges He gave us[32] so He provided a remedy. Marrying for love is a more mature approach, but to think love really conquers all is equally as immature. The fact of the matter is that sexuality plays a huge role in marriage, more so then in single life. An unsatisfied lover that is unmarried can simply replace their mate. However, in marriage there is no easy escape. Therefore, God instructs (reminds us) in Matthew to take whatever remedy is necessary to avoid sin and death. Sex as the reason for marriage sounds insane when stated from a biblical perspective, but is this not ironic since flesh/sex is the basis for most dating and the partial basis for marriage anyway? So, is there difference between marrying for sex and marrying not to burn?

Other marriage mysteries unfold pertaining to the actions of the flesh. From 1 Corinthians 6:18 we learn to that we should, "**Flee fornication. Every sin that a man doeth is without the body; but he that committeth fornication sinneth against his own body**. Later in Ephesians 5, we learn that, "…**no man ever hated his own flesh; but nourishes and cherishes it**." From Matthew 15:19 we find out that, "**OUT OF THE HEART PROCEED EVIL THOUGHTS, MURDERS, ADULTERIES, FORNICATIONS, THEFTS, FALSE WITNESS, BLASPHEMIES: THESE ARE [THE THINGS] WHICH DEFILE A MAN**…" Between these passages, we find another marriage mystery. We see that in God's way (marriage) the garbage that normally defiles us and makes us reprehensible unto Him He personally sanctifies through marriage.

Married Christians need not hate their flesh, nor defile their flesh by joining to a whore, nor leave their spouse to marry another this is a sign of self-hatred. In understanding that spouses are, sexual Band-Aids (patching up weakness in the flesh like lust etc.) we find that the truly given couple learns to give themselves completely to their spouse to keep them clean and present them without blemish. This means that the spouse that needs a lot of touching or sex should find in their mate an agreeable person who is always at the ready. Of course, we get sick and tired from the woes of life, but to give up the ability to bask in holy nakedness because we had a distressing day at work is folly. What else do we work for other than to enjoy what life has to offer, are not the gifts God gives the best life has to offer. Amazingly enough, humans think about sex all day according to researchers, we spend billions on porn and sex toys, yet one of the most common complaints in marriage is sexual dissatisfaction and infrequency. We know sex has not changed or cannot be deficient, so the problem must lie within us.

The spouse that withholds them self either sensually or sexually (physically) does not understand their ability and responsibility to keep their mate pure. In failure, we also do not love our mates as the woman in Songs loved Solomon with her soul. If we want our mates to be pleased physically then we need to put in the time with them, so they will never have to feel unloved or alone. Let the honeymoon never end, and there will be far less reason to divorce and far less time to argue.

When we find ourselves dissatisfied in our sex lives practice, practice, practice, it will work itself out. If we do not find that happy place with our spouses, then we should rethink what we need to be happy. No other human has different sexual apparatus; therefore, our dissatisfaction does not stem from the sex in our sex life, and it stems from some other aspect in our life or dissatisfaction with our spouse. Do not cheat, it will not work there either, working together with our spouses and with God to find out where the problem is in our happiness, and apply the marriage patch God said He made suitable for us.

A man once asked my counsel as he prepared to remarry. He asked did I think the new marriage would work, I said no. When asked why I responded, that the last marriage ended because he was stupid. Considering the fact that he was still stupid, how could the result have a better outcome? See, the outcome of a marriage is dependent on what we put into it. If we pour garbage into a marriage the only things we can pass out into the drought is the garbage we produce from the garbage we input. Therefore, we MUST change; sustained exposure to garbage promotes the growth of bacteria. As we learned from the idle Ages not until we get rid of the trash and live clean lives does disease and sickness finally leave the place we dwell. Most of the things that defile our marriages, like the things that defile our lives, come from within. Believers, when we clean up our lives we will clean up our marriages.

4.4 **The Shulamite mystery**

With this new understanding, we learn that some of the mysteries in the kingdom are not mysterious principles they are mysterious in application. In this, in this application of wisdom we see that, Deuteronomy 6:5[33]," is not legalism, but instead God's will applied. Where we failed is that we believed that Deuteronomy 6:5 is just another principle and never learned how to bring it to life.

Under the Law of Spiritual Reciprocity[34], we find that we can do the same going from spiritual to flesh as we can when going from flesh to spiritual. In other words, if a woman can love hard enough to transcend the bonds of the flesh, then we can learn to love God enough to allow our spirits to rule and feed our flesh. The Shulamite loved Solomon with her soul. This is by far the easiest part of our faith. The hard part is our understanding of what *lady* exemplifies. We must learn to take the same pleasure we find in fleshly companionship and apply that fervor to things of the spirit. Those of us who find life without sex an unpleasant prospect, in time should learn to feel the same way towards a life without Christ. Our pleasure is our meat, and Christ says to do the will of God is His meat. In Christ, we find the way to God through the flesh is in its renewing. Once we learn even to use sex to please God the rest falls into place. If we focused our marital energy towards pleasing God in our actions, we would find more joy in our marriages.

5.0
Marriage Needs Fortification

By night on my bed I sought him whom my soul loveth: I sought him, but I found him not. I will rise now, and go about the city in the streets, and in the broad ways I will seek him whom my soul loveth: I sought him, but I found him not. The watchmen that go about the city found me: to whom I said, Saw ye him whom my soul loveth? - (Songs 3:1-3)

5.1 Marriage fortifying concepts

As we look at biblical marriage/mystery models we unravel a mystery often missed--which is the mystery of why God ordained marriage. Understand as we study, all God's purposes glorify Him. Anything we believe exists to give us honor or glory is not of God. A pilot may fly a plane; or even the space shuttle but it is not his plane. The pilot of a crop duster we call a pilot just like the pilot of a fighter jet. The pastor of the largest church in the world is just a pastor; it is the God he serves that deserves the glory and honor. In the same manner, marriage helps us, but it serves God's purpose. Marriage is a vehicle used to get believers to righteousness though we still live in wretched flesh. We may enjoy the wife of our youth but the One Who gave us the reward still controls all.

In the following two scriptures, we find the marriage-fortifying concept that surmounts all other methods.

"Therefore shall a man leave his father and his mother and shall cleave unto his wife: and they shall be one flesh - (Genesis 2:24).

"I AND [MY] FATHER ARE ONE - (John 10:30).

In part, we must do whatsoever enables us to become one flesh and one spirit. Although the flesh and the spirit can never reconcile, the two can submit equally to the will of God. This is what God meant referring to Job when He said Job was righteous in all his ways.

In order to fortify marriage, it must have the requisite nutrients and nurturing. Since marriage is a delicate balance of body and soul both must have care. We see above that the spirit in a fortified relationship speaks of unity. We see that in a fortified marriage that the flesh also eventually becomes one.

Marriage ideally allows the body and soul to grow and learn simultaneously. In Wado-ryu karate, we learn both the left side and the right side of the body simultaneously. What this enables us to do in karate is maintain a balanced defense. If we earned a black belt on the right but held a yellow belt on the left, all the enemy would have to do to win is stay on our yellow side. Learning both simultaneously takes a little longer, but balance always does take longer.

Achieving the delicate balance requires years of practice and development. To see this model in perfection we go to Jesus. To see this model in practice we visit Songs.

"Jesus saith unto them, MY MEAT IS TO DO THE WILL OF HIM THAT SENT ME, AND TO FINISH HIS WORK - (John 4:34).

The watchmen that go about the city found me: [to whom I said], Saw ye him whom my soul **Loveth** - (Songs 3:3).

From Jesus we see that the flesh can take joy from spiritual control--this we call righteousness. We learn from the Shulamite woman that flesh can learn to make the things the soul loves a priority. This was always God's plan, since we live in the flesh. Through righteousness flesh attains spirituality, and through righteousness spiritually gains legs. Through marriage, God's will in the earth realm takes root and grows. Through marriage, an army of satisfied, righteous flesh develops to fight against the wiles of Satan's kingdom.

5.2 Satan's attack on marriage

As simple and stupid as it may sound, Satan attacks marriage because he understands spiritual potential. From the womb of one woman came forth a Son who destroyed Satan's power. Marriage in modern day poses two threats to Satan's plan. One threat is that from the model of marriage, men learn to better steward God's church. In addition, the permanent attack on marriage is an attack on righteousness. To understand why Satan attacks marriage, we look at six purposes of marriage.

5.3 How Satan wages spiritual war against marriage?

Here in I Corinthians 6:18 lies the most common method with which Satan attacks marriage, and the reason we must defend marriage. The Bible warns Christians about the danger of fornication, **"Flee fornication. Every sin that a man doeth is without the body; but he that committeth fornication sinneth against his own body."** Based on the 10 commandments, sexuality accounts for at approx. 30% of sin; it only makes sense that there would be a Godly solution. Marriage consequently, is a more important as a battleground than we realize. Not only does marriage potentially curtail 30% of our sin, marriage supports righteousness in the earth realm.

The reasons Christians are poor spiritual warriors, is because we fight the war as individuals. Nazi Germany learned that there is no way fight the entire world without allies. God gives each man: each warrior, an ally, and soft pillow. Ministers of the gospel often forget that marriage is part of the good news. Ecclesiastes 9:9 reminds us to enjoy the wives of our youth; they are our reward here on earth. Do not regard the woman as the weaker vessel when it comes to war, woman are our Balaam's mules. Wives carry husbands even as we abuse and underappreciated them. Wives lovingly bear us up to avoid the avenging sword of God.

God designed women to under-gird men in areas and places were men are weak, hurt, and frightened. The man with no wife finds the spiritual warfare impossible without the gift of singleness. The man with a wife finds a safe place to be weak yet be strong. Alone in the wilderness is not the place to fear, cry, or rest, which is why we have wives so that they journey through the wilderness does not give rise to sin and despair.

Unlike the members of the United Nations who use threat of nuclear war to keep peace, Satan wages conventional spiritual warfare. Satan uses the oldest, most lethal, and most potent weapon in the earth against God: human flesh. The reason flesh works well as a weapon is that flesh is self-serving and greedy. By Biblical standards[35] greedy and self-serving equates to evil. Satan therefore has no reason to update his arsenal he has the two things God detests in his favor, our flesh, and our imaginations.

God's commandments act to guide us and keep us from darkness. God's commandments exist to keep us focused. The *world* is as seductive as a woman is, but like Lucifer the beautiful, the world is evil. Satan's favorite fleshly attacks on marriage come in one of the following forms of adulteries and whoredoms.

1. Sexual adultery defined as fornication, whoredom, and homosexuality[36].
2. Spiritual adultery defined as idolatry, covetousness, and apostasy.[37]
3. *Adultery* defined by lust and or covetousness[38].

Men are visually stimulated, like King Herrod, we are vulnerable to the lust of our eyes. Proverbs 6:23-29 tells us a few useful things about adultery, "**For the commandment is a lamp; and the law is light; and reproofs of instruction are the way of life. To keep thee from the evil woman, from the flattery of the tongue of a strange woman. Lust not after her beauty in thine heart; neither let her take thee with her eyelids. For by means of a whorish woman a man is brought to a piece of bread: and the adulteress will hunt for the precious life. Can a man take fire in his bosom and his clothes not be burned? Can one go upon hot coals, and his feet not be burned? So, he that goeth in to his neighbor's wife; whosoever toucheth her shall not be innocent**." Because of the weakness of men, the Bible tells us that men fall prey to adultery. The Bible however, does not simply warn us about adultery it tells us that a whore[39] (male or female) ruins lives. The whore destroys because it is in their nature to have all, be all, and leave no one happy for they are not happy. The adulterer is selfish and destructive catering to their debase desires. The whore always looks for the precious life to feed off and eventually destroy.

We also look at Proverbs 7:11-27 as a further study of Satan's most common type of attack against marriage.

5.3.3.1. "**She is loud and stubborn; her feet abide not in her house**." Working spouses spend lots of time outside of the home trying to make ends meet. Although this does not necessitate adultery, it is necessary to separate the union in order to move on the vulnerable or greedy spouse.

5.3.3.2 "**Now is she without, now in the streets, and lieth in wait at every corner**." The whore's seductiveness is availability and willingness. It is difficult to walk past clearance signs and not look in the window, even if we do not need the product. However, what if we need a product from Home Depot to fix an air conditioning advertised at an 85% discount, or free would we not get it from them? Who among us would drive past the free products, we needed too and go to Wal-Mart to pay full price? The unhappy spouse has difficulty maintaining a home even with the needed tools. Without the tools at home, having to drive past free tools gets more difficult every day.

5.3.3.3 "**So, she caught him, and kissed him, and with an impudent face said unto him. I have peace offerings with me; this day have I payed my vows**." Impudence represents brashness and brazenness. For the whore to approach the married person knowing their condition in life shows a lack of regard for the marriage institution as well as the person themselves. A person that does not respect our marriage does not respect us. The whore offers gifts of flesh as a peace offering. The whore feels that they have paid their dues and are now above or at least beyond reproach. This is a common approach to make adultery desirable. Satan reminds the unhappy spouse that they have put in the time and have earned a respite.

5.3.3.4 "**Therefore, came I forth to meet thee, diligently to seek thy face, and I have found thee**. **I have decked my bed with coverings of tapestry, with carved works, with fine linen of Egypt. I have perfumed my bed with myrrh, aloes, and cinnamon. "Come; let us take our fill of love until the morning: let us solace ourselves with loves**." The whore has no shame, guilt, or fear because whores often have no obligations, and they do not take marriage seriously. Adultery often seems more pleasing and gratifying than the lack luster marriage because whores adorn themselves with whatever trappings necessary to seduce and appeal. A popular approach is *comfort;* the whore offers their services to ease woes and sorrows. The comfort trap is death for many. In the cradle of pleasure, where comfort and fragrance abound, death abounds! From the undefiled marriage bed, life is the result of lovemaking but here in the folded sheets of adultery death and accursedness are the offspring.

5.3.3.5 "**For the good man is not at home, he is gone a long journey. He hath taken a bag of money with him and will come home at the day appointed**. Verses 19-20 speak of the good man they say nothing of happiness. A good spouse should be trusted to come and go without incident. However, in the dark recesses of the human heart loneliness and unhappiness find fertile soil to plant seeds[40].

5.3.3.6 "**With her much fair speech she caused him to yield, with the flattering of her lips she forced him. He goeth after her straightway, as an ox goeth to the slaughter or as a fool to the correction of the stocks. Till a dart strike through his liver; as a bird hasteth to the snare, and knoweth not that it is for his life**." For many weak, foundation-less marriages, the ease of adultery is too much to defeat. Promises of happiness, fulfillment, and platitudes flow from the whore's mouth into the waiting heart of the unhappy. Eve decided that what Satan promised pleased her eyes. Like adultery, the temptation is always something we already want, nothing new enters the picture. No one cheats that does not want to, even if they do not really like the person, they want the promises. Adultery thrives where lust, sloth, and poor commitments exist.

5.3.3.7 "**Hearken unto me now therefore, O ye children, and attend to the words of my mouth. Let not thine heart decline to her ways; go not astray in her paths. For she hath cast down many wounded: yea, many strong men have been slain by her.**" This warning is set out for the weak and unsettled. The unsung victims of adultery are the next generation. Many blame God and Satan for multi-generational curses but this is far from the truth. The reason so many children seem to be accursed is that they are accursed according to Hosea 2:4[41]. When we set our flesh against itself, there can be no peace. God hates adultery because it allows our flesh to disobey His will. God also hates adultery because flesh is the proverbial genie in the bottle. Once we unleash the new happiness in our flesh, we must maintain the new happiness or return to sadness. How do we maintain the new happiness without the whore? What happens to the children while we play? They learn to let their flesh control their lives. The children become irreverent and disrespectful to their parents and to God. Sadly, Christian parents find themselves saying to their children, *I do not know where you got that from?"* They got it from the same place Cain got it from, his parents. The word warns us that we must not let our hearts decline to the dark paths of the whore, they destroy our families leaving behind broken virtue, broken dreams, and broken hearts.

5.3.3.8 **Her house is the way to hell, going down to the chambers of death**. Marriages result in offspring in the flesh, and they result in offspring in the spiritual realm. All adulterous relationships with the bride of Christ (church) and the world produce cursed offspring. Take heed and stop sharing our beds and hearts with whores, they do not love us, or themselves. The way of the whore leads to death, not just the death of the soul but the death of the family, the death of our church, and the death of the flesh.

5.3.3.9 The one thing sexual immorality loves is a place to express itself. Amazingly enough, many of the world's leading pornographers, sex symbols, and sexologists were homosexuals. The reason they encourage porn and free sex is to create an innocuous gateway for homosexuality to flow. They were so successful that lesbianism masquerading as bisexuality is a fantasy of 90% of men. This type of perversion has not only become acceptable this type of perversion becomes desirable.

5.3.3.10 The homosexual agenda against marriage is another brilliant attack by Satan. This attack is not actually against marriage. As with all of Satan's plans, the attack is against God. The reason homosexuality is not articulated in the 10 commandments is because it is covered by adultery[42]. The underlying reason homosexuals want to marry is not love or benefits, the real issue is simple. The Bible says in Hebrews that the marriage bed is undefiled. Marriage is the only institution in the earth realm that holds homosexuality in check. Therefore, if the homosexual concept legalizes, in their foolish minds this will stop homosexuality from being a sin and no longer wax great in the sight of God[43].

5.4 **Same-sex marriage**

We gloss over this topic because despite its pretense in society, even Jesus does not deal with this topic. Jesus does not speak on this topic because He has; any sex out of marriage is a sin. Therefore, either we are married (one man and one woman), or going to hell, God made it easy. The LGBT community confused the issues with their lies, chief among them that they can marry. They can marry, but God does not acknowledge man's foolishness.

Genesis 1:11 lays the plan out for all time, **"And God said, Let the earth bring forth grass, the herb yielding seed, *and* the fruit tree yielding fruit after his kind, whose seed *is* in itself, upon the earth: and it was so."**

5.4.1   God said - makes this law. Like creation itself, where He spoke, nature has not changed since then, nor has this law.

5.4.2   The fruit trees - we are His trees and the fruits we are to reproduce produce ONLY FRUITS AFTER THEIR OWN KIND.

5.4.3   The seed is in itself - humans only reproduce humans of like kind. Therefore, no human can produce anything other than a male of female child of normal characteristic and ability. We no more make aqua men than we can make human that function properly in the homosexual format. They cannot yield anything.

LGBTs cannot have it both ways, why lie about your orientation yet stick to gender functions. In other words, why is there a husband (masculine, dominant) and wife (recessive, submissive, feminine) even in their relationships? Why is there transvestism, and transgender except for a bastardization of God's template? The desire to do the wrong thing is not unique to homosexuals, they smiley have no shame, most creatures; even Adam and Eve hid the transgression from the God of Creation, not out of fear of punishment, but because Adam knew he was wrong and he was ashamed.

In this foolishness LGBTs believe if they feign marriage God will overlook their sin (Romans 1:22-23). This foolishness is the sheer definition of sin that leads unto death, for they know there is a bell that tolls, just as they know genitalia has a function which they reject (Romans 1:26). The stain in same sex marriage is actually not the sex; it is the reprobate mind. There is no amount of sex that bans us from heaven, for that there is forgiveness. However, from the reprobate mind, there is no convict and therefore no repentance, for God has cut them off.

So much of the LGBT lifestyle is a lie. Perhaps one of their greatest chinks in their armor if their lie about love. In order to remove the stigma from what they do sexually they pro port to be all about love. There are three major flaws in this theory found in scripture

    5.4.4 God is love (1 John 4:8) - **"Whoever does not love does not know God**..." We cannot love and hate someone at the same time, the two feelings cannot coexist (Romans 1:30). Be fruitful and multiply a Godly seed (Genesis 1:29), this is commandment which the LGBT cannot comply with thereby also violating John 8:44.

    5.4.5 Love is not puffed up (1 Corinthians 13:4,5) - The concept of 'Out Loud' and 'Gay Pride' fly in the face of this basic concept.

    5.4.6 Love doth not behave itself unseemly (1 Corinthians 13:4, 5) – Laying with men, forcing governments and business to conform to their will, these are examples of unseemly behavior.

6.0
Week I - Work Area
Spiritual Warfare & Marriage

6.1 What does undefiled mean?

_____
_____
_____
_____
_____

6.2 How can a union of flesh be undefiled?

_____
_____
_____
_____
_____
_____
_____

6.3 Can *life partners* have an undefiled bed?

_____
_____
_____
_____
_____

6.4 If we could change only one thing in our marriage, what would that be and why?

_____
_____
_____
_____

6.5 What things in your marriage bring the greatest pleasure?

_____
_____
_____
_____
_____

6.7 What do you feel is your greatest accomplishment in your marriage?

_____
_____
_____
_____
_____
_____

6.8 How does marriage control the flesh?

_____
_____
_____
_____
_____
_____

6.9 How does spiritual warfare affect marriage?

_____
_____
_____
_____
_____
_____

6.10 Why does flesh express itself best through sexuality?

6.11 Why is it important to be careful what you say to your spouse?

6.12 How does marital Loneliness parallel spiritual isolation?

Week II
Fortifying Marriage

7.0 - Building a marriage into a fortress
8.0 - Marriage and the spiritual warrior
9.0 - Fight right
10.0 - Establishing spiritual warriors through marriage
11.0 - Marriage and the use of Moats
12.0 - Week 2 - Work Area

7.0
Building a Marriage into a Fortress

"Thy neck [is] like the tower of David builded for an Armory, whereon there hang a thousand bucklers, all shields of mighty men. Thy two breasts [are] like two young roes that are twins, which feed among the lilies. Until the daybreak, and the shadows flee away, I will get me to the mountain of myrrh, and to the hill of frankincense - Songs 4:4-5."

The purpose of building forts and fortresses is safety. The purpose of marriage is safety and discipline. Marriage is the next phase in fortress building. Marriage is the spiritual fortress God designed as a forge, the workshop from which righteousness flows. Marriage is an expression of discipline and love. Believers; love is the ultimate discipline; therefore, God favors love because He is a God of love and order.

God's people are lazy, we do not like to read, learn, or love. As it was in the wilderness, we constantly complain against Christ and other men of God. When God does speak to us, we hide and refuse to take part. This cowardice reflects in our spousal relationships. A spouse that hides their true self cannot love their spouse or themselves according to God. Moreover, if our real self is dark enough to remain hidden, then by default God knows we do not love Him or our family because we refuse to change. The best way not to have to hide is to get rid of those things that thrive in the darkness. 'Operating in an atmosphere of love and forgiveness when handled properly promotes grow and happiness. Therefore, we draw strength from submitting to our spouse. Unfortunately, under the *Doctrine of Grace* many people abuse loving kindness at home and in the church.

_____
_____
_____
_____
_____
_____
_____
_____
_____

7.1 The blessed commandment

There are few fleshly things believers can offer God that are pleasing. There are only two things we can do with our flesh to please God;

    3.5.7   Purify out hearts thereby rendering righteous our flesh
    3.5.8   Produce Godly seeds in marriage

As a personal method to accomplish, His will in the earth God gave each human two drives specific to His purpose. Because churches do not teach spiritual literacy people mistakenly, believe pain in childbirth to be a curse, despite the verbiage in the passage. If we however look closely at the intricacies in the Garden judgment sequence, we notice that God was deliberate when He made sexual desire overwhelming. As a part of His plan, He made burning sexual desires, specifically for marriage.

We therefore find another marriage mystery hidden in the Garden of Eden. We see that God made celibacy undesirable for His people. In doing so, He ensured Godly seeds through marriage. To this end God made four things which are never satisfied, "**There are three things that are never satisfied, yea four things say not, 'It *is* enough': The grave: and the barren womb: the earth *that* is not filled with water; and the fire saith not *It is enough*** - Proverbs 30:15-16." It must be unbearably displeasing to be unable to produce children, but that is not why the womb moans. The empty womb moans just as the grave moans. As one empty chamber God meant for life and the other death, they both have to feed their purpose to survive and thrive. The grave longs for souls. Because of sin, the grave stays well stocked. As in all things fleshly, we misinterpret the gifts of God. The desire to reproduce serves God, as does everything He made. When we crave children, we see into the heart of God.

Love = God. Love one another therefore means to act like God. To love is to be like God. If we are His kids, then He should see Himself in us. As He once gave a Son, He understands what is to see the future in the lives of our children. When we look at our children and see their innocence and potential, we see what God sees in us[44].

7.2 **The fruitful marriage**

Psalm 8:2 - Children are a heritage From the Lord, offspring a reward from him.

Psalm 115:14 - Like arrows in the hands of a warrior are children born in one's youth.

Children are a blessing from God. To not have children or to be barren was once considered a curse. Puberty marks the maturation of a woman into fertility. Puberty starts around age 11 and menopause ends around age 55. The math looks like (#12 months) x (#2 eggs) x (#44 years). Considering a woman produces on average #1056 eggs with a single purpose of fertilization. It begs the questions, what are they for, we cannot scramble them and lesbians cannot fertilize them? If the spilling of seed (wasting) which differs from pouring it out displeases God, why would we assume that wasting eggs does not. This forum does not deal with birth control, because that is not the issue. A couple that has too many children to feed does not please God, therefore He organized the menstrual cycle to allow married couples to stay on the honeymoon and not produce. IT IS A LIE FROM HELL TO SAY THAT GOD ONLY MADE SEX FOR PROCREATION. We find ample bible verses that speak of recreational sex; but God gave these rewards to married people, to balance their spiritual life.

How does sex balance our spiritual life? It helps to control the flesh, so we can be spiritual. Nothing is fun when we are horny. When married, we get to go home and spend as much flesh time with our own spouses as we can so that we can function in society without lusting and fornicating.

Alas, the planting of the seed, in due time (the right season), produces a tree of like character. God's people produce Godly seed. Though flawed, the apple tree bears the fruit God honors. The flawed apple, ugly and spotted, has many uses as food and organic compounds. Apple have another use, far more important than food, they have in them seeds; of like kind. Satan fears these seeds; the seeds of Godly marriages. "Apple seeds contain a plant compound known as *amygdalin*. It is harmless when intact, but when the seeds are damaged, chewed, or digested, *amygdalin* degrades into hydrogen cyanide. This is very poisonous and even lethal in high doses (4, 5). Cyanide has been used as a poison throughout history[45]." Remember, Satan fears the Godly seed because it is poison to him. The Godly seed has enmity for him always. One such seed, had he understood he never would have crucified. Moreover, of this Seed scripture says, other seeds will come after Him that will do greater things than He did. We need to have kids, Godly kids because they are poison to Satan and his kingdom. Why does the LGBT community not want to have kids normally; because they do not want to produce Godly seeds[46].

LGBT kids are seeds of hatred, they are designed by Satan's prideful ones to be poison to God's kingdom; a plan he stole from God's kingdom.

7.3 **Six purposes of marriage**

7.3.1 **Companionship** (Amos 3:3) - God did not ordain for His people to be alone in the spirit or the flesh. Just as God made a suitable mate for our Spirit He gave suitable mate for our flesh.

7.3.2 **Enjoyment** (Hebrews 13:4) - What greater joy is there than to be able to revel in the flesh with our spouses without consequences.

7.3.3 **Completeness** (Genesis 2:23) - Whatever God needed to make the woman, He ordained for the return of same thing (flesh) to complete the man. When the two become one flesh, they both finally become whole.

7.3.4 Fruitfulness (Genesis 1:28, 9:1: 1, Peter 3:7) - A Godly seed produces Godly fruit.

7.3.5 Protection (Ephesians 5:25; Titus 2:4-5; Malachi 2:15; Psalms 112:1-2) - A good wife guards the spirit and flesh against a multitude of problems we encounter in this life.

7.3.6 Exemplify Christ and the Church (Ephesians 5:31-33) - The parallel between the church and marriage is a great mystery. When people see a blessed marriage, they see the fruit of God's work in both the spirit and the flesh.

To abate an absurd argument, we use the term righteous to imply God's will and unrighteous the opposite. Satan's attack on marriage is not an attack on morality it is an attack on righteousness. The two concepts are cousins not identical twins. Righteous is God's design and morality man's design. The righteousness of God is absolute. Morality finds it roots in righteousness, but morality is not absolute. Satan knows the weaknesses of the flesh and the power of the flesh. Satan attacks marriage because he knows that men who cannot obey the laws of men have no chance of obeying the law of God.

Satan also fears the potential of the united/righteous church. God's bride in the earth realm bears children. One child gave Satan power; the other child took it all away. Jesus foretold that many (children) would come after Him that would do even greater things. Satan fears the offspring the church has the potential to bear--he cannot stand another Jesus.

8.0
Marriage and the Spiritual Warrior

"Behold, I have graven thee upon the palms of [my] hands; thy walls [are] continually before me. Thy children shall make haste; thy destroyers and they that made thee waste shall go forth of thee. Lift up thine eyes round about, and behold: all these gather themselves together, [and] come to thee. '[AS] I LIVE, saith the Lord, THOU SHALT SURELY CLOTHE THEE WITH THEM ALL, AS WITH AN ORNAMENT, AND BIND THEM [ON THEE], AS A BRIDE [DOETH]' - (Isaiah 49:16-18)."

8.1 The discipline of marriage

"Wives, be subject to our own husbands, as to the Lord. For the husband is the head of the wife, and Christ also is the head of the church, being Himself the Savior of the body. But as the church is subject to Christ, so let the wives also be to their own husbands in everything. Husbands, love our wives, even as Christ also loved the church, and gave Himself up for it; that He might sanctify it, having cleansed it by the washing of water with the word, that He might present the church to Himself gloriously, not having spot or wrinkle or any such thing; but that it should be holy and without blemish. Even so husbands also ought to love their own wives as their own bodies. He who loves his own wife loves himself. For no man ever hated his own flesh; but nourishes and cherishes it, even as the Lord also does the church; because we are members of His body, of his flesh and bones. "For this cause a man will leave his father and mother, and will be joined to his wife. The two will become one flesh. This mystery is great, but I speak concerning Christ and of the church. Nevertheless, each of you must also love his own wife even as himself; and let the wife see that she respects her husband - (Ephesians 5:22-33).

Like everything in God's Kingdom, success relies on discipline. Marriage like every other discipline has rules, requirements, and parameters. Ironically, we again look for marital advice to the man who said that marriage was a burden. I think however, we should examine the context in which Paul made the comment. It is important for us to realize that this is Paul's opinion, not the word or will of God[47]. Paul, *by way of advice* explains to ministers the ramifications of spreading the gospel. "**But I would have you without carefulness. He that is unmarried careth for the things that belong to the Lord, how he may please the Lord: But he that is married careth for the things that are of the world, how he may please [his] wife. There is difference [also] between a wife and a virgin. The unmarried woman careth for the things of the Lord, that she may be holy both in body and in spirit: but she that is married careth for the things of the world, how she may please [her] husband** - (1 Corinthians 7:32-34). It is difficult to find the necessary time to serve the Lord fully. The cost, the bitter cup of sacrifice, takes its toll on every Christian. The added strain of marriage makes the task almost impossible. It is to the requirements of the relationship with God that Paul implies can be devastated by marriage.

8.2 A list of marital traits

8.2.1 **Need** - Like every living thing, marriage has needs.

8.2.2 **Drive** - Because marriage has purpose, it also has drive. Through drive, marriage achieves purpose.

8.2.3 **Discipline** - In order for a marriage to remain equally yoked, both spouses must employ discipline.

8.2.4 **Heart** - Marriage has heart, vows illustrate this fact. It takes determination to last a lifetime.

8.2.5 **Temperance** - In tolerance, we find companionship.

8.2.6 **Patience** - In our patient love towards each other, we find joy.

8.2.7 **Subjection to the Lord and our spouses** - Spouses must submit to God, and the marriage or neither relationship flourishes.

8.2.8 **Life** - Marriage is a new life, it needs room to override the old ways.

8.2.9 **Sanctification** - God commands sanctification, I recommend sanctification, for it makes a purer heart and a cleaner marriage.

8.2.10 **Love** - Sadly, we do not understand that a marriage needs love because a marriage needs God and God is love.

8.2.11 **Sacrifice** - Love promotes sacrifice for it is through sacrifice that we attain the greater **good**.

8.2.12 **Narcissism** - We cannot love another if we do not love ourselves. Christ tells us that loving ourselves is prerequisite to loving others.

8.2.13 **Unity** - The only purpose of marriage is unity, without unity there is no marriage.

8.2.14 **Forgiveness** - How can we refuse to forgive one we claim to love? Forgiveness is the gateway to Godly love.

8.2.15 **Maturity** - Marriage is a difficult, time-consuming journey it is not a joy ride.

8.2.16 **Revelation** - Stale food is of little nutritional value. Daily revelation keeps the spirit in and of marriage in charge of the flesh.

8.2.17 **Reverence** - Revere the marriage as a thing of God, cherish, and guard it as such.

8.3 <u>The mind, marriage, and spiritual warfare</u>

Many of the traits of the warrior make marriage untenable. The warrior feels, hurts, and cries deeply, and they mourn constantly. There is little joy in the heart of a warrior. There is little joy in the life of a warrior. The life of a warrior requires discipline. This same discipline requires walking away from the things that make marriage great. The joys of life, which are a distraction to the warrior, are the little things that make marriage a wondrous journey. A warrior does 90% of their living in their minds, this leaves little room for a spouse and children; but the concession <u>must</u> occur, or the marriage is doomed. Many ministers do not realize that God considers their family a priority. How we treat our family directly reflects how we treat His family.

8.3.1 **The married warrior hates in the mind** - Hatred in most people is an emotion. Hatred implies emotional involvement. Logical disdain does not function well within the wall of a marriage because it offers no solution. Much marital tumult results from the spiritual warrior's mental construct. Spouses often feel the need to push the warrior until they make some type of emotional outburst. This is a ridiculous policy especially since synonyms for outbursts include eruption, explosion, and flare-up. By design, all these sudden occurrences cause emotionality. Then our spouses claim they cannot understand why we explode on them or result to violence. To this folly Proverbs asks, "**Can a man take fire in his bosom, and his clothes not be burned**?"

8.3.2 The married warrior loves in the mind - Love needs more attention than the warrior allows. The warrior loves and makes love in their mind and can immerse in whatever part of the love they desire. This method assures safety for the warrior and a delicate balance in which a warrior lives does not leave room for puerile change. All these traits negate romance, intimacy, and passion--without which a married couple becomes roommates. We cannot love our spouses in our minds. God made the she-creature of soft flesh, soft needs, and soft giving, but WIVES MUST BE TOUCHED. Paul did not mention that the natural opposite of the Gospel of the Eunuchs[48] is marriage.

    8.3.2.1 We cannot love God in our minds. Like a woman, God too must be felt and held; slowly, tenderly, and close to us. Only in intimacy does love flourish, it needs closeness to bind and bond.

8.3.3 The married warrior forgives in the mind - Forgiveness to a warrior simply maintains fluidity of movement. Spouses need frequent, complete, and often repetitive forgiveness. The logical type of forgiveness does not work in marriage because marriage is an emotional bond. Unemotional resolutions and interactions do not work well with the softer half of the couple.

8.3.4 The married warrior fights in the mind - The married warrior wages warfare in the mind. For most wives this is annoying because women crave verbal communication. Countless days and evenings spent running scenarios, schemes, attacks, and defenses bore most spouses because this seems to be time wasted. Constant strategizing forces the married warrior to stay sober, sharp, adept, and consequently aloof. The silent treatment and denying physical attention does not work on the married warrior. The married warrior practices self-denial so there is no added strain caused by the spouse cutting the other person off from physical pleasure. However, the irritated spouse becomes problematic because they feel ignored. The mind's eye prepares the warrior to war under any situation; this sometimes means that war is often indiscriminate. An overly aggressive spouse often meets the insurmountable spirit of the warrior; the resulting civil war is often unrecoverable. Many Christian marriages fail due to this conflict - the inability of two spirits and two hearts to become one. The reason God made the woman from the man's ribs is so the piece (she) can fit perfectly when replaced (married).

8.3.5 The married warrior loses in the mind - Although the warrior is fully prepared to fight to the death, this type of preparedness does not create peace in a marriage. There is a distinct difference between defeat and surrender; however, the operative word in marriage is *comprise*. For the warrior, comprise equates to *acceptable loss*. Therefore, the married warrior can form the issue though unresolved abates. The warrior's training enables them to overlook marital strife, but they have difficulty placating their spouse, because they seem indifferent. For the disgruntle spouse, indifference produces anger, resentment, and hostility. The warrior can handle each disdain in turn with little to no effort, but the true battle for the warrior is to engage their spouse emotionally--yet keep their sphere of self-control.

8.3.6 **The married warrior kills in the mind** - Efficiency hardens the necessary parts of the warrior's psyche, which make marriage pleasant and functional. Normal people are born with an innate desire to share life, not so for the married warrior. Sharing to the warrior is uncomfortable and requires subtly and gentleness from their spouse. The warrior, although honed, knows their weaknesses and this is what they withhold from their spouses. Unfortunately, the good things the spouse desires end up in same files as the undesirable traits. Consequently, when the warrior exposes the self we invariably get the good, the bad, and the ugly escape.

8.3.7 **The married warrior dies in the mind** - Marriage takes planning. Warriors plan for death that they may better learn how to avoid this end. This is not fear, but their lack of concern for the prompt demise concerns the spouse. It must be challenging to live with someone who does not mind death and would welcome it under the right circumstances. The average spouse would feel overshadowed and intimidated by the fact that their life partner does not relish life. The invariable conclusion is that their partner does not relish life with them. Who finds happiness in a life spent in the valley of the shadow of death? The warrior does not dislike their spouse; they just did not plan for marriage in their first training, now the change is difficult; albeit not impossible.

_____

_____

_____

_____

8.4 **The warrior's heart in marriage**

We previously discussed the warrior heart; now let us look at how marriage affects that heart.

8.5.1 **The warrior hurts in the heart** - Years of warrior training dulls the normal pleasures of an emotional life. The joys of life are only important of they are recognizable. The warrior does not understand most of the emotional eventualities of life because they do not spend time considering them. Despite the veneer of confidence, and contentment, the warrior's heart holds darkness, loneliness, and fear. Pain in the warrior grows exponentially because the warrior does not develop normal channels for emotional control.

8.5.2 **The warrior cries in the heart** - Many warriors cry about what they create in their hearts and eventually become. The spouse does not understand that their cold spouse feels a level of compassion they will never understand. In a life designed and spent in service there is little room for selfish love. This paradigm places the warrior in a tailspin because, a spouse, kids, and a family need a selfish type of love. When a spouse wants to love they do not want the compassionate, service type of love, they want us to want ONLY THEM. It is possible: but for warriors it is a long arduous journey of hues.

8.5.3 **The warrior needs in the heart** - Despite years of discipline and denial the warrior has needs; ironically, safety is one of them. Prior to marriage, many warriors indulge in frivolous relationships. The superficial relationship offers safety and obscurity. The warrior does not worry about their true find emerging; they have no intention on growing close to the person. The problem with this course of action is that this facade cannot continue in a successful marriage.

8.5.4 **The warrior fears in the heart** - Once the warrior morphs into a weapon, the concept of relinquishing control is horrific. The simple fact is that many warriors cannot make the transition. Relinquishing control to our spouses seems idiotic and unsafe. Even if the fear is not abuse, who wants to suborn their will to another? Ergo, what the warrior fears from marriage is personal *change*. The warrior fears what the spouse wants them to become.

_____

_____

8.5 Phases of the married warrior

8.5.1 **Phase one: The needful student meets the newly wed** - The needful student wanders out into the wilderness and seeks all training available. This drive and ambition soon become problems in marriage because it is neither contentment nor satisfaction; it is mindless motivation. The useless energy comes across originally as passion but soon thereafter reveals itself. Ambition becomes an excuse to avoid intimacy and commitment. After the passion of the honeymoon wears off reality kicks in, the spouse soon finds that, the warrior's energy is not intended to grow them together, but instead to keep them apart.

8.5.2 **Phase two: The artesian and the spouse** - With the artesian, philosophy and the practical marry. The artesian learns that the warrior and his weapon are one; there is no separation. Marriage is a craft, a work of hearts. A study of the human body makes the warrior appreciate the marital state as the two develop physical unity. As we learn to please our spouse, we also learn about our own inner desires. As we look at the way we treat our spouse, hold our spouse, and make love to our spouse, we learn to see what we believe to be love. When there is a hole in the physical, it is often because the same hole exists in our mental construct of love.

The warrior has 10 weapons used for combat. The artesian has 10 weapons, which he learns to use to show love.
- 8.5.2.1 Hands to hold our lover close
- 8.5.2.2 Arms to keep our lover safe
- 8.5.2.3 Forearms to pull them along gently into the new life
- 8.5.2.4 Elbows to rest on and dream together
- 8.5.2.5 Shoulders to cry upon
- 8.5.2.6 Knees to pray for each other
- 8.5.2.7 Shins to bear up the weight of the new life
- 8.5.2.8 Feet to stand patiently in service
- 8.5.2.9 Ankles to run behind the spouses of our youth
- 8.5.2.10 The head to plan the route to righteous bliss

The artesian also learns to apply their healing arts to marriage--few things in this life cause more internal strife, heartache, and pain as marriage.

- **8.5.3 Phase three: The master and the mistress** - The warrior learns to live compassionately and to love at the same time. The master learns that compassion and love flow from the same Spirit. In marriage, compassion elevates love to sharing and motivates intercession. In this phase, the master pushes all their desire to the rear and interlocks their will with the will of God. Regardless of what we understand, adoring our spouses is in the will of God. What better way to gauge the way we will treat His bride than by observing the loving kindness we show our spouses.

8.6 Marriage and the spiritual warrior

The spiritual warrior forces discipline into their life, this trade off manifests itself in a reserved sensuality. The spiritual warrior is human, a human under control. The spiritual warrior has sensual releases, usually refined, sedate, uncharacteristic releases. Unfortunately, in marriage reserved sensuality does not appear to be an act of self-restrain and often comes across as rejection. It requires a great deal of effort to bring the flesh under control. Going back and forth between restraint and indulgence creates an imbalance in all humans.

8.7 The Sampson Principle as it applies to marriage

As we discussed in From a Fortress in Patmos, in order to retain power, WE MUST MAINTAIN RIGHTEOUSNESS. Like Sampson once we find ourselves confined to the dungeon the Holy Spirit blinds us to the characteristics of light. After we have put our lives to His plough[49]: God builds in us His strength and vision, making us useful to His kingdom. The main difference in marriage is that whereas Sampson's submission to sexuality cost him power and time, married people are encouraged to give themselves sexually to each other. Instead of sexuality conquering the spiritual warrior, marriage conquers the negative aspects of a heightened sexual lifestyle.

8.8 Marriage and the traits of the spiritual warrior

8.8.1 Marriage and spiritual need - All spiritual warriors have needs. The spiritual warrior needs sexual fulfillment; it too is part of his design. Sexuality is not unrighteousness fornication is unrighteous. Therefore, the spiritual warrior through marriage is free to grow in leaps and bounds. While of the unmarried God needs waiting, the spiritual warrior is encouraged to be free. With this freedom, the spiritual warrior serves at a higher ability, because the flesh is more easily controlled. Freedom from the normal pull of sexuality allows the married spiritual warrior to be one of the most trustworthy members in the church. With satisfied flesh, there is little reason to covet anything.

8.8.2 Marriage and spiritual drive - The spiritual warrior does not afford themselves gratification or happiness, but a family man has no choice. Spouse or parent must indulge in emotions because they have children and each other to love. To this responsibility, Paul also spoke when he said that marriage was a hindrance to the gospel. There is one thing God and the family both demand--time! Proverbs 3:1-2 reads, "**MY SON, FORGET NOT MY LAW; BUT LET THINE HEART KEEP MY COMMANDMENTS: FOR LENGTH OF DAYS, AND LONG LIFE, AND PEACE, SHALL THEY ADD TO THEE**." Although there are only 24 hours in everyday, the Father of time removes many times wasting events from the spiritual warriors' day. To the married warrior the length of days, peace, and long life are indispensable to family.

8.8.3 Marriage and spiritual discipline - The spiritual warrior directs most of their energy to discipline. The married warrior is no less disciplined, they simply have fewer restrictions. Like the spiritual warrior, the married warrior is also;
8.8.3.1 Judgmental
8.8.3.2 Does not have many friends
8.8.3.3 A zealot

Neither of these three qualities make for a happy marriage. The wife really shines when contrasted with the unpalatable traits. It is the grace softness and patience of the wife that tempers the callousness of her husband's discipline. As in the case of thank-you cards and birthday cards men forget to send, the wife takes up the slack and encourages her husband to find a kinder way to deliver the truth.

8.8.4 Marriage and spiritual heart - All that exists in the spiritual warrior's heart is the raw essence of need. Rigidity makes it easy to fail, where the unmarried warrior use sheer strength of will to change, the married warrior does not have to change. The key to understanding this is applying the purpose of salvation to marriage. Just as God sent Jesus to make straight the way, He ordained marriage to make straight our hearts.

8.8.5 Marriage and spiritual temperance - Because of the struggle beneath the surface, the spiritual warrior resembles the alternating current electricity designated ac/dc. Alternating current makes for an unhappy spouse, all spouses want warmth and consistency. Temperance is for everybody in God's kingdom. The problem is that the unmarried spend hours trying to indulge in what they perceive as happiness. Many hide behind closed doors activity of which they should not partake. In marriage, many of these activities[50] we find no longer forbidden. The stomach that leaves the feast satisfied no longer looks for food. The soul that finds itself in the presence of God no longer craves companionship. In addition, flesh that leaves the bedroom fulfilled no longer seeks fulfillment.

- 8.8.6 **Marriage and spiritual patience - In your patience possess ye your souls** - Luke 21:19, nowhere is this more essential than in the blessed union of souls where we tie our soul to the soul of another. The wife is subject to the husband, but God required the husband to submit to the wife. In other words, the woman is a *subject* and the man *subjected*--in the will of God. In this paradigm, we find that the two must learn to wait not only upon the Lord but also on each other. Without my wife, my soul has a hole[51]. When we stand before the judge, our wives must be able to stand pure and unblemished, and Husbands must be able to stand blameless. We must not stand before the throne naked and guilty like Adam and Eve. Eve tarnished herself because she sinned intentionally, Adam was not blameless because he harkened unto Eve rather than God. We must work within out marriages to stay equally yoked and unified. Men must be patient and women yielding else the mystery of marriage never expresses itself.

_____
_____
_____
_____
_____

8.9 Marriage and the heart of the spiritual warrior

A spiritual warrior does 30% of their living in their hearts. The spiritual warrior hurts deeply and mourns constantly. The horrors of the world weigh heavily on their hearts. This does not change once we marry. On the contrary, new troubles occur unique to marriages that do not affect the unmarried.

- 8.9.1 **The spiritual warrior hates in the heart -** Hatred is an emotion, and the spiritual warrior meets this emotion often. In most spiritual warriors, this emotion directed at evil compels them to act. The problem with hatred is that it invariably leads to anger. Anger is a weapon that takes years to master. In marriage, this paradigm always lends itself to marital strife. The warrior immersed in righteous indignation when pulled back to the concerns of this world has trouble transitioning back into the husband. Like a skunk, our spouses usually drag us into the bedroom with our tails raised. There is a time under the sun for everything. Rarely however, is there a Godly cause to adopt hatred into a marriage, this cannot produce superior results.

- 8.9.2 **The spiritual warrior has to learn love in the heart -** Of all the spiritual traits this condition in the spiritual warrior is the most useless. The spiritual warrior knows they cannot to be like and with God without love. The spiritual warrior's use of love eventually develops into acceptance, understanding, and finally a need to love. The spiritual warrior loves and makes love in his mind because they do not cherish material and physical things. Despite many possible wonderful applications, the excessive use of the mind renders marriage inert. A common complaint of minister's wives is the perceived holier than thou mentality. There are no immaculate conceptions in the flesh; we must touch our wives. NO WOMAN MARRIES A MAN WITH HER SPIRIT. No matter if you are Billy Graham; Mrs. Graham expects Billy to come home for supper and snuggle with her at night.

The religious preoccupation of the spiritual warrior does not allow the wife due benevolence. The good wife is all women; and requires all of her man. In her patience, she may not complain about apathy, so I will complain for her. Most of the world is going to hell by choice; God's missions take little time because He does most of the work. Ministers: Go home to the family; He will call us when the time arises.

8.9.3 **The spiritual warrior forgives in the heart** - Forgiveness to a spiritual warrior maintains fluidity. The problem with forgiveness in humans is that it is emotional. Because the spiritual warrior hates, true forgiveness is not easy. True love requires forgiveness. Trust needs forgiveness and marriage requires forgiveness. The unforgiving are often unloving. Who wants to love a person that dislikes them?

8.9.3 **The spiritual warrior fights in the heart** - The spiritual warrior wages all warfare in the heart. Unlike the warrior, the spiritual warrior is sensitive and easily offended. They pretend not to be sensitive, but sensitivity is required to love. Many husbands go out of their way to hide their sensitivity. Sadly, it is this sensitivity, which kids and wives need to develop and maintain their security. Even sadder is the fact that this sensitivity we need to stay attuned to the whispers of God. Since spiritual warrior's wage war in their hearts, they seem calculating and cold. This is not the case; they are not cold they are simply prepared. Women are emotional fighters, planning angers them. Married warriors should refrain from useless banter and bickering because it leads to insecurity in the wife.

8.9.4 **The spiritual warrior loses in the heart** - Another characteristic of the spiritual warrior is that they accept loss stoically. Again, this trait does not sit well often because it gives the appearance of indifference. Because of their emotional makeup, women force emotionalism into every interaction, this is one field in which they will always come up short.

8.9.5 **The spiritual warrior kills in the heart** - If we want to kill a woman simply ignore her. Training and experience like the armor of God allows spiritual warriors to stand as they battle in the wilderness. Most spiritual warriors feel more comfortable in their armor than without. To this end, spiritual warriors often keep their armor on, even in the bedroom. It is difficult to make yourself feel what another person feels empathy is also learned. If we learn to be sensitive to our wives, we learn to be more sensitive to the Spirit and vice versa. In the manner, we quench our wives; we also quench the Holy Spirit. The Bible reminds us that a man who hates in their heart is a murderer. Do not let bitterness into the bedroom, it will find fertile soil in between the emotional folds of a marriage.

8.9.6 **The spiritual warrior hurts, cries, and dies in the heart** - My wife has no idea how many tears I shed during our marriage. Some of the tears were due to marital issues and many spiritual issues. Remember however, that ALL issues we bring into our marriages become marital issues. Sometimes I look at my wife and see the hurt in her face, and it hurts me too, but I cry inside. It is not that I fear crying in front of my wife; I trained myself to press the fight. For this purpose, I will probably die crying internally; for this I apologize to my wife.

8.9.7 **The spiritual warrior needs in the heart -** The only thing I do more of than cry is need. My wife; my Band-Aid, has no idea of how badly I hurt. Tsunamis are a common occurrence out to sea, it is not until they strike land that we see the true horror they wield. For the average person life is tough enough without tossing back and forth in the wilderness. I have as many needs as anyone; however, I spend more time in the wilderness than most. Wilderness journeys are demanding on the body, mind, and soul. For those of us who think our life is tumultuous, we have not seen rough seas if we do not spend time in the deep ocean.

8.8.7 **Spiritual warriors fear in the heart** - I fear few things. My wife has no idea (had no idea) that I fear the darkness. I do not fear the dark as a child fears the dark; I fear the shade. What makes the darkness dreadful is that it often finds company within the chambers of our hearts. The truth of the matter is that I fear the darkness that lies just beneath the surface of our hearts. The delicate balance of warrior and war only exists in those who control their darkness.

All the Bible greats had a dark side, even Jesus. There is NO WAY to live in the flesh and not have a dark side. The more potential for darkness we wield, the greater the power we potentially yield. Rarely understood, is that Jesus had the potential to be darker than Satan. Jesus knew the potential for darkness. For forty days, Jesus fought the potential in His own flesh to accept all the power Satan offered. Satan fell as he stood in the presence of God. Jesus suffered to learn obedience. Jesus suffered to control the darkness in His heart. Jesus killed His-*self* so that the love the world desperately needed would spring forth. Fear of the Lord is the beginning of wisdom. I believe fear (respect) of the darkness in our hearts is the application of wisdom.

_____
_____
_____
_____
_____
_____
_____
_____
_____
_____

9.0
Fight Right

According to most experts, the major causes of marital conflict occur due to hardness of our hearts, in other words, it is not ailing health, sexual dysfunction caused by health, or aging. The natural issues of life, which should cause failings due to physical changes etc., are not the problem they just pass out into the draught. The major #12^{52} issues that defile marriage seem to be;

- Overstepping boundaries
- Lacking complete communication
- Declining occurrences of sexual intimacy
- Wandering focuses
- Emotional infidelity
- Fighting about money
- Waning appreciation.
- Technology interference
- Lacking trust
- Losing control of anger
- Changing future ambitions

The destruction of most marriages Christian or not start from within. We are going to fight, but if we must fight let us fight right.

9.0.1 **Overstepping boundaries** - Trying to change each other, and not respect personal and heart space.

9.0.2 **Lacking complete communication** - Communication is not just information transfer, it is about reaching into both persons and finding the message.

9.0.3 **Declining occurrences of sexual intimacy** - Loss of sexually appetite or frequency or not wanting to spend time with spouse or finding happiness elsewhere.

9.0.4 **Wandering focuses** - Finding things and people to fill the voids from home. Sadly, children also fall into the category of dividing issues in marriages.

9.0.5 **Emotional infidelity** - Giving our hearts and finding happiness with someone other than our spouses.

9.0.6 **Fighting about money** - This is a common occurrence, especially when a party is already unhappy.

9.0.7 **Waning appreciation** - Taking each other for granted.

9.0.8 **Technology interference** - Porn and electronics become companions.

9.0.9 **Lacking trust** - Once a partner's interest and attention diminish, it is a natural inclination to believe our spouse is unfaithful. After all nobody wants to be unhappy, and they are not getting their happiness at home.

9.0.10 **Losing control of anger** - Feeling trapped produces panic and anger in any animal. Once marriage gets sour, and a partner becomes desperate to leave the marriage or just be left alone anger boils. Another source of the anger is resentment, as couples tend to blame each other for the marital failing and condition.

9.0.11 **Changing future ambitions** - Nothing angers like betrayal. Marital planning is part of the covenant after all. Part of the reason a couple marries is their shared vision for the future. When one party changes that future with no regard to the other lifelong party, anger is the natural reaction.

The strength of a rope is determined by how much tension it can withstand. The ties that bind marriage are not ropes, they are arms, legs and other specially crafted appendages. God, in His design saw that the man was alone (without) that which he needed to be complete. The solution was a creature made not only for him but from him. The design, like the milk of a mother's breast is to foster intimacy, trust, and partnership.

The bible does not say to be bound by hearts of souls; it says we become one flesh. The method to become one flesh, he made special between a man and a woman. There is no part of the man's body designed to please another man. Likewise, there is no part of a woman made to please another woman. The flesh was made to join face-to-face, bare chest to breast eyes fixed on the future. No man hates his own flesh, it gets hard to hate the woman we join with every night.

This is why premarital sex is devastating; it takes the intimacy out of sex. Everyone wants a car, and a free car is better. However, no one wants the car with high mileage and maintenance issues. What is so special about a used car?

Understanding our imperfections, we must learn to handle each other out of respect and genuine concern about the happiness of our spouse. So, fight right, learn to love another day.

_____
_____
_____
_____
_____

9.1 Peace talks- for beginners

9.1.1 **Discern our feelings**[53] - If our have no relationship with our emotions, they are in control, we must control our feelings so that cannot harm our spouse.

9.1.2 **Manage anger** - Be angry, only sin not, do not hate or hurt your spouse, we must share a bed and a future with them. Hate is murder, which is a sin (1 John 3:15). No man hates his own flesh; do not let yourself dwell in anger, for it is directed at self.

9.1.3 **Negotiate and compromise** - One flesh; does ye right hand argue with the left over a meal, or a trinket. Why do we quibble about that which is ours? We must agree that to win we must surrender, in doing this we save both our marriage and our souls.

9.1.4 **Cool-off** - Take time after or during a conflict to cool off. Prior to the explosion of insults and venom is a time to cool off.

9.1.5 **Quick resolutions work best** - Do not drag an issue out, this allows it to fester and boil.

9.1.6 **Fight by mutual consent** - Try not to start a fight when our spouse is sick, or tired, or already in a bad mood. All that will follow is personality conflicts.

9.1.7 **Stick to the subject** - try deal with one issue at a time and resolve one thing before moving onto another. This is not always easy as many times areas of contention overlap but try.

9.1.8 **State the issue honestly and clearly** - communication is about clarity, there can be no resolution if the problem is not clear. This will also help our prayer life, be specific when our cast our cares upon the Lord.

9.1.9 **Do not camouflage** - Red Herring discussions, are a waste of time and often make matters worse as they open areas in a contentious manner that are really not problems. Too many problems, at one time will make anyone despair, because they task seems insurmountable.

9.1.10 **Afraid to fight**? - Do not attack each other as part of the process attack the problem. When working with Bleach gloves are suggested for safety, this is because Bleach is a caustic substance. Out marriage has enough problems, there should be not toxicity in the way we treat each other.

9.1.11 **Do not hit below the belt** - The object is to repair damage, do not use their past, or vulnerabilities as weapons. Even if these issues the problem, diplomacy, diplomacy.

9.1.12 **Do not label** - No name calling, sarcastic insult or diminutive titles, these just incense the situation, and often cause harm.

9.1.13 **Grant equal time** - The issue must be resolved on both sides; else it will continue to resurface and or cause problems. Both parties must agree to the solution, liked or not; this is the essence of compromise.

9.1.14 **Feedback and clarification** - Speech 101, discuss and resolve the issues do not just banter about them and vent, this opens other problems and fosters anger.

9.1.15 **Gain new understanding**. Extract enough additional information and insight from a fight to permit growth. Do not waste a good fight by not learning from it.

9.1.16 **Implement changes** - Once derived, a solution should be implemented in the least injurious manner. There should be no push back, as this is an agreed solution. If there is push back, there is no agreement and the peace talks must resume.

9.1.17 **Develop humor** - Laughter makes the time together more pleasant, without it there will always be friction. Friction never leads to good things; it wears down both sides and produces needles heat.

9.1.18 **Keep your fights to yourself** - The say keep fights private. I do not necessarily agree. If there is nothing uncommon to the brethren, then this should apply to marital issues. If our do not seek council from more successful married couples, then where do we get it from? When we do seek counsel, be open, objective, and fair state the problem, not our opinion of our spouse.

9.1.19 **Manage anger in front of children** - Try not to argue in front of kids. This is not realistic, unless our whisper or discuss matters when they are not home. As long as we can be heard, we are in front of kids - next room, door closed or not. If our genuinely want to accomplish this then sneak around like we do when we are trying to have sex, then our will not be in front of kids.

9.1.20 **'Touch' can begin dialogue** - Remember the flesh is always alive; most humans crave touches. If the Peach Talk is going the wrong way, find a neutral touch to calm them or stop the negative progress until, the peace talk can resume.

9.1.21 **Exclude violence** - There is no room in love for physical abuse, and no MAN resorts hitting his bride to resolve anything. If there is abuse THERE IS NOT LOVE, no one hates their own flesh. God judges us, convicts us, even condemns us; yet He never abuses us. This is the model. Before we physically abuse our spouses, we should leave.

9.1.22 **Is the problem elsewhere**? Make sure we are discussing the actual problem, not triggers or symptoms.

9.1.23 **Respect crying** - Crying implies pain, ease off for just a moment. Then when there is a cessation, resume the peace talks.

_____
_____
_____
_____
_____
_____
_____
_____

9.2 We fight with prayer

"**AGAIN, I SAY UNTO YOU, THAT IF TWO OF YOU SHALL AGREE ON EARTH AS TOUCHING ANY THING THAT THEY SHALL ASK, IT SHALL BE DONE FOR THEM OF MY FATHER WHICH IS IN HEAVEN** - (Matthew 18:19)."

In <u>From a fortress in Patmos</u>, we discussed steps to establish prayer warriors. These laws also apply to spiritual combat.

    9.2.1   We cannot worship the Spirit unless we are in the spirit
    9.2.2   We cannot fight spiritual wars in the flesh
    9.2.3   We cannot be a part of Christ' army unless we are part of Christ

There is something the Paul did not discuss when he said that marriage is a hindrance to the Gospel. The thing Paul did not discuss was the relationship between marriage and prayer. To explore this mysterious relationship, we have to jump around the scriptures and construct our picture.

_____
_____
_____
_____
_____

9.3 The mysterious power of prayer

If we trained to compete in the Olympics whatever it took to get us there, we must maintain in order to stay there, as it is with our relationship to God. I watched a Health-watch program at her OBGYN. According to that program, after the birth of a child, women lose and average of 90 minutes a week exercise and men lose and average of four hours. When translated this means the most powerful part of the marriage loses at least four hours from their spiritual relationship.

In prayer, unity is the key. The mystery of praying spouses is that the two parts make a whole. The way the mystery works is that the wife and the husband pray for the same things and the time the other loses from their single life they make up jointly. In other words, the man may lose four hours, but his wife makes up the other two hours. If the two pray with singleness of heart, they can maintain some level of relationship with God.

To make the best use of the unified, undefiled bed thus far. Look at the following scriptures;

9.3.1 **"Again, I say unto you, that if two of you shall agree on earth as touching anything that they shall ask, it shall be done for them of my Father which is in heaven** - (Matthew 18:19)." The prayers of the unified couples gain access more readily to God.

9.3.2 **"Pray without ceasing"** - (I Thessalonians 5:17). Rather than leaving home to find another to touch and agree with, all we have to do is roll over.

9.3.3 **"For whoremongers, for them that defile themselves with mankind, for men stealers, for liars, for perjured persons, and if there be any other thing that is contrary to sound doctrine"** - (1 Timothy 1:10). A husband can have the company of a beautiful, fully sexual woman, in his bed enjoying her flesh and it not make of him a whoremonger.

9.3.4 **"Likewise, ye husbands, dwell with [them] according to knowledge, giving honor unto the wife, as unto the weaker vessel, and as being heirs together of the grace of life; that your prayers be not hindered"** - (1 Peter 3:7). Look; see, men are not the only heirs; our wives also inherit the gifts, as she is part of us. Therefore, when the couple prays, they have twice as many voting shares when they approach the throne.

9.3.5 **"Having eyes full of adultery, and that cannot cease from**

sin; beguiling unstable souls: a heart they have exercised with covetous practices; cursed children" - (2 Peter 2:14). I can lust after my own wife, and think all manner of sexual thoughts about her, and my children are not cursed, nor my practices covetous.

Yet another wonderful mystery unveils a beautiful wisdom in marriage. DO NOT STOP PRAYING AND DO NOT STOP TOUCHING. This principle, this marital mystery is the highest level of intimacy humans achieve. In the *Touch* mentioned in Songs, the woman says she sought him who her soul loved. This is why touching is imperative to marriage; it elevates prayers into a *spiritual touch*. How could there be any greater blessing than to never have to leave the bosom of our mate, yet still be able to enter the Holy of holies? We should cling to our spouse and never stop touching. When will we learn that the true pleasures of the flesh do not stem from sin, the stem from intimacy and sharing? This mystery elevates our fleshly undefiled lives into spiritual intimacy with God. In the *spiritual touch* we learn not to leave our souls unloved and unkept. Through the *spiritual touch,* we learn what God intended for our relationship with Him, continual, uninterrupted, close contact with His Spirit.

Many misunderstand the story in Luke chapter 11 about prayer. Pastors usually teach this in terms of the way in which Jesus attained power. However, the closer look reveals a marriage mystery amidst this most important message. Jesus does not tell the disciple ANYTHING about power, nor does He teach them anything about power. Instead, what the Master teaches is about **relationship**. Kingdom Mystery--**power does not derive from anointing it derives from RELATIONSHIP**. The same applies to the

Lord's Prayer in Matthew 6. In both cases, Jesus taught about RELATIONSHIP.

Power in marriage also derives from relationship. Intimacy is the key to reaching and maintaining power. In reading what Jesus says, He never gives us a secret key to unlocking God's power. What Jesus gives us is the key to God's heart. Prayer in and of itself yields little[54]. Effective fervent prayer yields more (James 5:16). However, a relationship with God through prayer yields the mysteries of the kingdom and crowns of Glory. Therefore, Paul admonishes us to pray unceasingly, because He understood the benefits of relationship with God. Maintain intimacy with our spouses unceasingly and see what power we can walk in together.

In Acts chapter 16, we learn from Paul and Silas the power prayer yields. Though not married, Paul and Silas met on one-accord and yields results. How much easier it should be for a couple that shares a bed to share a heart. Paul and Silas found unity easy because Paul and Silas knew the power of prayer. Paul and Silas prayed down walls, as any married couple can do as well. There is no such thing as a problem in a Christian marriage that prayer cannot remedy. If the results do not exist or are slow coming, the fault is in the couple not God. If my wife and I cannot reach an accord on a familial decision, should God rush to take an inappropriate action?

There are many hours in the night, many of which we need to spend whispering into each other's ears. However, married people at some point the bedroom should also yield prayer. No family can withstand or survive all Satan throws against it without prayer. We can tithe all we want to and go to every service in the universe, unless we engage in prayer and fasting as a couple there are MANY demons that we will not be able to fight, and many temptations for which we will fall.

As a couple grows, the things they pray for should mesh into one streamlined set of needs and wants. As a couple, parents should want the same thing for their kids, and they must agree upon a way to get those things or they will not reach their goal.

9.4 **Hitting is quitting**

Allow me to break tradition and pass judgement. Because of my job, I spent more than 20 years of my life fighting almost every day. I have 20+ years in Martial Arts and have been hit during lots of fights. However, I say this; any male that finds it necessary to strike his wife is of no value to her. An empty plastic bottle he uses, but not value unless we are in a desert environment and find potable water. Like this bottle, the abusive man has uses, but no value, unless we live life in a desert. When we find ourselves in need of a plastic bottle reach out to God first, for He is the master of all things including rain. If the righteous do not have to beg for bread, He will not sit by and watch them beg for a husband; BUT WE HAVE TO WAIT, AND WAIT WITH ALL OUR CLOTHES ON.

10.0
Establishing Spiritual Warriors Through Marriage

"**O magnify the Lord with me and let us exalt His name together**" - (Psalms 34:3).

Previously we set up that one of the basics of spiritual warfare is that we must train junior saints that the foundation for warfare is prayer. We learn from the book of Peter that a married man cannot prosper without prayer. If a marriage cannot prosper without prayer, then married spiritual warriors that do not pray will find spiritual warfare increasingly difficult. It is sad to see newlyweds engage in spiritual warfare, so many have fallen. There is a reason for this, which we find in scriptural application of the parable of the 10 talents. The reason many Christian couples have '*peace*' is because they are not involved in kingdom building. Many Christians are satisfied with putting their talent into the bank so that God can draw interest. Therefore, it is easier to grow and maintain a Church than it is to make disciples and forge out into Satan's kingdom. As members of churches, we give money and sit quietly in the pews as the preacher talks. We then wonder why we have no power. We have no power because we relinquished personal power to the church and the pastor. As a result, we look to the pastor and the church for healing and strength. **Married people should never submit their union to the church**; Matthew 19 says clearly, "...**what God has joined**...." ergo, <u>the church should not be a part of our marriage; marriages should be a thriving part of church</u>. God did not design the church to give to us, but the converse is true. The church is the bride because we are to take care of her.

We must pray in and for our marriages to keep unity, integrity, and power. The power in a marriage leaks out through discord and bickering. Even worse, as our power leaks out satanic influence over our flesh creeps in and increases. We do not understand the power of the flesh. More importantly, we do not understand the power of married flesh. Here is another kingdom mystery--happily, married flesh is virtually immune to satanic attacks. In the years I have waged in spiritual warfare, I learned many satanic inroads. The most common inroad into a happy marriage is the children because each new generation moves further from God. Even if spouses are united, the attacks continue, but through unity and prayer, we have the power to withstand and conquer.

10.1 A guide for establishing married spiritual warriors

We learned that a strong man is integral to a successful Christian marriage. We also realized that the woman is not *weaker* in the literal sense but more attuned to her flesh. Therefore, we need a man to be both a lover and a fighter.

Most common complaints about lack of sexuality come from males. We misinterpret this data; not only are the men dissatisfied. There is a reason the woman is withholding her favor. Address the underlying reason and the issue ends. When Christian couples fail at warfare, it is because they lack unity. When Christian couples fail at sexuality it is because the woman does not feel unified. No one, especially a person that values self wants to give themselves to abuse, misuse, and indifference. Women married us because they loved us, if that is the case why do they avoid us? **Often wives avoid husbands to preserves themselves**. Often in a failing marriage, virtuous women do not commit adultery they simply withdraw themselves. When we counsel failing marriages look for body language between the couple, a cold woman often indicates a bad marriage. If a woman withholds her earthly gifts, that same person will often withhold her prayers. The prayers she sows issue often are for salvation of the marriage. When the anchor of the marriage must spend their time praying just to hold the marriage together, there is little room for power and warfare.

10.1 **The battle is not our own -** Most of the things God gives us are not for our fleshly delight but for His work. Marriage is no different. Although marriage manages fleshly delight, marriage's primary function is kingdom work. Look again at Genesis 1:29, where can we get Godly seeds from if not Godly unions. God does not need marriage to keep saved people saved; He uses marriage to make more righteous seeds.

10.2 **We do not choose spiritual warriors -** Although we do not choose spiritual warriors, we do choose our spouses. Let our future spouses know that we are spiritual warriors they may change their minds about marriage. As spiritual warriors, we must choose mates that can and will battle with us. If a mate is not battling for us, they are working against us. This is a common fault in Christian marriage; we choose unequally yoked partners and then cannot figure out why we tire easily. We cannot successfully fight Satan with dead weight around our neck. Even the Christ had to free Himself from the dead weight of the cross to gain the victory. This does not mean divorce; it means use Godly wisdom when we marry.

10.3 **There are more well-intentioned people than there are true warriors -** Many marry for love; others have assorted reasons. In our Christianity, we must love the Lord our God primarily. When I married, I made sure that my wife and I agreed upon the importance kingdom building in our life. King Arthur discovered that if we live to serve the King, then we must also LOVE TO SERVE THE KING. If we serve God's kingdom we must also be willing and able to protect God's Kingdom.

10.4 **No matter our relationship, the training of a wife that God did not call WILL NOT SUCCEED -** Mercy has it place. If God does not call our wives to warrior status, be patient, be kind, and love our wives anyway. However, do not go into war with our wives nor use them in direct combat--our marriages and souls may depend on it.

10.5 **Those God does not ordain for a task, will not have His protection in that task.** In spiritual warfare, understanding what God anointed us to do is where we find favor and power. In what the church anointed us to do, we find death and misery. In marriage, the same principles apply. What God ordains He empowers and protects. If God tells the husband to go to Indonesia and witness, the order applies to the wife as well. However, it is in the application many couples fail. Our wives do not have to go to Indonesia to help us in this effort. A praying wife does wonders before her husband even arrives. Artillery should always precede the infantry. Our praying wives may well save our foolish lives as we jaunt across the world leaving them unprotected.

10.6 **A prayer warrior must be both strong and armored to succeed -** Prayer is an act of discipline. No matter who we are, prayer takes effort. Prayer is like foreplay for the flesh; we do not see or feel the results immediately. The translation of prayer takes time. I do not refer to translation in the linguistics I mean the implementation process.

We send our petition or prayer to the Holy Spirit. We do <u>not</u> pray to the church, pastor, saints, the pope, or Jesus we pray only to our Father which art in heaven. The Holy Spirit intercedes on our behalf in a language we do not understand. When the Father answers, He sends His will He sends to the Holy Spirit who is the power in the earth realm[55]. The Holy Spirit translates God's will. We pray to through the Holy Spirit because the Holy Spirit intercedes on our behalf in a language that we do not understand. The Holy Spirit dwells in the earth realm so He understands the nature of humans. The Holy Spirit also dwells in heaven and He understands God's nature[56]. Therefore, intercession is a conversion of our needs and petitions into a format God will accept. I did not write understand because God knew what we needed before we asked, but our prayers must occur in a manner to which God can respond. God's only limit is His word. In other words, He cannot give us things that belong to others, He does not make people fall in love with us, and He is not our magic Genie. Once God responds, the Holy Spirit then translates that information into a format we can understand and use.

10.7 **An un-armored warrior becomes a victim -** Nowhere does the Bible more accurately display this than Adam and Eve. Since Satan once worked in heaven, he understands the power of covenant relationship. Is it a wonder why Satan took the time and the risk to destroy the first marriage? In doing so, Satan hoped to stop the production of Godly seeds. Adam left Eve to fend for herself. Eve had neither flesh nor word to protect her. Had Adam either been present or trained his wife adequately in the word of God she would have at least known enough to respond to Satan's query to the orders from on High. Since she was without armor she fell, but the fault was not her own. How was Eve supposed to understand that which her husband had charge over?

What we should learn from this couple is that men who have kingdom responsibilities should explain their duties and skills to their spouse, as she bears a portion of those same responsibilities. Moreover, in the description of the virtuous woman we see the proper application or being the man of the house. To rule our house well requires the agreement, participation, and respect of our wives. Hence, God tells women in Ephesians… 'nevertheless wives respect your husbands.' A man cannot rule a house well if the lady of the house is against him.

10.7 **Power play** - Many couples make the mistake of trusting in their gifts instead of the Spirit that sent the gifts. Do not trust in the gifts of God, put our trust in the God of the gifts. Marriage is a gift; a tool to control our flesh, we should care for it. Sometimes the boundaries of marriage are all that causes us to remain righteous. There is nothing wrong with fidelity due to fear. Our spouse would rather we come home out of love…but most accept a return due to fear. In time, this fear will grow into fondness and eventually love.

10.8 **Loss of a battle costs us more than it costs God. Satan cannot steal from God** - Satan cannot put Christian marriages asunder, even at the threat of death. Even if we live in Sodom and Gomorrah, we must stay the course of righteousness. When judgment falls, all those found in sin perish. God does not care why we choose to sin. If we allow trend, peer pressure and the homosexual agenda to sway us we become part of a group destined to fail. Those put to the sword have a blessing, those that take the mark of the beast in their hearts and hands take into themselves and their marriage, death.

10.9 **To die in the service of God is to die free and blessed**[57] - What greater love has a man than he lays down his life for his wife? We have to die to the old ways when we accept Christ. For the old fleshly ways that we cannot kill, God gives us marriage. Within marriage, our sexuality must still follow God's rules. This excludes; homosexuality, bestiality, incest, bigamy, polygamy, and wife swapping, the undefiled bed only consists of a husband and wife[58].

If it takes us, a lifetime to master ourselves so that we may present our spouse without spot or blemish then that is a worthy feat. If we die in the arms of our spouse, after struggling to keep us both in the will of God, then we die safe and secure. Upon death, those who die in a righteous marriage leave the bosom of the one that loves our flesh and enter the bosom of the One that loves our soul.

11.0
Marriage and the Use of Moats

"Husbands, love your wives, even as Christ also loved the church, and gave himself for it; That he might sanctify and cleanse it with the washing of water by the word, that he might present it to himself a glorious church, not having spot, or wrinkle, or any such thing; but that it should be holy and without blemish" - (Ephesians 5:26-27).

11.1 Short reasons

    11.1.1 **Moats provide marital protection**
    11.1.2 **Moats provide marital irrigation**
    11.1.3 **Moats provide marital food**

11.2 Long reasons

    11.2.1 **Marital protection** - In Ephesians 5, we see that unlike a regular moat, which consists of regular water, the marital moat flows with Living water. The stillness in these waters does not imply lifelessness but instead peace. God is not the author of confusion; ergo His waters should not toss His people back and forth but make it, so they never thirst. With Living water, we wash our spouses and our families, the Living water that cleanses our hearts and drowns our flesh.

    11.2.2 **Marital irrigation** - Irrigation keeps pastures green. There is no way to keep marriage green and young without infusing water our gardens of secrets. Solomon tells his bride as they cuddle. **"Many waters cannot quench love, neither can the floods drown it**[59]**,"** Solomon goes on to tell her[60], **"A garden enclosed [is] my sister, [my] spouse; a spring shut up, a fountain sealed. Thy plants [are] an orchard of pomegranates, with pleasant fruits; camphire, with spikenard, a fountain of gardens, a well of living waters, and streams from Lebanon."** Solomon describes well the value of irrigation, and he waters his garden well. As a junior farmer, I learned gardens unlock their secrets when watered and maintained. It is amazing how grass and trees respond to seasons. The right temperature, fertilizer, and water promote growth, fruit, and hardiness.

    11.2.3 **Marital food type one:** *Soul food* - Paul admonishes couples to walk in the same calling but achieving this is not easy. Many people do not heed or understand their calling until late in life. Some people do not arrive at their call until fulfilled by marriage. Consequently, it is difficult to marry in the same calling. Paul's advice about spiritual gifts gives us the answer. 1 Corinthians 12:6-7 reminds us that the same Spirit gives all gifts for the benefit of His body. Therefore, the Spirit maintains the yoke between His married oxen. God's yoke is light; it always has been light, it is the yoke of the church hold marriages in chains[61]. Two with the gift of healing is good, but two with different gifts working together do twice as much for the kingdom.

_____

_____

_____

Consequently, equality in our yoke MUST BE IN THE TIME SPENT WITH GOD. Adam and Eve DID NOT have the same responsibilities, but they both had access to the same Spirit. Had Eve spent more time with that Spirit or had Adam spent more time with Eve in the Spirit the world would be a better place.

12.0
Week II - Work Area

12.0 What is the discipline of the temple?

_____

12.1 Why must Christians have discipline?

_____

12.2 Why does the Bible encourage to pray with us how does this parallel constantly touching each other?

_____

12.3 What is the Kingdom mystery regarding power and where does it derive from?

_____

12.4 We do not choose spiritual warriors and the church does not make spiritual Warriors where do they come from?

12.5 Why does an unarmed spiritual warrior?

12.6 Why does boredom creep into so many marriages?

12.7 How do married Christians maintain togetherness even when they are apart?

12.8 What is the natural marital defense?

12.9 Research and List the things the Bible says you can do when your spouse commits adultery.

12.10 Explain the 2-tiered mystery why so many marriages fail in your own words.

Week III
The Walls Within Marriage

13.0 - Marriage and the use of walls
14.0 - Marriage and the use of supplies & stores
15.0 - Marriage and the use of barracks
16.0 - Marital discipline
17.0 - The marital armory
18.0 - Marriage and the use of sanitation
19.0 - Marriage and the use of God's armor
20.0 - Week 3 - Work Area

13.0
Marriage and the Use of Walls

"If she [be] a wall, we will build upon her a palace of silver: and if she [be] a door, we will enclose her with boards of cedar. I [am] a wall, and my breasts like towers: then was I in his eyes as one that found favor" - (Songs 8:9-10).

13.1 Short reasons

13.1.1 Marital walls keep people inside the marriage
13.1.2 Marital walls keep people outside the marriage
13.1.3 Marital walls allow for rest in the marriage
13.1.4 Marital walls natural marital defense

13.2 Long reasons

13.2.1 **Marital walls keep people inside the marriage -** The wall or boundaries set by marriage have within their function retention. Marriage is difficult; it is a siege on our flesh imposed by our new King. We cannot easily walk away from marriage, God uses His and man's law to *help* us stay in our marriages. Do not forget however that most women seek the safety of that wall in marriage.

- Short story: The first winter of my marriage, I was stuck because of snow. Rather than follow my own advice and *water my garden* I tried to escape that plush, green, soft soil. As a result, I ended up wrecking my car in the snow. The fault is not all mines. My garden was young, but she also did not understand that she grows best when watered. Now, equipped with this understanding we welcome the snow each year and all it has to offer.

13.2.2 **Marital walls keep people outside the marriage -** One of the worst influences in marriage is the influence of in-laws. Although simple honesty would abate this issue readily, God did not rely in this. The reason honesty would abate these issues is of we honestly asked ourselves if we want a marriage like our parents or to end up like our parents how many of us would honestly say yes? That being that case why take their advice, they are steering us into the same problems they had. One of the first '*buts*' of Godly advice on marriage is that we NOT INVOLVE OUR IN-LAWS IN OUR

MARRIAGE[62]. Married people; by way of advice do not keep single friends they are not trying to accomplish the same things.

13.2.3 **Marital walls allow for rest in the marriage** - I had trouble sleeping for many years in my marriage. It was not until a friend asked did I trust my wife did it dawn on me that I had the problem. My wife gets close to me and she can fall asleep in moments, I misinterpreted this as sloth. As I matured, I understood, she found comfort behind the walls of marriage. I had trust issues, so like most Guerrilla fighters I do not function well in enclosures. I had to learn to stay behind the wall and take advantage of the safety and luxury marriage affords.

13.2.4 **Natural marital defense** - The wedding band and the marriage dot on Indians exist as warning markers. However, I suggest we do not rely on the wedding marker to maintain our fortress, one day at the beach or pool, and our marriage maybe over. The safety behind marriage walls, the intimacy, and the garden we cultivate is what should call home.

Gluttony is the reason for the media's success with advertisement. Advertisers fill our mind with their products and ideas so that we crave nothing else. Believers, what do we think large breasts, firm muscles, pretty feet, and nice lips are? They are GOD'S COMMERCIALS FOR MARRIAGE. **To pretend that sexuality in marriage does not matter is to throw away marriages.** Spouses should think about each other's *naked favor* often. God wants and encourages us to dream of our wives breasts all day, every day[63]. In this way, we can keep our minds and hands off everybody else's wife. Is not a reward good? Do not all good things come from above? To think of the wives of our youth all day is a good thing because God gave them to us. Men lift weights, women takeoff the weight; married people advertise, advertise, advertise!

14.0
Marriage and the Use of Supplies & Stores

"**She riseth also while it is yet night, and giveth meat to her household, and a portion to her maidens. She considered a field, and buyeth it: with the fruit of her hands she planteth a vineyard. She girdeth her loins with strength, and strengthened her arms. She perceived that her merchandise [is] good: her candle goeth not out by night. She layeth her hands to the spindle, and her hands hold the distaff** - (Proverbs 31:15) -19.

14.1 Short reasons
  14.1.1 **Marital food supplies & stores offset marital hunger**
  14.1.2 **Marital food supplies & stores forestall marital panic**
  14.1.3 **Marital food supplies & stores sustain marital life**
  14.1.4 **Marital food supplies & stores delay marital infighting**

14.2 Long reasons
  14.2.1 **Marital food supplies & stores offset marital hunger** - Marriage has two food sources. Since the typical marriage is tepid, it is obvious that believers do not nourish their marriages fully with either source.
  14.2.2 **Marital** *food type two* - One of the mysteries of marriage is its control of the flesh. It stands to reason, that one type of food for marriage is for the flesh. To this Paul has the following to say, "**Now concerning the things whereof ye wrote unto me: [It is] good for a man not to touch a woman. Nevertheless, [to avoid] fornication, let every man have his own wife, and let every woman have her own husband. Let the husband render unto the wife due benevolence: and likewise, the wife unto the husband. The wife hath not power of her own body, but the husband: and likewise also the husband hath not power of his own body, but the wife. Ye not one the other, except [it be] with consent for a time, that ye may give yourselves to fasting and prayer; and come together again, that Satan tempt you not for your incontinency. But I speak this by permission, [and] not of commandment. For I would that all men were even as I myself. But every man hath his proper gift of God, one after this manner, and another after that. I say therefore to the unmarried and widows, it is good for them if they abide even as I. But if they cannot contain, let them marry: for it is better to marry than to burn** - 1 Corinthians 7:1-9." Let us clear up verse one before we proceed. Paul is responding to the church at Corinth in verse 5. The issue in verse 5 is fornication, so Paul tells them to stay away from sex. However, by way of advice, Paul reminds them that this is not possible, so he suggests we marry.

_____
_____
_____

Continuing, we see Paul understands that the best way to crucify the flesh is not to deny the flesh pleasure but to redirect pleasure. Who would not rather make love to their spouse than undertake a fast? We need to understand that crucifying the lusts of our flesh is a fast. If we forsake all other flesh for righteousness, that is a fast. Christians routinely fast from food, television, sweets, and all manner of ceremonial fasts. If; however, we spent more time lusting after our spouses, making love to them, and basking in nakedness together there would be little time for the other follies from which we hide.

14.2.4 **Marital food & stores forestall marital panic** - How many of us remember the days of our youth when we made love in places we should not have, when we probably should not have? We needed money and food back then, but did we not have stress and worry. What changed is the importance we place on these things. When we were young, and passion abounded, we wanted to make love all day and night. As we age, we sought other forms of pleasure for assorted reasons. Now we seek material things over marital pleasure. An adequate supply of love and affection coupled with plentiful intimacy makes the woes of life smaller.

14.2.3 **Marital food supplies & stores sustain marital life** - My first serious girlfriend once asked me a very adult question. I was a tender 16 years old in college and not concerned with adulthood or adult relationships. She asked me how to keep the music playing in a relationship. The answer to the question we find in every discipline; those that excel at music and art- PRACTICE. Stop putting down hardwood floors and snuggle with our wives on the floor. Stop washing and waxing our cars and wash and wax our spouses. If we find mountain biking more pleasurable than close tender moments with our spouses, we need more practice.

4.2.4 Marital food & stores delay marital infighting - "**...No man hates his own flesh**," is another mystery of marriage. Once we marry all of the problems of the flesh stem from the flesh. As men mature, they learn to see their flaws in their families. Even though wives come with baggage, the old submits to the new in marriage and the problems that emerge cause the hardships. As we find flaws in our wives, look to ourselves. As she is suitable for us, we are therefore suitable to lead and be responsible for her. For our suitable mate, the flaws in her reflect a lack of husbandry in us. Remember Jesus told us that His majesty as a bride was due to the good husbandry of His spouse.

Life is a journey. Marriage is a journey within parameters. In a balanced marriage, we find spouses who exercise maturity and their gifts to make their lives work in unison. The Biblical example of this we find in the story of the virtuous woman. In these excerpts from that passage, we find that the couple benefits from their unity, "**The heart of her husband doth safely trust in her, so that he shall have no need of spoil. She is like the merchants' ships; she bringeth her food from afar. She stretches out her hand to the poor; yea, she reaches forth her hands to the needy. She is not afraid of the snow for her household: for all her household [are] clothed with scarlet.**' The balanced couple therefore has a better grasp of money, and they retain more together.

The couple is able to achieve more as a unit than they both could individually. Like a chariot, the two pull together because their yoke binds them. They therefore tackle problems, as one powerful team not two competing horses. Let our team ride like the stallions of the east, upon the winds of the arid desert of this life. A blessed couple, like two beautiful steeds at full gallop together, unencumbered by a heavy yoke, enjoying the beauty of each other's strength. Satan will come against us, but he will have to contend with a 2-

15.0
Marriage and the Use of Barracks

"Thy wife [shall be] as a fruitful vine by the sides of thine house: thy Children like olive plants round about thy table - (Psalms 128:3).

15.1 **Short reasons**
    15.1.1 **Marital barracks provide a place to train**
    15.1.2 **Marital barracks provide safe place to rest**
    15.1.3 **Marital barracks afford fellowship**
    15.1.4 **Marital barracks provide moral support**

15.2 **Long reasons**

15.2.1 **Marital barracks provide a place to train** - What better place to learn about trust and resisting temptation than in our marriages. Even the most loathsome spouse has to pay some attention when at home. However, we need not waste time teaching them to live a Godly life, for them there is no hope. In martial arts higher belts practice fight at three speeds; 1/4, 1/2, and full speed (with control). This scenario allows students to warm up, to stretch, and to practice new techniques without fear of harmful retaliation. As the body conditions itself the speed and force intensify. At full speed, power, and speed maximize, but the focus changes from deep penetration of the opponent to simply *'touching.'* In martial arts, sparring the term for light or superficial contact is *Touch*. In marriage, the same scenario regarding development of the relationship should occur at the same tempo. The marital prayer life is vital to combat; it must develop for the couple to wield power. When married couples pray they must learn to pray at full speed and with focus. This is important for the same reason; lovemaking takes time to learn because it is difficult for two to stay in the same place for the same length of time. Mature couples learn that foreplay becomes the major part of their happy sex life. Foreplay, like praise and worship prepares us to give and receive. Foreplay in our prayer life does the same it focuses our attention so when the time comes to give and receive we are ready, willing, and able.

15.2.2 **Marital barracks provide a safe place to rest** - After spiritual combat, the need for rest is more important than many realize. As it was in the wilderness with Moses[64], regardless of whether or not we are winning, there comes a time when we get tired. The Biblical model proves that this is the fleshliest time for Christians. Remember, flesh seeks to please itself and righteousness is tiresome. Satan waited until Jesus tired before offering Him the pleasures of this life. Satan does this same thing to us because we are more likely to make mistakes or give in to lust when we are tired and unfocused.

    The more fatigue sets in the more careless we become. This tendency is one of thing the Marine Corps trains against constantly. Loosing strength does not cause carelessness but this is often the by-product. After a long day, we come home to bond, to rest and enjoy safety.

15.2.3 **Marital barracks provide a place for marital fellowship** - Part of the bonding at home is the unifying of the couple. As the years grow, the couple should learn to see the benefits of the others input and respect them. This type of planning requires minimal distraction and intrusion. It is ill advised to plan our family's future at a nightclub. The visual and auditory stimulus does not foster intimacy. The bedroom and the closet are quiet isolated places that allow vulnerability, and nakedness. Nakedness in this sense implies raw and without covering, not nudity. We cannot develop intimacy with God or our spouses from behind curtains, secrets, and lies.

16 Marital barracks provide a place for moral support - We learned about moral influence in <u>From a Fortress in Patmos</u>. In marriage, the inverse becomes imperative. In battle, warriors must influence each other externally, but spouses must influence each other internally. A spouse must undergird us morally or we lose more than just ground forces.

A wife should not encourage her husband to seek pleasure outside the home. The Bible warns against annoying, nagging wives, but a lack of hygiene, poor appearance, and apathy are equally as harmful to a marriage. Husbands, we must not abuse the reward God gave us in this life. We must be good stewards over money yet spend adequate money her happiness.

15.3 <u>Moral influence</u>

One of the greatest means of moral support is a satisfied mate. A mate that finds home a place of favor and a place they are welcome cherishes the time spent in the home. When a spouse weakens in terms of the flesh or spirit it often takes a few well-placed kisses or words to rectify the situation. Moral support does not have to take the form of words; it can just as easily be a hand pulling us away from the liquor store, crack house, or adult bookstore.

One of the greatest hindrances to moral influence is that it requires the person to be moral. When we consider some of the synonyms for moral, we begin to understand why it poses a problem in many families. Moral has as synonyms, ethical, honest, decent, proper, and honorable. The one thing moral is not it politically correct. Christians are in the midst of a war for eternal life. Why would we risk our family's eternal security in order not to offend a person of low moral fiber? A man that steals should not take offense at the label of thief, and if they do so what. What does the message resonate to a child that we allow to hang out with their drug dealing, abusive uncle then mummer about them behind their back? The appropriate manner in which too handle the matter is to denounce the behavior, leave a door for reconciliation upon cessation of the behavior and bid your uncle good day. When we choose to try to separate the person from their actions, we create confusion. Whatever idiot said *that a man should not be defined by their actions* was attempting to justify bad behavior. Moreover, as Christians, God requires us to abide by His commands not the clichés of the world. To that end, the Bible says of moral influence, "**Even a child is known by his doings, whether his work [be] pure, and whether [it be] right** - (Proverbs 20:11)" and "**EITHER MAKE THE TREE GOOD, AND HIS FRUIT GOOD; OR ELSE MAKE THE TREE CORRUPT, AND HIS FRUIT CORRUPT: FOR THE TREE IS KNOWN BY [HIS] FRUIT** - (Matthew 12:33).

To influence our family morally, they must perceive our actions and us as, ethical, honest, decent, proper, and honorable. Then when we take our stand, as all Christians eventually must we will be able to do so with a clear conscience, and fluidity, because this is how we live.

_____
_____
_____
_____

16.0
Marital Discipline

"And the man said, 'The woman whom thou gavest [to be] with me, she gave me of the tree, and I did eat.' And the Lord God said unto the woman, 'WHAT [IS] THIS [THAT] THOU HAST DONE?' And the woman said, 'The serpent beguiled me, and I did eat'," - (Genesis 3:12-13).

16.1 Short reasons
- 16.1.1 **Discipline establishes marital parameters**
- 16.1.2 **Discipline prevents hasty marital responses to attacks**
- 16.1.3 **Discipline minimizes marital dissent**
- 16.1.4 **Discipline diminishes marital fear**

16.2 Long reasons

16.2.1 **Discipline sets marital up parameters** - The Christian walk is a walk of discipline, in the flesh. God fashioned men in a peculiar way, and He made a peculiar people. In making men who love God enough not to follow their flesh, God established His way. Under the same authority, men enter marriage, which is a thing of God. We enter marriage with the intention of becoming something better, something Godly. The subtle beauty of marriage is that it reinforces parameters in righteous living without adding misery. Rigors of celibacy weigh on single Christians because physicality is a large part of a relationship. In prolonged dating the chances of sexuality increase. To pretend that teen Christians do not face this dilemma or can simply pray through this dilemma denies the obvious statistics.

The flesh abhors righteous living; it longs for lavishness. I prayed for a wife. Even before encountering sex, I prepared for a wife, training to stay faithful, remain patient, and avoid temptation. Until the inevitable happened - I encountered sex. Then I realized that I wasted years at home alone. Denial was a waste of time, so I told God, "Give me a wife or send me to hell now." There was no reason to waste time fiddle farting around. I was not going to spend my life living alone and sexless.

I once asked a friend why she was so determined to marry. She responded, "Because I want to have sex." I laughed but I understood her well. Marriage is the cure for most of what ails. Once married, we do not have to sleep alone, and we do not have to stop at kissing; most importantly, our fleshly actions do not cause us to go to hell.

16.2.2 **Discipline prevents hasty marital responses to attacks** - Patience can win more battles than skill. Although martial artists train for skill, the main purpose of discipline is endurance. When an attack occurs spiritual or physical, the right response will always win. This means that in unity: in the preservation of peace and safety in marriage there is strategy not weakness. A woman flirting with your husband is an attack, but it does not necessitate an immediate response. In the heart of the good husband, there is no fertile ground.

16.2.3 Discipline minimizes marital dissent - My friend Walter Harris told me that love was a decision, once I decide to love my wife he said I had to walk that out. He never told me how difficult that was, or that it does not necessarily get easier. What I did take from that is that it is not love that carries couples through the better or worse, discipline makes the difference. Love does not bring us home we make a choice. Although love factors into the choice, many people that love their spouses do not live together. It is not that they do not love the other they simply do not have the discipline to change enough to make the relationship work. The same discipline that brings us home has to enable us to keep our home. Learn the discipline to shut our mouths[65] and maintain the peace.

16.3 The appropriate use of 'silent treatment'

Under normal circumstances, the silent treatment is an immature method to resolve a problem or get selfish needs met. The proper application of the silent treatment comes from Proverbs 29:11, "**A fool uttereth all his mind: but a wise [man] keepeth it in till afterwards**," wherein we learn not to let unpleasant or unwholesome words proceed from our mouths. In marriage let sweetness and edification flow between lovers. However, when we find that the words we wish to utter are injurious; this is the time to use the silent treatment. Use silence to calm down and let the anger subside. Before we speak evil to each other remember a fool utters their whole mind and there is always and way to discuss things without ugliness.

Hebrews 3:13 continues to tell us why we must be nice to our spouses, "**But exhort one another daily, while it is called Today; lest any of you be hardened through the deceitfulness of sin.**" It is plain to see that there is a window of opportunity in relationship building. The Bible warns us that kindness during the beginning of the relationship keeps the day alive. After the divorce or the affair is not the time to be considerate. Nevertheless, there comes a time in every relationship that darkness rears its ugly head: pray that the darkness is not within our families.

16.3.1 **Discipline diminishes marital fear** - When spouses trust each other it reduces tension. My wife can ask anything about anything I do, wherever I go, and with whom I go. The key to this relationship is not to do things we do not want to answer for. When we discipline ourselves to succeed, then we find fewer distractions in life.

16.4 Marital discipline

"**Every vow, and every binding oath to afflict the soul, her husband may establish it, or her husband may make it void** - (Numbers 30:13). Like all Godly disciplines marriage has responsibility. The husband is morally responsible for the family. Despite rhetoric about individual rights and choice, these do not extend to the children in a Christian family as indicated in verse 30:16. That being the case, husbands/fathers how can we live a substandard immoral existence and expect to have moral influence? Decide what we want, according to Matthew 12:33 are fruit is what we make it to be, if we want moral fruit, we must live a moral life.

My beautiful son David was stillborn. After a little 'jumpstart' from the hospital, he was all right. My wife asked why I was not afraid, to which I responded, "God told us we were having a son, does not matter what the hospital said we were having a son." The tree of ambivalence (good and evil) never has yielded anything other than death. My son is fruit from the Tree from which I eat. The Tree of Life bears nothing except Life; therefore, I had no doubt. The discipline of marriage God designed to bring life into a family, but this depends on the family eating from the right tree.

17.0
The Marital Armory

"**Behold, thou [art] fair, my love; behold, thou [art] fair; thou [hast] doves' eyes within thy locks…Thy neck [is] like the tower of David builded for an Armory**" - (Songs 4:1-4).

17.1 Short reasons
  17.1.1 **The marital armory is a common place to store marital weapons**
  17.1.2 **The marital armory gives a place to keep marital weapons safe**
  17.1.3 **The marital armory is a place to hide marital mysteries**

17.2 Long reasons
  17.2.1 **The marital armory is a common place to store marital weapons** - The marital armory like the regular armory exists, to store weapons. The difference is that the marital armory is requires careful balancing at times. Adam took half the kingdom and played in the garden, he failed because he did not leave his wife what she needed to protect the home he left unguarded. The fact is that kingdom work does not work, as quickly through married people as single people, in this Paul was correct. Marriage does not make kingdom building easier; parents have a lot more to maintain than just self-discipline. Eve was not weaker, she was untrained and unprepared; Adam left her unprotected. The same man that blamed her for failing in the garden left her unprotected. Adam took all the weapons with him, he did not even tell Eve what to do in case of attack. The fault is not entirely Adam's he was unaware of Satan's subtly, and more concerned with kingdom building. To the husband, kingdom building only works within the bounds of our marriage. God does not want the husband that leaves his wife to favor another man's wife (or His church).

  17.2.2 **The marital armory is a common place to go for marital weapons** - Either Adam did not leave weapons for his wife or Eve apparently did not know where to go to find weapons. When Satan appeared, Eve did what every unprotected woman does, fend for herself. Protection in marriage extends internally and externally. Adam should have kept Satan away from Eve's body. Adam and Eve should have kept Satan away from Eve's heart. Unity and intimacy protect hearts in marriage. When we pray together, the faults in individual hearts lose their power to the strength of the marital life[66]. In this loving manner, Jesus teaches us how to protect our wives/lives.

  17.2.3 **The marital armory is a place to keep marital weapons safe** - The most sacred place in marriage is not the dinner table it is the bedroom; control central. From this place, (the only place sanctified by God) much of the family's future begins. The bedroom is where families have private conversation, where mom and dad wake and fall asleep, and where forgiveness begins and ends.

  In the garden, Satan walked into the bedroom and spoke to Adams wife. I find this repulsive, but beautifully intricate. What daring Satan showed to walk into a man's bedroom in broad daylight and whisper to his wife? Adam was so pathetic that he did not even get angry at the discovery; instead, he joined in the idolatry/adulterous affair.

17.2.4 **The marital armory is a place to hide marital mysteries** - Adam made the same mistake ministers make every day, he was out doing what he thought was his primary duty and neglecting his bride. **Marriage is sanctified ministry is not sanctified**. God did not give us wives, so we could neglect them and run off to name animals. We cannot be trusted with God's bride if we neglect our own. Scarecrows stuffed with straw do not make good husbands. The reason many ministers fall prey to their flesh is that they do not maintain their marital responsibilities in priority.

_____
_____
_____
_____
_____
_____
_____
_____
_____

17.3 Sex Toys

I get this question many times, 'Can Christians use sex toys?' My answer is '*No married Christians are sex toys*'. But I do not refer to the not the ones you buy at Adult Stores. Christians have Gods permission, not to use sex toys, but to be sex toys. "**Drink water from your own well - share your love only with your wife. Why spill the water of your springs in the streets, having sex with just anyone? You should reserve it for yourselves. Never share it with strangers. Let your wife be a fountain of blessing for you. Rejoice in the wife of your youth. She is a loving deer, a graceful doe. Let her breasts satisfy you always. May you always be captivated by her love**," (Proverbs 5:15-19).

The Bible tells us why we do not need to buy sex toys.

17.3.1 Undefiled Bed Clue #1 - This is not a slight suggestion, this is a deep sexual suggestion and euphemism at the same time. The Clue is not in his response, but that her well should always respond to her spouse. The water should not dry up for her spouse; she should be the recipient and the only recipient of our fleshly outpourings.

17.3.2 Undefiled Bed Clue #2 - An admonishment to keep our pants on until we reach home. The *whore* (referred to as a street) produces nothing of value and since she is a street, reminds us that anyone may travel on her. A biblical way of demeaning the person that lends themselves to another person's spouse.

17.3.3 Undefiled Bed Clue #3 - Keep your sex toy (spouse) germ free. If we are going to use set toys, at least care enough to use the one we know is clean.

17.3.4 Undefiled Bed Clue #4 - *Fountain* is another euphemism for arousal in a female. The Bible encourages the woman to find a way to enjoy and become aroused for their spouses. After all, despite all the stupid articles, woman cannot be as emotional about sex as they claim; otherwise, there would be no one-night stands.

17.3.5 Undefiled Bed Clue #5 - **'Rejoice'**…SEX IS SUPPOSED TO BE FUN-REMEMBER!

17.3.6 Undefiled Bed Clue #6 - Sex is flesh; change your batteries. Stop the lying - Sadly, the same people that would not keep their hands off each other now cannot find a reason to touch. More than likely you are doing something wrong. She is a loving deer, a graceful doe. Always does not depend on emotions, or finances, or work, or headaches.

17.3.7 Undefiled Bed Clue #7 - People change, bodies change, but the components of sex do not, it may just take more to get the fires burning. But as long as we breathe (**Always**), we are flesh, and the flesh God made to experience and enjoy pleasure. He gave us marriage to have more sex not less sex.

18.0
Marriage and the Use of Sanitation

"Husbands, love your wives, even as Christ also loved the church, and gave himself for it; That he might sanctify and cleanse it with the washing of water by the word, that he might present it to himself a glorious church, not having spot, or wrinkle, or any such thing; but that it should be holy and without blemish" - (Ephesians 5:25-27).

18.1 Short reasons
- 18.1.1 **Marital sanitation improves marital hygiene**
- 18.1.2 **Marital sanitation stops marital diseases**
- 18.1.3 **Marital sanitation depraves the enemy of weapons**

18.2 Long reasons

18.2.1 **Marital sanitation improves hygiene** - There are two important ways to end a soccer game: score points or stop the opponent from scoring points. Most marital training focuses on what not to bring into a marriage, but that is less than half the battle. The real focus should be on **what to remove from the marriage**. The problem for most marriages is not what happens after the marriage begins; it is how the new life clashes with the old life. The alcoholic who marries adds marital problems to their alcoholism, not the other way around. The reason much marital counseling is flawed is that it approaches the problem as though the marriage brought out the drunk. Not true, the drunk got married. Now the person that could not manage one set of problems suddenly faces two, then three etc. as the family grows. How can a drunk not rely on their only coping skill to survive? The problem is that most alcoholics do not make good spouses; therefore, the marriage was in trouble before it began. It is therefore of great importance to allow God to tell and shows us what we need to remove from our marriage.

18.2.2 **Marital sanitation stops marital diseases** - Diseases, especially social diseases, are the most common sign of unhealthy human contact. Sadly, many people marry spouses that carry diseases. Some spouses carry spreadable diseases like *strep*, and yeast infections while others carry HIV and TB. There is one disease deadlier than any other diseases, and that disease is sin. Not only unsaved people spread sin; in fact, sinners spread less sin to Christians than other Christians spread. The sinful spouse can do more damage to a soul than to a body. God requires that we pour purity into her heart, even if we have to find it outside ourselves. In filling our wives, God says we show we love her, and ourselves. Moreover, in over filling our spouse's heart, purity flows out into our lives, through our clean vessels.

18.2.3 **Marital sanitation depraves the enemy of weapons** - Had Adam spent less time naming trees; and more time loving and talking to his woman under the tree, Satan would not have had a chance to get Eve's ear.

Look at another marriage mystery compiled between Genesis and Songs, "**The eyes of both of them were opened, and they knew that they were naked. They sewed fig leaves made themselves coverings. They heard the voice of the Lord God walking in the garden in the cool of the day, and the man and his wife hid themselves from the presence of the Lord God among the trees of the garden. The Lord God called to the man, and said to him, 'WHERE ARE YOU?'** - Genesis 3:7-9." We see that God *walked* about the garden in the cool of the day. As we discussed in the book <u>From a fishing trip in Patmos</u>, this is a peculiar usage of the verb *walked* considering the context. Some translations use *sound* instead of voice[67]. However, when we apply one of the meanings of the verb walk it lends much more reason to the passage. We also look to Songs 2:3, "**As the apple tree among the trees of the wood, so [is] my beloved among the sons. I sat down under his shadow with great delight, and his fruit [was] sweet to my taste.**"

Another reference to lovers in a garden comes from Songs 8:12-14, "**My vineyard, which [is] mine, [is] before me: thou, O Solomon, [must have] a thousand, and those that keep the fruit thereof two hundred. Thou that dwellest in the gardens, the companions hearken to thy voice: cause me to hear [it]. Make haste, my beloved, and be thou like to a roe or to a young hart upon the mountains of spices.**" Had Adam learned about spending quality time *true loving* his woman. Adam and Eve would have learned they were naked a lot sooner, and not lost Eden.

Unfortunately, Adam did not learn as God intended. Between the two passages, we uncover what Adam did not learn. The time God spent walking with Adam in the cool developed bonds and closeness. Therefore, God knew Adam's solitude was not good, because Adam's flesh separated them.

19.0
Marriage and the Use of God's Armor

"**Wherefore they are no more twain, but one flesh. What therefore God hath joined together let not man put asunder** - (Matthew 19:6)."

There is another thing of interest regarding armor in marriage. When a man leaves his family to cleave to his wife and the two become one flesh, armor goes on them both. This does not mean that there are two helmets etc. What it means is that the helmet goes on the unified head, the boots on the unified feet, and the loin protector on the unified loins. This is why unity is crucial in the fortress of marriage. A fortress cannot be safe with missing walls neither can a marriage. Many of the chinks in the armor are not in the use or placement of the armor they are in the marriage itself.

19.1 **Short reasons**
    19.1.1   **Armor produces unity**
    19.1.2   **Armor produces strength of command**
    19.1.3   **Armor produces defense**
    19.1.4   **Armor produces fortified positions**

19.2 **Long reasons**
    19.2.2 **Unity** - There is nothing in marriage or Christianity that is as important as unity. In Acts, the Holy Spirit added people to the church because of unity. Failures in Christian marriages run parallel to Christian relations. The phrase **Marriage is a mystery**; is not an idea it is a paradigm. The reason Christians marriages fail is that Christian fail. Paul states over 2000 years ago that there were divisions among Christians. The divisions have grown since then and spread out into the marriages. How can a disjointed people have unified marriages? If we want to fix our marriages, we need to fix the practices of the faith or vice versa.

    19.2.3 **Strength of command** - Marine training is replete with the unified chain of command. The chain of command enables communication between ranks. The purpose of unity is unity; it has nothing to do with correctness. A unified couple that is wrong is better than a couple divided over an issue. Which is easier to correct, a bicycle or skates? The bicycle is uni-body construction, which means no individual parts. Skates are similar except they are a bifurcated unit. It takes both skates working together at the same speed and direction to make the unit function.

    19.2.4 **Defense** - The defensive posture of unity is perplexing to an attacker. The reason Islamic fundamentalism is successful is because Islamic fundamentalists are unified in mission and commitment. Unity is present in every pagan religion and every cult. Gangs also utilize unity as a tool. The reason cults and gangs recruit people more successfully than Christianity is definitely not because gangs are beneficial, it is because gangs are appealing. Social trends in the animal kingdom show us one thing; Strength in numbers is a powerful attracter. Even against helpless creatures like deer and pigs, lions and tigers hunt stragglers, or cut the prey off from the pack. 500 pigs attacking a lion is a losing battle for any lion, even lions will not attempt this battle. Unity makes the defender more powerful and more versatile.

- **19.2.5 Fortified positions** - There is security engaging in a battle with an ally. In the marines, I dreaded being stuck in fighting holes or dangerous missions with certain others because they were inept. This may sound strange, but I figured my partner would handle the flank. I never worried about losing; it was betrayal or disappointment I feared more.

Lethargy is a common Christian problem. Most Christians will not stay awake during the night. Jesus returned from prayer in the garden and He was sorely disappointed that the disciples did not stay awake with Him in His last hours. When the battle comes, even fewer Christian intend to stay and fight. No matter the foolishness men teach, God ordained for Christian to succeed as a team.

_____
_____
_____
_____
_____

19.3 Armor basics

Before we continue let us remember together some basics concerning Armor. Once we reestablish the basics, we then look to Saul and learn the proper application of Armor in a covenant relationship.

- **19.3.1 *Armor - Is a defensive covering, as a safeguard, or protection*** - armor serves to protect the wearer, but it is just as effective as a weapon, especially against the unprotected.

- **19.3.2 *Spiritual Armor - is a safeguard or protection for our spirit*** - armor serves to protect the believer, but it is just as effective as a weapon, especially defending the weak and captive.
    - 19.3.2.1 The Loin Protector of Truth[68]
        - a. The loins protect the groin.
        - b. The loins protect our ability to reproduce.
        - c. The loins protect what we reproduce.
        - d. The loins protect future.

    - 19.3.2.2 The Breastplate of Righteousness[69]
        - a. Righteousness protects heart.
        - b. Righteousness protects the breast.
        - c. Righteousness protects lungs.

    - 19.3.2.3 Feet shod with The Gospel of Peace
        - a. Gospel of peace guards where we walk.
        - b. Gospel of peace keeps crud off our feet.
        - c. Gospel of peace allows us to walk on something other than the earth.

        d. Gospel of peace protects feet when kicking.

   19.3.2.4 <u>The Shield of Faith</u>
        a. Faith covers and offers concealment.
        b. Faith defends others.
        c. Faith makes us move.
        d. Faith makes it more difficult to attack us.
        e. Faith protects the parts of the body not armored.

   19.3.2.5 <u>The Helmet of Salvation</u>
        a. The helmet protects from blows
        b. The helmet protects from sounds
        c. The helmet protects thoughts and imagination
        d. The helmet keeps things in or keeps them out.

   19.3.2.6 <u>The Sword of the Spirit</u>
        a. The sword is a lethal weapon.
        b. The two-edged sword.
        c. The sword is an effective for defense and protection.

   19.3.2.7 <u>Prayer</u>
        a. Through prayer gives God permission to act.
        b. Prayer moves flesh out of the way.
        c. Prayer allows us to hear from God.
        d. Prayer helps us match our thoughts to God's thoughts.

   19.3.2.8 <u>Alertness</u>
        a. Alertness keeps us out of danger.
        b. Alertness helps us hear the still small voice of god.
        c. Alertness helps us to be good watchmen.
        d. Alertness helps us to be good stewards.

_____
_____
_____
_____
_____
_____

19.4 **<u>The proper way to put armor on</u>**

"Then Saul dressed David in his own tunic. He put a coat of armor on him and a bronze helmet on his head. David fastened on his sword over the tunic and tried walking around, because he was not used to them, "I cannot go in these," he said to Saul, 'Because I am not used to them.' So he took them off" - (1 Samuel 17:38, NIV)[70].

We read in the book of Samuel that Saul took his own armor and put it on David. David wisely tried the armor but when he realized that, he could not fight while wearing it he took it off. David learned that covenant relationship DOES NOT AUTOMATICALLY TRANSFER TO SPIRITUAL MATURITY. In other words; just because we marry and our spouse is now joined to us, does not mean that we are the same size spiritually.

We find that out in 1 Corinthians 12:12, and Ephesians 5:31 that a married couple though desired, must achieve unity, it is not automatic. 1 Corinthians 12:12, "**For as the body is one, and has many members, and all the members of the body, being many, are one body; so also is Christ. For in one Spirit we were all immersed into one body, whether Jews or Greeks whether bond or free; and were all given to drink into one Spirit. For the body is not one member, but many. If the foot would say, 'Because I'm not the hand, I'm not part of the body,' it is not therefore not part of the body. If the ear would say, 'Because I'm not the eye, I'm not part of the body,' it is not therefore not part of the body. If the whole body were an eye, where would the hearing be? If the whole were hearing, where would the smelling be? But now God has set the members, each one of them, in the body, just as he desired. If they were all one member, where would the body be? But now they are many members, but one body. The eye cannot tell the hand, 'I have no need for you,' or again the head to the feet, 'I have no need for you.' No, much rather, those members of the body which seem to be weaker are necessary. Those parts of the body which we think to be less honorable, on those we bestow more abundant honor; and our unpresentable parts have more abundant propriety; whereas our presentable parts have no such need. But God composed the body together, giving more abundant honor to the inferior part, that there should be no division in the body, but that the members should have the same care for one another. When one member suffers, all the members suffer with it. Or when one member is honored, all the members rejoice with it. "For this cause a man will leave his father and mother and will be joined to his wife. The two will become one flesh. This mystery is great, but I speak concerning Messiah and of the assembly. Nevertheless, each of you must also love his own wife even as himself; and let the wife see that she respects her husband,**" (Ephesians 5:31).

After reading these two verses and seeing the information about armor does it not make sense why Paul suggests we do not marry unequally yoked (those who are armor does not fit) people. In a normal training environment where the armor is the correct size all that is necessary is practice. Many Christian couples find themselves behind the curve because they have to redesign their armor to make it fit before they can ever effectively use it in battle. Some couples do not stay married long enough for the new armor to come back from the Dealer before they divorce. If two cannot walk unless they agree, how much more difficult for two to fight in a suit of armor that fits poorly?

_____
_____
_____
_____
_____
_____
_____

20.0
Week III - Work Area

20.1 What is moral influence?

20.2 Why is marriage a storehouse what type of hunger does marriage offset?

20.3 How do marital food and stores minimize panic?

20.4 What are marital barracks for?

20.5 What is due benevolence?

20.6 List the chinks in spiritual armor that marriage corrects?

20.7 Why does spiritual armor have chinks?

20.8 List your strongest and weakest pieces of your marital armor.

20.9 What type of spiritual discipline do you employ?

20.10 How do you spread hope when you have none?

20.11 Why is a crisis of faith so devastating to a marriage?

Week IV
God's
Armor
and
Marriage

"For the weapons of our warfare [are] not carnal, but mighty through God to the pulling down of strong holds; For though we walk in the flesh, we do not war after the flesh - (2 Corinthians 10:3&4).

        21.0 - Marriage and the loin protector of truth
        22.0 - Marriage and the breastplate of righteousness
        23.0 - Marriage and the boots of the gospel of peace
        24.0 - Marriage and the shield of faith
        25.0 - Marriage and the helmet of salvation
        26.0 - Week 4 - Work Area

21.0
Marriage and the Loin Protector of Truth

"**She girdeth her loins with strength, and strengthens her arms** - (Proverbs 31:17)."

21.1 Short reasons
- 21.1.1 **Truth develops trust**
- 21.1.2 **Truth is easy to remember**
- 21.1.3 **Truth is a way to bond**
- 21.1.4 **Truth maintains integrity**
- 21.1.5 **Kids are less confused**

21.2 Long reasons

21.2.1 **Truth develops trust** - A marriage without trust fails. Faith in God depends upon on the level of trust developed during the faith walk. In marriage, most people fear adultery. The overwhelming complaint about adultery is that it violates trust. Once we abrogate this trust, it is difficult to rebuild. There is a common fallacy that adultery has saved marriages, this could not be true. What is most probable is that the fear of losing something taken for granted supersedes immaturity. In other words, stupid people let small problems go on because we would rather be right than happy. When we realize that, our spouse no longer wants to play that game we grow up and do what we should have done before our spouse felt it necessary to cheat.

21.2.2 **Truth is an easy to remember** - They say we never have to remember the truth. When we tell the truth, we do not have to try to remember what lie we told last time. No matter how good a liar, eventually we slip. There is One who remembers all nothing slips past God. When we stand before judgment, it is better not to need a defense attorney than to rely on grace for forgiveness.

21.2.3 **Truth is a way to bond** - The benefit of protecting our loins and saving ourselves for our mates is it enables our spouse to open up to us more. No one wants to be vulnerable with someone untrustworthy. The reason Paul says in Corinthians that he wishes that we all prophesied is that **prophesy requires trust from God.**

God does not reveal Himself to those He does not trust. It is for this reason those that sought God in the bible said to Him, *if I have found favor in your sight.*

When asked how he ensured that his messengers relayed his message accurately Chaka Zulu is fabled to have responded, "Because if they do not, I will kill them." Fortunately, God does not use this extreme measure; He exacts a different type of toll. God only uses those He trusts for prophecy because prophesy requires the messenger to deliver the message unchanged. The reason for the trust is that God gives us information on the future, if misused it could be devastating. If we dilute the message as Jonah wanted to deliver, the result can be equally devastating.

21.2.4 **Truth maintains integrity** - The ability of our spouses to respect us speaks volumes to our integrity. Our wives should not follow us if we are unrighteous. God does not require us to sin or exist outside His will. God requires her to submit, within the bounds of His will. Men do not think we are exempt for our wives' behavior. Adam thought if he blamed Eve, God would mitigate his responsibility; we now know better. Men, if we abuse our wives, neglect them, cheat on them, or are too pathetic to provide for them do not think when we point a finger at them God He will overlook our reprehensible behavior. Men, if we have learned nothing from Adam and Eve remember we are tasked with the crown and therefore responsible for the happenings in our domain. Only boys cannot control their gifts, however, through God all things are possible. If we married a nonbeliever or we drove our believer away…repent and make it right before we lose[71] more that we dreamed possible…Verily, verily, the Bible says unto us that <u>not</u> dwelling with a woman according to knowledge HINDERS OUR PRAYERS.

21.2.5 **Kids are less confused** - The other benefit of truth is that lies drive wedges between families. A common occurrence in the Old Testament was favoritism. Favoritism tore apart families and kingdoms. A lack of integrity does the same thing to our children. Children raised around drugs, abuse, lying, cheating, pornography etc., are thrown for a loop when the person that introduced them to the bad stuff punishes them for the same behavior. The only thing worse for a person than confusion is diffusion. When Godly children learn that mom and dad cannot be trusted, they soon learn that the God that mom and dad worship is also not to be trusted.

21.3 **Training our children**

There must be a reason for the Bible to admonish us to train a child in Proverbs 22:6. There must also be a concomitant reason the same passage assures us that the children will not stray but so far from the truth. Children of saint's fall the Bible, and the world is full of evidence of this. However, what the story of the prodigal son exists to do is to also reaffirm that if parents instill the right basics in the child, when (not if) they stray they will only go so far before the Holy Spirit reigns them back in. As the story shows, there comes a point in the degeneration of the children that they come to their senses. This assumes that we put the right information for them to draw from in the first place.

In order to train the child in the way they should go parents must learn that way and agree on that way. If we want to protect the fruit of our loins feed it good food, make it healthy, and anchor it to God. Then when they do need to sup, they will pull from the one source of nutrients in the universe better for them than even their parents.

The other part of this training is that we need to leave the wayward children a way to come back. If we are the lights in the world, we should also be the lights in their lives. Like our relationship with God, no matter how far we go He awaits and allows us to return. In the case of the fallen angel, they too must have a home to which they can return. What is the point of representing God only as long as they do what we want them to? This is not the standard to which we are held, therefore this is not the standard He expects us to hold them to? The truth is truth we were all darkness, and only the repentant heart returns to God. As part of our truth, we must discipline our children and training them to accept the harshness of the truth whether they like it or not for there is nothing easy in the truth of God and there are no lies in God.

22.0
Marriage and the Breastplate of Righteousness

"**But let us, who are of the day, be sober, putting on the breastplate of righteousness; and for a helmet, the hope of Salvation** - (1 Thessalonians 5:8).

22.1 Short reasons
- 22.1.1 **God honors righteousness**
- 22.1.2 **Righteousness produces less infidelity**
- 22.1.3 **Righteousness protects family**

22.2 Long reasons

22.2.1 **God honors** - God honors righteousness and a righteous family. Righteousness also helps stave off marital friction because the mercy and humility of God thwarts the fleshly desire to belittle and degrade.

22.2.2 **Righteousness causes less infidelity** - This blessing needs no explanation, except to say that desire is natural, righteousness[72] helps to curb that appetite. It is not that Godly men are not tempted they learn the appropriate application of *Three Fingers of Temptation*.

_____
_____
_____
_____
_____

22.3 The three fingers of temptation

22.3.1 **Resist temptation** - Temptation for everyone is different because we want different things. Learning to resist or ignore temptation is the first finger.

22.3.2 **Replace temptation** - Replacing the things that tempt us with things of God is the most difficult finger because the things of the spirit rarely, placate the flesh.

22.3.3 **Remove Temptation** - Learn to think as God does and to love what God does and there will be on more room for temptation in our hearts.

22.2.4 **Righteousness protects family** - We may not want to believe it but righteousness has certain built in benefits. The Bible is full of promises to the righteous. One of the greatest benefits is the constant teaching, comforting, and intercession of the Holy Spirit. People lie about God constantly, pretending as though there are not different levels of interaction between God and His people. These people are not lost; they do not want to change. These people want God to accept them as they are, so they can continue sin. This is not the case; salvation is a gift freely given, but intimacy and power take work.

If we want to provide the best for our family in this and the next life righteousness is a good start. Ever wonder what the best anniversary gift is, the gift of righteousness. For in this gift we learn to let all other gifts flow.

23.0
Marriage and the Boots of the Gospel of Peace

"And He said, 'DRAW NOT NIGH HITHER: PUT OFF THY SHOES FROM OFF THY FEET, FOR THE PLACE WHEREON THOU STANDEST [IS] HOLY GROUND'" - (Exodus 3:5).

23.1 **Short reasons**
- 23.1.1 **Peace stomps out conflict**
- 23.1.2 **Peace maintains control**
- 23.1.3 **Peace allows rest**
- 23.1.4 **Peace helps with fear**
- 23.1.5 **Peace determines what we take home**
- 23.1.6 **Peace determines our family's future**

23.1 **Long reasons**
- 23.1.1 **Peace stomps out conflict** - Peace should relax the spirit. Restlessness and struggle in the Old Testament arose because people were unsure about their relationship with God. The cross assured people peace, safety, and intimacy with God. The peace of God's might and His grace flows into marriage, not to overlook flaws and shortcomings, but so we survive them. Mercy is not accepting adultery, but through the Spirit working in us, adultery is forgivable. The Gospel of peace transcends lying, defrauding, intolerance, and hard heartedness. Without peace, there is no unity, and without unity there is no marriage, people are simply roommates.

- 23.1.2 **Peace maintains control** - The desire to maintain peace in a home solves and subjugates strife, issues, immaturity, and friction. It is easier to live in a peaceful environment with a roommate than a harsh environment with a spouse. Many people shack up because they agree with this conundrum, but they are shortsighted. A troubled marriage still falls under the covenant of God. Shacking-up leads to fornication, which is a sin, and it has no reward, understanding, or help in God's kingdom. Look at it this way, if we live in Florida and a hurricane destroys our house our homeowner's insurance rebuilds for us. This is what God is He is our insurance.

23.1.3 **Peace allows rest -** When it is time to come home, the home should be a place of rest and tranquility. No one learns in a burning classroom. Passion has its place, but peaceful foreplay, kissing, petting, and loving that creates the strongest bonds in marriage. *Quickies* have a place, but the basis for marriage is gentleness. Because of peace, there is even a little room in marriage for selfishness. The quickie is just such an animal, quickies are for selfish gratification, and lovemaking is about sharing and bonding. There are things that quickies never bring to light.

23.1.4 **Peace helps with fear -** I once heard that the definition of love was that it meant knowing the worst thing there is to know about a person and it does not matter. Most people have dark patches before marriage, but none should arise afterwards. **Husband and wife should not develop secrets after they marry**. This does not mean there is no temptation, anger, strife, fighting, or lying, but these issues ALL need to be resolved inside the home. The rationale behind all of the world's greatest martial arts is a return to peace. From anger good things can arise, but only if the anger stays in its rightful place. A man that is displeased with his sex life has the right to complain to his wife and request updating the relation: but he has no right to hit, or cheat. A woman that feels underappreciated has the right to cry and entreat her husband to pay more attention to her: she also has NO right to cheat or deny her husband. This type of vigilante behavior only fosters more problems.

23.1.5 **Peace determines what we take home** - The fool goes home drunk is an old parable. NEVER TAKE INTO THE FORTRESS A THING THAT CAN DESTROY THE FORTRESS. Liquor is not an enemy unless one of us has a drinking problem. The drunken fool is a thing in the marriage that is fearful. Food, gambling, pornography, in-laws, work, church, or anything inimical to peace in the home MUST remain outside the home. This is the easy approach; the best approach is that these things must remain outside the marriage; The Godly approach is that they remain outside our lives.

23.1.6 **Peace determines the family's future** - Matthew 10:13 is of particular interest, "**AND IF THE HOUSE BE WORTHY, LET YOUR PEACE COME UPON IT: BUT IF IT BE NOT WORTHY, LET YOUR PEACE RETURN TO YOU**". Often, we overlook the hidden mystery when we speak of dusting our feet and leaving. In this passage, we see that we carry peace with us and can take it back. If we can carry peace into someone else' home, we can certainly determine the future for our family. Go ahead of our families in prayer and lead them onto the peaceful shores of God's hand. There will always be storms, but storms rarely move earth.

There are few things in marriage and family as important as peace. Peace is important for prayer, intimacy, trust, friendship, and safety. Although, Paul speaks of a peace that defies all understanding, this does not automatically to apply to family. That peace Paul spoke of applied to peace in the storms of life and spiritual warfare this is not the peace God plans for marriage. The peace God plans is the peace David spoke of in the 23rd Psalm; a peace that leads us to still waters and green pastures and as boundaries His rod and His staff. The peace in our homes is the peace of security provided by strong righteous parents.

In a Christian family, parents wear the boots, so we bring the peace. There can be no peace in a home where parents refuse to wear the boots of the gospel of peace. Many parents decline this arduous joy because they have to shed their shoes before they can wear the boots born by God. In these boots, we learn to walk a new way and our paths God guides into a new plain of existence. Many parents are too selfish, too scared, or just too plain stupid to use this gift. As a result, they go to God constantly to give them the peace they already have at their feet. I pray that before we try to attempt to establish peace in our homes lest every time we raise our feet to bruise his head Satan bruise our delicate, unprotected, ill-prepared feet and like the sons of Schevia send us home naked. Matthew 5:9 says, "**BLESSED [ARE] THE PEACEMAKERS: FOR THEY SHALL BE CALLED THE CHILDREN OF GOD**." The gospel is not an act of surrender, but a righteous dispensing of His will. Without our boots, we cannot carry the gospel of peace very far bare feet get tired. Once shod with the boots God gives the Bible promises that we will run and not grow weary.

24.0
Marriage and the Shield of Faith

"**That the trial of our faith, being much more precious than of gold that perisheth, though it be tried with fire, might be found unto praise and honour and glory at the appearing of Jesus Christ**" - (1 Peter 1:7).

24.1 **Short reasons**
    24.1.1 **Faith enables trust in each other**
    24.1.2 **Faith God helps with tough problems**
    24.1.3 **Faith makes marriage easier to endure**
    24.1.4 **Faith fills in gaps in kingdom mysteries**

24.2 **Long reasons**

    24.2.1 **Faith enables trust in each other** - Faith; like love, hopes for good things. Through faith, we hold to God's promise that in our mates are the things that will make us both happy and fulfilled. It is easy to trust when God does the driving.

    24.2.2 **Faith and problem resolution** - Two adults unable to resolve internal conflict are pathetic. No matter the flaws discovered during dating, many stayed around for good sex, money, or free stuff. Once we married, we suddenly become too stupid to figure out how to compromise. Compromise results in victory for everybody. Both parties get what they need. Problems outside the home that we cannot control, we allow faith to walk us through--together. The story of Abraham, Hagar, and Sarah is proof positive that God expects us to resolve marital problems that we create. God told Abraham to fix the problem that Abraham created.

    24.2.3 **Faith makes marriage easier to endure** - Despite our spouses' shortcomings; our partners can become great in our eyes. The beauty of faith is that holding on to it allows us to change, with minimal suffering. The promise of the new life helps us to endure the growing pains.

    24.2.4 **Faith fills in gaps in kingdom mysteries** - "**This thing marriage is a mystery I speak concerning Christ and the church**." Believers, the mysteries of the kingdom are too complex for us to understand at once. Kingdom mysteries require study, patience, personal growth, and sacrifice: as does marriage. The mystery to this relationship is how and what we learn in marriage translates to kingdom mysteries and vice versa. Problems in marriage are actually lessons to develop kingdom usefulness.

        "**The Lord [is] my strength and my shield; my heart trusted in him, and I am helped: therefore, my heart greatly rejoiceth; and with my song will I praise him** - (Psalms 28:7). As we discussed many times in the Patmos wilderness series, most people do not realize the high degree of spiritual insight (wisdom) David possessed. When David spoke of his heart trusting God he spoke parenthetically of faith. This phrase is the epitome of what faith is. It is not our minds or even our souls trusting God it is our hearts that trust in God. Therefore, faithfulness in marriage is necessary. Faith is the hearts trusting condition. In marriage, two hears must trust each other of there is no intimacy. When we hold our faith in God, hold it in front of our family, and trust in our heart that He is God. Then the Husband of all Christian spouses shall defend His bride and their children.

24.2.5 **Faith protects our dreams -** The dreams of a lifetime, no matter how stupid, need nurturing. Many times, combined dreams show hidden talents in us. Someone once said *that a man without dreams dies*. This is not far from the truth. God often communicates with us through dreams. Faith becomes more believable in the dream world where the impossible happens every day. Dreams are often visions of what God wants brought it to life in our small minds.

Once God gives dreams, He protects them from becoming plans used by the enemy.

_____
_____
_____
_____
_____
_____
_____
_____
_____
_____
_____
_____
_____
_____
_____
_____
_____
_____
_____
_____
_____
_____

25.0
Marriage and the Helmet of Salvation

"**Ye shall not [need] to fight in this [battle]: set ourselves, stand ye [still], and see the salvation of the Lord with we, O Judah and Jerusalem: fear not, nor be dismayed; tomorrow go out against them: for the Lord [will be] with us**" - (2 Chronicles 20:17).

25.1 Short reasons
- 25.1.1 Salvation helps guards from lust
- 25.1.2 **Faith keeps our words chaste**
- 25.1.3 **Faith helps to maintain faith**
- 25.1.4 **Faith protects our dreams**

25.2 Long reasons

25.2.1 **Salvation guards from lust** - '**Blessed are the pure in heart for they shall see God.**' The pure heart has as either a partner or opponent in the human mind. If we keep a pure heart, we learn to imagine pure things: eventually the heart and mind unify. Meditation in Shaolin Monks is supposed to produce this response, but the fact is that they cheat. Living in closets our entire lives is not purity it is isolation. Only the renewing of the mind by the Holy Spirit produces purity.

25.2.2 **Salvation keeps our words chaste** - The renewed mind works with the pure heart to produce pure words. Nothing sucks so much as sharing our bed and future with a person the hates us or that we hate. Chaste conversation is a woman's weapon against men, but women respond even better than men do to sweet words. The kingdom mystery to this is that out of the abundance of the heart the mouth speaks. The words we share with our spouses tell them what is in hearts[73] and our minds. Speak chastely, edify, exhort, and build up our spouse with kindness and love.

25.2.3 **Maintaining faith** - Reassuring ourselves like the little engine, makes the hardships of life bearable. Allow me to state the mystery of strong faith. **IF GOD SAID IT WILL BE, IT WILL BE; IF HE DID NOT SAY IT WILL BE...SO BE IT**. What this means is that what He says He will do He will do, but He is not obligated to do anything He did not say He would do. Be sure we actually hear God, not our hearts. When we learn to hear God's two voices, we will never mistake His for any other voice.

25.3 God's two voices

25.3.1 The staff - God like any father has two voices, the friend, and the king. The friend is the Holy Spirit and it educates, exhorts, and comforts. We hear this voice most often because there is constant teaching and correction needed.

25.3.2 The rod - This is the voice of the King. When we hear this is usually short and to the point, it DOES NOT REPEAT, and it is usually giving instruction or response in an authoritarian manner.

26.0
Week IV - Work Area

26.1 What type of spiritual discipline does your family employ?

_____
_____
_____
_____
_____

26.2 If you were Satan, where would you attack yourself?

_____
_____
_____
_____
_____

26.3 If you were Satan, where would you attack your family?

_____
_____
_____
_____
_____

26.4 Why is marriage often lonely?

_____
_____
_____
_____
_____

26.5 How do we keep our marriage is clean?

26.6 How do we build walls around our marriage and what is their purpose?

26.7 What type of attitude does sexual impurity create?

26.8 How do both spouses wear one suit of armor?

26.9 How does the married couple administer first aid?

26.10 Why is Satan focused on destroying marriage what is his ultimate goal?

26.11 List of ways civil war damages marriage and how to fix them?

Week 5

Marital Armor

"So ought men to love their wives as their own bodies. He that loveth his wife loveth himself. For no man ever yet hated his own flesh; but nourisheth and cherisheth it, even as the Lord the church" - (Ephesians 5:28:29).

    27.0 - Marriage and the sword of the Spirit
    28.0 - Prayer and marriage
    29.0 - Alertness in marriage
    30.0 - Marital armor
    31.0 - Subjection to the husband as a piece of marital armor
    32.0 - Subjection to the Lord as a piece of marital armor
    33.0 Week 5 - Work Area

27.0
Marriage and the Sword of the Spirit

"**Howbeit when He, the Spirit of truth, is come, He will guide us into all truth: for He shall not speak of Himself; but whatsoever He shall hear, [that] shall He speak: and He will shew us things to come**" - (John 16:13).

27.1 Short reasons
- 27.1.1 **Truth helps maintain respect**
- 27.1.2 **Truth helps maintain romance**
- 27.1.3 **Truth educates**
- 27.1.4 **Truth exhorts**
- 27.1.5 **Truth chastens and guides**

27.2 Long reasons

27.2.1 **Truth maintains respect** - Truth: no matter how harsh is respectable. No matter whether people want to hear the truth they should learn to honor the truth. I have swords in my home they are beautiful. At no time however do I forget they are swords, at least not now. Once I forgot my sword was a sword. I had the sheath of my Katana (Japanese sword) around my waist. As I kneeled to bow, the sword slipped from its sheath. Instinct overrode training and I reached to catch the falling sword. I was able to grab the blade as it slid through my hands slicing my hand. The sword of God is no less deserving of respect. Rest assured when we start slipping; God has no problem cutting us to make His point.

27.2.2 **Truth maintains romance** - Lying is not romantic to anyone. Nothing ruins romance as much as giving our all to a liar. Sometimes our spouses grow cold and we cannot figure out why. Perhaps it was what we said; the little lie about where we were resonated somewhere in their past. Sometimes our words open old wounds we knew nothing about.

27.2.3 **Truth educates** - There is no greater use of the truth than teaching. Many of the lies we learned in school tainted our views of the truths. Lies about Christopher Columbus, creation, dinosaurs, victimless crimes, and alternative lifestyles create doubt in humans. It is hard to trust a liar, remember the dentist that gave our first needle? The doctor that tells his patient it is going to hurt makes for a healthier patient because they become accustom to the brief discomfort associated with healthcare. The child told *there is no pain*; never wants to return to any type of doctor or dentist because they no longer trust the profession. Because of distrust, many people get no healthcare. Spiritual healthcare is the same thing. When we lie, sleep with, fleece, or mislead the sheep, they also shy away from God's healthcare because they are not sure what else spiritual doctors lie about.

27.2.4 **Truth exhorts** - A truthful lesson or exhortation promotes growth. Many people want the truth; it allows them to set boundaries. All people needed truth because it is life. If we deny the truth, we deny the Spirit of truth. We cannot deny God yet expect to benefit from His blessings.

Most Christians overlook the harsh truths of God like judgment, wrath, and vengeance and settle for the Sesame Street version. This is why so many Christians have bad relationships with the rod and staff because they think of God as Ronald McDonald--their own personal clown.

28.0
Prayer and Marriage

"Likewise, ye husbands, dwell with [them] according to knowledge, giving honor unto the wife, as unto the weaker vessel, and as being heirs together of the grace of life; that our prayers be not hindered" - (1 Peter 3:7).

28.1 **Short reasons**

    28.1.1 **Prayer guides future**

    28.1.2 **Prayer protects against the evil one**

    28.1.3 **Prayer manages the unseen**

28.2 **Long reasons**

    28.2.1 **Prayer guides future** - Prayer allows God to assist and direct our lives. The other thing prayer does is allow God's will to intermingle Christian lives so that He can use His people to help each other.

    28.2.2 **Prayer protects against the evil one** - Prayer does one thing that is indispensable in any relationship, especially marriage. Prayer keeps wicked imaginations and lustful thoughts at bay. As is written in Proverbs about the good man going away from home, it has not changed. Most men do not meet their adultery partner at home, the exception being house cleaners, and baby sitters. When spouses are away, the Holy Spirit aids them in resisting the wiles of the evil one. It is not that spouses should not be trusted, none of us is trustworthy, and without the help of God, no flesh would attempt righteousness.

    28.2.3 **Prayer manages the unseen** - The most important part of deliverance from evil is deliverance from the unseen evil. There is no way to count how many attacks by satanic forces God resolves or helps us to avoid. Think of all the unprotected premarital sex Christians have engaged in over the years--how much of it has resulted in kids and diseases. Now think of that same amount of sex that went unnoticed because there was no result. Every day of our life after salvation, Satan's kingdom attacks. In the cold war between USA and the USSR, there were many casualties of that unseen war, but there are far more success stories and rescues.

In spiritual warfare, there are also many casualties of that unseen war. The Bible says that if we were to tell of all God's mercies, there would not be enough room on the earth for the books[74].

29.0
Alertness in Marriage

"Now the serpent was subtler than any beast of the field which the Lord God had made. And he said unto the woman, Yea, hath God said, YE SHALL NOT EAT OF EVERY TREE OF THE GARDEN" - (Genesis 3:1).

29.1 **Short reason**
    29.1.1 **Alertness stops demonic encroachment**
    29.1.2 **Alertness protects kids**
    29.1.3 **Alertness manages attacks**
    29.1.4 **Alertness maintains unity**

29.2 **Long reasons**

    29.2.1 **Alertness stops demonic encroachment** - Do we remember the song, *who's making love to your old lady while you were out making love*? Adam proved that this attack stills works. The fact that our spouse is not actively engaged in adultery does not mean that we are not under attack. Remember anything we hold dear is subject to satanic attack[75]. We must always be sober because our adversary is always on the attack. Remember, demonic influences manifest in many ways. A wife that bankrupts her husband is the result of demonic influences. A husband that denies his immigrant wife papers is the result of demonic influences; domestic violence is the result of demonic influences, etc.

    29.2.2 **Alertness protects kids** - I was on a school field trip to Disney. I was a teenager and concerned with popularity. As I sought to be friendly with to be popular kids one of my friend Scott Thompson said, "*Donaldson, dude trying to make a move on your brother.*" I looked over and an older guy was sitting at the table attempting to sweet talk my brother. Some big brother I was, I was so busy living I let my guard down and left my younger brother unprotected. Rest assured that I never let my guard down again. I miss nothing now, except I occasionally do not see the subtle wretchedness in my own heart.

    29.2.3 **Alertness manages attacks** - We must always be involved with our families, because we of the need to immediately diagnose change. Alertness assists in managing demonic attacks. Logistics is part of combat. Not all changes are bad. However, nothing good comes from Satan. If our family is not in God's kingdom, they are lost. God's stadium is the only stadium in the universe without seats; there are no spectators in God's war.

    29.2.4 **Alertness maintains unity** - Combat has a unifying effect, survival an even more unifying effect. A couple fighting each other will probably not notice the enemy slip into camp. Though we are on the winning side, the battle is not yet over.

As a young marine, I found myself in North Carolina. My squad earned liberty that weekend. There were six of us in two adjacent rooms. The guys went to get drunk, so I stayed at the room. When I got hungry, I went for food. I walked down to the closest eatery and dined alone. Upon returning, I realized I had no key and could not get back into either room. Neither room was in my name, so the manager would not let me back into the room.

As fate would have it, a young woman came out of her room approximately 30 minutes after I returned. I was cold, but not hungry. She made pleasant conversation and we stood outside for a long time talking. Abruptly she remarked how cold it was and invited me to wait with her and watch television. I accepted after all I had been waiting outside approx. 90 minutes and had no idea when they would return.

We walked into the room and sat down. We watched television for a while then she started to remark about the relative comfort of her room. I agreed her room was better than outside. She continued to explain to me the benefits of staying with her in the room verses standing outside. She even offered the comfort of her room for the night to assuage any possibility of me missing my friend upon their return.

I was young and naive, but at this point, I was beginning to sense something peculiar about her platitudes. It was not until she asked how much I was willing to pay for all that comfort did I realize that I had stumbled into the waiting arms of a *working girl*. I politely thanked her for her hospitality and waited outside until my drunken friends returned.

Satan is always subtle, I did not sleep with her, but it would still have been difficult to convince my wife that I did not. Had I been drunk; or so inclined, or perhaps even if she was prettier, I may have fallen. Had I remained alert and perceived the danger at the onset I would have never had to finagle my way out of her boudoir. Cold as the outside was I was not interested in her dark, warmth. Alertness helps abate many problems, sometimes problems we do not even discern.

30.0
Marital Armor

*"**And what man [is there] that hath betrothed a wife, and hath not taken her? Let him go and return unto his house, lest he die in the battle, and another man take her**"* - (Deuteronomy 20:7).

It makes sense that soldiers in an active area of combat stay prepared for battle. Although women in combat are not the preferred method, God neither neglects nor overlooks females when it comes to battle. God; being the good Father, realizes that MEN CANNOT FIGHT FOR WOMEN'S SOULS. No matter how we try to interpret Ephesians, the way we accomplish the *blemish less* wife is by LIVING TO SAVE HER--NOT FIGHTING WITH HER.

Spiritual warfare is a fight for eternal life, and for the right to choose. This does not mean that a wife is at the mercy of her husband. Although God ordained for Godly men to lead their wives to Him, He does not send women to hell that have pathetic husbands[76].

30.1 How does marital armor work?

Martial armor is extremely complicated because it requires unity. Just as in the three-legged race, two cannot function, as one until they suborn their personal needs to each other. We cannot fight a battle if our left side falls asleep. The wife and the husband need to unite to live. The way unity works creates complexity. Imagine a pocket size wife. Once I put her in my pocket and then put on my armor, she is inside the armor and part of the fight with me. The man takes the warrior posture and goes to the fight wearing the armor. The woman on the other hand has two battles to wage. She too is in the armor, so she has to stay both submitted and committed to the husband. As long as they stay together, he fights in her stead and protects her because the two are one.

The reason God honors this approach is because He only has to deal with one team of two unified, submitted souls.

The other battle the woman has is the battle to stay in the right place with/in her husband. An un-submitted wife creates more problems than most marriages can withstand. Spiritual warfare in a disjointed marriage is more severe. Satan needs permission to enter a home or family. In a marriage, the husband and the wife are one; this means either spouse can allow demons inside the home[77].

When police respond to a domestic and find that there is a third party at the house that one of the married persons wants to leave the police cannot make them leave. The police cannot usurp either person's authority. Do not be deceived, Adam was the head of the household. Sampson was also the head of the household. The wife can bind the strongman just as easily as drugs, demons, or fornication.

It behooves men to take care with our other half because she can do as much damage to the family as we can. Although Eve did not have authority over Adam, she destroyed life, as we knew it; and her idiot husband stood by and helped her do it. Who was the weaker vessel?

31.0
Subjection to the Husband as a Piece of Marital Armor

"*Who can find a worthy woman? For her price is far above rubies. The heart of her husband trusts in her, He shall have no lack of gain. She does him good, and not harm, all the days of her life*" - (Proverbs 10:31).

31.1 Short reasons
- 31.1.1 **Subjection makes decision making easier**
- 31.1.2 **Subjection satisfies the tender male ego**
- 31.1.3 **Subjection helps nullify insecurity**
- 31.1.4 **Subjection leaves less room for Satan to work in the marriage**

31.2 Long reasons

31.2.1 **Subjection makes decision making easier** - Subjection means *compromise*. Only an immature person sacrifices peace just to be *right*. In marriage there is no right or wrong, there is peace and conflict. I routinely make command decisions in my household. I jokingly say to my wife, "I command you to make a decision." I am man enough to share decision making with my wife. If we have a difference of opinion, the welfare of the family determines the decision; on this approach, we unify.

31.2.2 **Subjection satisfies the tender male ego** - Like most men, I hate when my wife is right. However, if she chooses the better course of action we abide by it. To use the stupid half-scripture that the woman is the weaker vessel, only shows men's stupidity. If the woman is that stupid, why did we marry her?

31.2.3 **Subjection helps nullify insecurity** - A husband does not need a strong independent woman he needs a wife. If men wanted to sleep alone, and argue all the time, they would not get married. A man wants a woman he can hold and take care of. A man wants a charming-woman strong enough to get the job done but not too hard to squeeze. A woman subjected to her husband has a gentler, caring man because he does not have to fight with her.

31.2.4 Subjection leaves less room for Satan to work in the marriage - With the peaceful resolution of conflict, and less friction Satan runs out of places to hide attack. Urban warfare is difficult because there are so many places to hide.

The stony heart of humans is urban terrain. Subjection to our husband makes subjection to God easier because we already have the habit. When men learn the responsibility of a submitted wife, they learn to understand the relationship between Christ and His church.

32.0
Subjection to the Lord as a Piece of Marital Armor

"**And if it seem evil unto you to serve the Lord, *choose* you this day whom ye will serve; whether the gods which our fathers served that [were] on the other side of the flood, or the gods of the Amorites, in whose land ye dwell: but as for me and my house, we will serve the Lord,**" - (Joshua 24:15).

32.1 **Short reasons**
    32.1.1 **Subjection to the Lord is better than sacrifice**
    32.1.2 **Subjection stops God's anger when we challenge Him**
    32.1.3 **Subjection to His word obliges Him**

32.2 **Long reasons**
    32.1.1 **Obedience is better than sacrifice**[78] - As proof that obedience is better than sacrifice; God forbade David's completion of the temple. God denied David's sacrifice because he broke the law. The reason obedience is better than sacrifice is simple. Every year for my birthday, my wife insists on giving me what she wants me to have -- whether I like it or not. I constantly remind her that a gift for me should please me. It is this way with God. Cain and Abel sacrificed but Abel's obedience was better. To do what God wants is always more pleasing than to give what we think He deserves. The reason David pleased God was that David wanted to do God's will, the fact that David failed is not as important to God--He expects us to fail. It was not God's idea for David to build the temple.

    32.1.2 **God gets angry when we challenge Him** - God has no problem with questions but He warns us in Isaiah & Job not to quarrel with Him. If we have a quarrel with God He tells us to take it up with another human[79], He has the right to what He wants with everything He created. Job quarreled with God and God summarily put Job in his place[80]. Besides, as all happily married people know comprise is the fastest way to any solution.

    32.1.3 **God's word obliges Him** - ONLY GOD'S WORD BINDS HIM. I once heard a man foolishly teach that if we tithe 15% we force a God to raise our salary. Having read the Bible cover to cover, nobody ever forced God to do anything. In fact, the hardest thing God had to do He did because He so loved the world.

33.0
Week V - Work Area

33.1 Why is it imperative to administer first aid together?
_____
_____
_____
_____

33.2 Why did Jesus send the disciples out in pairs?
_____
_____
_____
_____

33.3 How do you handle the un-submitted spouse?
_____
_____
_____
_____

33.4 What does it mean for a man to rule his house well?
_____
_____
_____

33.5 What things do you imagine that are harmful to your marriage?
_____
_____
_____
_____

33.6 What is a spiritual causality?

33.7 What is spiritual first aid?

33.8 Explain three traits of a spiritual warrior.

33.9 What does discipline have to do with marital parameters?

33.10 What is the definition of adultery in the Bible?

33.11 What is your definition of adultery in your marriage?

Week 6
More about the Armory

34.0 - Sanctification as a piece of marital armor
35.0 - A Husband's love as a piece of marital armor
36.0 - A husband's sacrifice as a piece of marital armor
37.0 - A husband's self-love as a piece of marital armor
38.0 - Unity as a piece of marital armor
39.0 - Forgiveness as a piece of marital armor
40.0 - Week 6 - Work Area

34.0
Sanctification as a Piece of Marital Armor

"That every one of you should know how to possess his vessel in sanctification and honor"

- (1 Thessalonians 4:4).

34.1 Short reasons

- 34.1.1 **God meets us in the Holy of holies**
- 34.1.2 **Blessed are the pure in heart**
- 34.1.3 **Less sin produces more blessings**

34.2 Long reasons

34.2.1 **God meets us in the Holy of holies He detests sin** - When God slew the man for touching the ark the concept was plain[81] -- the earth is cleaner than flesh, let the ark fall. Sanctification is necessary so that we can communicate with God. If it were not for the shed blood of Christ, NO MAN would see God. Sanctification blots out human contamination. God does not dwell in putrid fleshly places, for this He sent His Son. Jesus dwelt among human garbage, so Gods Holy Spirit would not have to. Just as a lobotomy blocks brain function, God does not have to see sin, because as far He is concerned all He sees is blood.

34.2.2 **Blessed are the pure in heart** - Few things in the Bible represent a regard for righteousness as beautifully as a pure heart. In one of the shortest verses in the Bible, we find one of the greatest blessings. This blessing is among the greatest because unlike Paul's or the prophet's promises this promise comes from the mouth of God. The other reason is that unlike many other blessings and rewards this ultimate reward is to be close to God--for eternity.

34.2.3 **Less sin produces blessings** - Exercise benefits little, but the Bible reminds us that exercising the spirit yields eternal blessings. The benefit of sanctification is that there are fewer inroads for satanic encroachments, which means less time waging war at home. The one thing America's war policy was brilliant at was exporting war. The brilliance behind this is that the toll is less costly than almost any other country. There is no damage to the land, culture, and less damage to the citizens, the only thing that really suffers in the U.S. war policy is the budget. This is a splendid example for spiritual warfare; let Satan pay of the high cost of real estate.

35.0
A Husband's Love as a Piece of Marital Armor

"**And Jacob loved Rachel; and said, 'I will serve thee seven years for Rachel thy younger daughter'**" - (Genesis 29:18).

35.1 **Short reasons**
    35.1.1 **Love builds a wife's security**
    35.1.2 **Love makes a better home**
    35.1.3 **God requires a husband's love**
    35.1.4 **Children that feel loved are more balanced**

35.2 **Long reasons**

    35.2.1 **Love builds a wife's security** - Most agree that love produces comfort and security. Security is the underlying reason for most marriages on both sides of the fence. As a former single man, I freely admit that being married is simpler. There is only one set of problems, one birthday and no lies to remember. Not to mention that Valentine's Day when we are married is not a nightmare.

    35.2.2 **A happy wife makes a better home** - The Bible gives numerous descriptions of the effects of a nagging wife[82]. The Bible says that it would be better to live in a barren wasteland. The opposite is true for a marginal wife; a good wife is even better.

    35.2.3 **God requires love** - There are few things required by God, love is one of them. The reason God requires us to love is because this is not the natural order of fleshly things. Many people lust, some admire, and some develop a fondness--but flesh is not capable of true love. This is why God allows the pleasures of sex, because we understand pleasure. We do not understand the rewards of intimacy with God, so we do not find gratification in serving God with our spirit. The best of us still serve God in our flesh, but revelation requires intimacy.

35.2.4 **Children that feel loved are more balanced** - Once I took my son to get an MRI. My son and I get along like twins, either he is advanced for his age, or I am way behind. After staying the lengthy time to get the MRI a person walked up to me and shook my hand, "Thank you for spending time with your son." I took what she said with a grain of salt, until I thought about it. She was able to tell by his behavior that he knew someone loved him. In that moment, I changed again. I understood that I could get the same result from my wife if she knew that I loved her. To know love requires action. *Faith without works is not the only thing that is dead--love without works is dead.* We learn from God that love is not passive; it is active, growing, and responsive.

36.0
A Husband's Sacrifice as a Piece of Marital Armor

"AND THE SECOND [IS] LIKE, [NAMELY] THIS, THOU SHALT LOVE THY NEIGHBOR AS THYSELF. THERE IS NONE OTHER COMMANDMENT GREATER THAN THESE" - (Mark 12:31).

36.1 Short reasons
- 36.1.1 Sacrifice teaches a family how to govern flesh
- 36.1.2 Sacrifice is a show of love
- 36.1.3 Sacrifice keeps material things in balance

36.2 Long reasons

36.2.1 **Sacrifice teaches a family how to govern flesh** - The failing in churches is not a failing of the FAITH; it is a failing of the application of faith. The reason fellowship is important is because **there is nothing spiritual churches can teach**. In order to swim we MUST get into the water. No matter how many land-locked classes we take, we cannot swim until we get into the water. **We cannot learn spiritual lessons in the flesh**. The Bible tries to explain spiritual lessons through fleshly examples because we cannot see in the spirit. This does not mean that the spirit and the flesh are the same; it means God communicates Himself in a manner that fleshly students can understand.

36.2.2 **Sacrifice is a show of love** - When people see love in action, they imitate it because they like the results. Godly love produces Godly results. Ungodly love produces abuse, mistrust, and pain. When a father sacrifices, he shows that love understands that there are things that it is willing to make sacrifice for.

36.2.3 **Sacrifice keeps material things in balance** - Sacrifice teaches that material things are less important than the people that own them. It is a nice gesture to buy a child a car, but to love the child in the car in a way that they appreciate the giver more that the gift produces longer lasting relationships.

Reverse application of the scripture in this cease yields benefit to our understanding. In the story of Abraham and Sarah, we note that there was an absence of children in their marriage, but it was balanced. God promised them a child, and all the while, they waited and mourned the absence of the child they had balance. Not until Sarah conceived of a way to hasten their parenthood did they begin to run into turmoil. Because of selfishness, the world still suffers unrest from the offspring of the children.

Many times, the famines in our lives exist for our sakes not as punishment. I assure you, that a marriage in trouble develops more problems upon the introduction of children. As wonderful as they are I would lie if I did not admit that parenting is difficult at requires sacrifice and patience. But through the process, like Jesus we too learn obedience.

37.0
A Husband's Self-Love as a Piece of Marital Armor

"**...LOVE THY NEIGHBOR AS THY SELF**" - (Matthew 19:19).

37.1 Short reasons
- **37.1.1 Difficult to stay faithful without self-love**
- **37.1.2 Hard to be the head of the house without self-love**
- **37.1.3 Makes the hard times easier**
- **37.1.4 Family can see the love of God through this love**

37.2 Long reasons

37.2.1 Difficult to stay faithful without self-love - The Bible reminds us that no one hates their own flesh. The popularity of abusive, reductive, cosmetic surgery leads us to believe this incorrect. The truth is these people do not hate their flesh they hate the image of themselves, the flesh is the only thing they can cut. A spouse that does not love them self finds faithfulness difficult. Even in the Marines where *Semper Fidelis* is the motto, they try to instill a love for what Marines affectively refer to as, "*Our beloved Corps.*" The Marines do not actually want us to love the Corps, but without that love for the corps it is virtually impossible to stay loyal--why would we? If we do not love ourselves enough to want the best for our families, that little affair is just around the corner.

37.2.2 Hard to be the head of the house without self-love - Many people regard head of household as just a tax designation. The head determines the direction the house takes. If we want to gauge the house, look at the head. The reason many families are messed up is not because of multi-generational curses [83], it is because the heads if the houses are messed up. Without a positive experience, most children from dysfunctional families end up dysfunctional.

37.2.3 Makes the hard times easier - The husband that demonstrates giving and sacrifice makes for his children a way to survive the worst life has to throw at them. The sacrifice of the husband also ensures that the family will be cared for and feel loved. The hardest part of sacrifice is the accompanying humility that God requires.

37.2.4 **A family can see the love of God through a husband's self-love -** Through the loving father; the family sees they can be happy with what things they have. The beauty of the fleshly lesson of sacrifice is that kids see the reason God does what He does. Through sacrifice we learn to appreciate the love it takes to give up dreams, needs and desires to make sure that the family has what they need and what they want.

38.0
Unity as a Piece of Marital Armor

"*But while he thought on these things, behold, the angel of the Lord appeared unto him in a dream, saying, 'Joseph, thou son of David, fear not to take unto thee Mary thy wife: for that which is conceived in her is of the Holy Ghost*" - (Matthew 1:20).

38.1 Short reasons
- 38.1.1 **Unity makes Decision making easy**
- 38.1.2 **Unity minimizes bifurcating kids**
- 38.1.3 **Unity Increases power**
- 38.1.4 **Unity Decreases chinks in armor**

38.2 Long reasons

38.2.1 **Unity makes decision making easy** - A unified couple, whether right or wrong is a much stronger unit. If Christians modeled their unity after Bonnie and Clyde, Butch and Sundance, Starsky, and Hutch, or the Long Ranger and Tonto we could walk in power. Instead, many Christian couples are more like Popeye and Bluto, or Tom and Jerry. Antagonistic behavior is not love; it is the result of two people living together and the resulting growing pains. The way unity works through this tumult is with the understanding that trials produce a stronger couple.

38.2.2 **Unity minimizes bifurcating kids** - Two parents create a child. God ordained for two parents to rear the child. The makeup of the human body is head and body. The church also consists of a head and body. The child with two parents has a head and body. Under normal circumstances, this works out to mold the child into a Godly seed. We know that single parent homes struggle and divorce negatively affects children. It is not that a single parent cannot rear a good child, but the woman is the body and the man the head. The missing head severely alters the child's future. Many paraplegics live useful lives without bodies. No one in the history of mankind survived without a head.

38.2.3 **Unity increases power** - In order that believer's prayers do not encounter hindrances, the Bible tells us to dwell with a woman according to knowledge[84]. One morsel of this knowledge is that there needs to be unity throughout the marriage.

    38.2.3.1 **Spiritual unity** - Do not be unequally yoked in the relationship. This does not mean that there is no growth; it means couples should grow together.

    38.2.3.2 **Fleshly unity** - Do not physically defraud one another the Bible warns least people there be a cause for adultery[85]. Physically means in affection and sexuality, and it depends on the individual relationship.

    38.2.3.3 **Bodily unity** - The Bible tells us that married people's bodies do not belong to themselves, and we should submit to one another. This submission is not in the subordinate sense it is in the unity sense. The difference is that women are not under the man or vice versa, what is actually suborned are the two contrary wills.

The husband and wife suborn their individuality so that they produce a stronger union.

38.2.4 Unity decreases chinks in armor - Satan's arrows work against armor by finding their way into the body through chunks in the armor. Chinks, open spaces, or weakness in armor usually occurs at joints or in the folds of the armor. It is at these places Satan likes to attack. Chinks Satan likes to attack within;

38.2.4.1 *Sex* - The joining of a man and a woman
38.2.4.2 *Kids* - The joining of the seeds of a man and a woman
38.2.4.3 *Prayer* - The joining of spirit and flesh
38.2.4.4 *Money* - The joining of material desire and ability
38.2.4.5 *Imagination* - The joining of desire and ability

When Satan fires arrows, he fires a hail of arrows, not just one the hail of arrows increases his chances of success.

39.0
Forgiveness as a Piece of Marital Armor

"TO WHOM YE FORGIVE ANY THING, I [FORGIVE] ALSO: FOR IF I FORGAVE ANY THING, TO WHOM I FORGAVE [IT], FOR OUR SAKES [FORGAVE I IT] IN THE PERSON OF CHRIST, LEST SATAN SHOULD GET AN ADVANTAGE OF US: FOR WE ARE NOT IGNORANT OF HIS DEVICES" - (2 Corinthians 2:10-11).

39.1 Short reasons
39.1.1 **Forgiveness makes decision making easy**
39.1.2 **Forgiveness protects kids from scars**
39.1.3 **Forgiveness enables healing**
39.1.4 **Forgiveness decreases chinks in the rear of the armor**

39.2 Long reasons

39.2.1 **Forgiveness keeps relationship moving forward** - When there are no conflicts in marriage decision-making moves smoothly. If the past constantly affects the present and the future, issues never become part of the past and they never heal, consequently, forgiveness is important.

39.2.2 **Forgiveness protects kids from scars** - When we divide children with petty bickering and childish behavior, they invariable have to choose sides. When kids have to choose sides, they have to use their own rationale to choose. How can a child make a sound decision when the two components of their decision-making process are flawed and disjointed?

39.2.3 **Forgiveness enables healing** - The healing power of love and laughter flourish when a person learns that their mistakes are over looked. How much easier it is to try when we do not have to fear failure and derision.

39.2.4 **Decreases chinks in rear of the armor** - My wife and I have a forgiveness policy. As part of our annual New Year's resolution, we forgive each other for anything said or done in the previous year that gave offense. In doing this we enable each other to heal and to grow. The thing we have noticed is that the list of stupid things said and done decreases each year.

There is no nice way to condemn other believers, so I will let God do that. After all that is God's province anyway. However, I say in passing that the majority of the marriages I watched fail had their failure in the issue of forgiveness. It is not infidelity, immaturity, or even stupidity that destroys most marriages. Unforgiving spouses destroy more marriages than anything else. We have to forgive our spouses for tumult not just transgressions. Whatsoever angers us in our marriages we must learn to forgive.

40.0
Week VI - Work Area

40.1.1 What is a Spiritually Transmitted Disease?
_____
_____
_____
_____
_____

40.1.2 What is the most common STD found in marriage?
_____
_____
_____
_____
_____

40.1.3 What is the purpose of armory?
_____
_____
_____
_____
_____

40.1.4 What type of weapons do we store in the armory?
_____
_____
_____
_____
_____

40.1.5 What causes most chinks in marital armor?

___

40.1.6 What is lethargy and why is it a common marital problem?

___

40.1.7 What are the uses and benefits of spiritual Armor?

___

40.1.8 What is a covenant relationship with God?

___

40.1.9 Does a covenant relationship with God automatically transfer to marriage?

40.1.10 What is Satan's goal or method of using incest and child molestation designed to accomplish?

40.1.11 Demons are far more resourceful than they are strong what does this mean in terms of the way they attacked your marriage and your family?

Week 7
Maintaining the Armory

41.0 - Maturity as a piece of marital armor
42.0 - Revelation as a piece of marital armor
43.0 - Reverence as a piece of marital armor
44.0 - Prayer as a piece of marital armor
45.0 - Marriage as a weapon
46.0 - Week 7 - Work Area

41.0
Maturity as a Piece of Marital Armor

"For when for the time ye ought to be teachers, ye have need that one teach you again which [be] the first principles of the oracles of God; and are become such as have need of milk, and not of strong meat." - (Hebrews 5:12).

41.1 **Short reasons**
    41.1.1 **Maturity makes marriage easier**
    41.1.2 **Maturity makes wilderness trials difficult**
    41.1.3 **Maturity makes helping others more important**

41.2 **Long reasons**

    41.2.1 **Maturity makes marriage easier** - Nobody likes a fool and being married to one is not easy. Who wants to have kids with a fool, or share finances and plans with an immature, selfish individual? Maturity allows men to keep their tender egos under control. Immature men do not handle, stress well, nor do they survive rejection. Immaturity makes pregnancy unpleasant for men, because they do not go without sex for the 9-month period without complaining. I am not a woman, but a baby kicking me inside and a man groping me outside would not turn me on either.

    41.2.2 **Maturity makes wilderness trials easier** - The two worst components of the wilderness trials are time and silence. Immaturity makes success almost impossible. If the silence does not drive us crazy, the length of time will. The key to the wilderness is maturity, because maturity is the purpose of the wilderness experience, time and silence promotes growth.

    41.2.3 **Maturity makes helping others more important** - The good Samaritan showed maturity when he decided to overlook tradition and help a person. The mature Christian MUST learn to look beyond tradition, prejudice, and fear to help people in need. The Spirit of the Lord came upon us to help the poor, sick captive, homeless and lost. If we are not going to help people, why do we need an anointing? After all, the purpose of ointments, balms, and oils are healing properties. The purpose of the anointing is to spread the Holy Spirit's healing properties throughout the world. If we do not function to carry the healing, God does not need to cover us in His anointing oil. The gifts and the call are still without repentance. However, God does not have to give us anointing power, just look at Sampson, Saul, Eli, and Aaron.

42.0
Revelation[86] as a Piece of Marital Armor

"**The secret [things belong] unto the Lord our God: but those [things which are] revealed [belong] unto us and to our children forever, that [we] may do all the words of this law**" - Deuteronomy 29:29.

42.1 Short reasons
- 42.1.1 Revelation keeps families moving forward
- 42.1.2 Revelation informs church
- 42.1.3 Revelation maintains a righteous lifestyle

42.2 Long reasons

42.1.1 **Revelation keeps families moving forward** - Revealed knowledge maintains healthy growth[87]. As we mature in the Lord He shows more of Himself. We found a peculiar thing happens when we give water to men parched by the sun. If we give them too much water, too fast, they get sick. Men parched by sin cannot receive too much of the Lord and live either, so God spoon-feeds us. The other reason He takes His time, is so we do not develop arrogance and alienate Him and His people.

42.1.2 **Revelation informs church** - Revelation knowledge edifies the church through prophecy[88]. The purpose of God's wisdom is to help His people. God did not give revelation and revealed wisdom for personal benefit and hording, it is all for His people. Personal revelation the Bible calls *word of wisdom, word of knowledge and the gift of tongues*[89]. The Bible clearly goes on to inform us that prophecy edifies the church (entire body of believers). The God that owns the cattle on a thousand hills maintains large a herd because God provides for all His children.

42.1.3 **Revelation maintains a righteous lifestyle** - The blessed revelations of God allow our spirits to stay attached and intimate with the Holy of holies. Through continual revelation, God uses vessels to warn people, correct behavior, and to direct lifestyles.

Mark 4:11 gives yet another reason to maintain intimacy in marriage. The reason intimacy (close relationship) is important in marriage is that from intimacy secrets generate. Whispering into the ear of our spouses we find hidden in the folds of this scripture, "**And He said unto them, UNTO YOU IT IS GIVEN TO KNOW THE MYSTERY OF THE KINGDOM OF GOD: BUT UNTO THEM THAT ARE WITHOUT, ALL [THESE] THINGS ARE DONE IN PARABLES**:" there are many secrets needed to make a man successful. Many more secrets exist in successful marriages, and Kingdom secrets are the vastest of the three. Stay close to God to gain wisdom, use that wisdom in our marriage by staying close to our spouses. A chink in either relationship allows secrets to escape.

43.0
Reverence as a Piece of Marital Armor

"**But he seemed to his sons-in-law to be joking. When the morning came, then the angels hurried Lot, saying, 'Get up! Take our wife, and our two daughters who are here, lest we be consumed in the iniquity of the city.' But he lingered; and the men grabbed his hand, his wife's hand, and his two daughters' hands, the Lord being merciful to him; and they took him out and set him outside of the city. It came to pass, when they had taken them out, that he said, 'Escape for our life! Don't look behind you, and don't stay anywhere in the plain. Escape to the mountains, lest you be consumed!' Lot said to them, 'Oh, not so, my Lord. See now, our servant has found favor in our sight, and we have magnified our loving kindness, which we have shown to me in saving my life. I can't escape to the mountain, lest evil overtake me, and I die...But his wife looked back from behind him, and she became a pillar of salt**" - (Genesis 19:14-19, 26).

43.1 **Short reasons**
    43.1.1 **Mutual respect aids longevity**
    43.1.2 **Teaches kids how to respect authority**
    43.1.3 **Keeps maintain a Godly lifestyle**

43.2 **Long reasons**

43.2.1 **Mutual respect aids longevity** - Reverence creates a bond that many do not understand. People who revere each other tend to be gentle, compassionate, and patient. Admiration lends a level of caring and sharing not found in the newlywed stages of life and spirituality. The Japanese have a tradition when sharing a meal, if we want more tea; we pour a glass of tea for our companion. Courtesy lends itself to sharing and inspires our companion to pour tea for us. This gentle lifestyle may lack passion, but it is easier to sustain lovemaking than the energy required for a quickie.

43.2.2 **Reverence teaches kids how to respect authority** - A child that admires a parent finds obedience easier. John 14:15 says when we learn to love God we obey His commands. This is why children must learn to admire their parents, because it teaches them how to serve God lovingly. Parents, this necessitates that we make ourselves into people worthy of respect, love, and admiration.

43.2.3 **Reverence keeps a Godly lifestyle a float -** Fear of the Lord is the beginning of wisdom[90], but _love for the Lord is evidence of wisdom_. To fear the Lord is to have a slave's relationship with the King. Nevertheless, to serve the Lord out of love is to show understanding of Him as Savior.

I once flew in a storm. However, the storm outside failed to compare to the storm between my fiancée and I. The man next to me sensed something wrong and gave me some free advice. He advised to never let go of the respect in the marriage, once it left everything else important was sure to follow. Two men in a fighting in a foxhole that hate each other have little chance of survival because they are too stupid to understand mutual need. Spouses share spiritual battles, regardless if they are speaking or not. If we have to fight, anyway one less enemy to fight is always a good thing.

44.0
Prayer as a Piece of Marital Armor

"Likewise, ye husbands, dwell with [them] according to knowledge, giving honor unto the wife, as unto the weaker vessel, and as being heirs together of the grace of life; that our prayers be not hindered" - (1 Peter 3:7).

44.1 Short reasons
- 44.1.1 **Prayer opens spiritual communication**
- 44.1.2 **Prayer quickens spirits**
- 44.1.3 **Prayer builds power through unity**

44.2 Long reasons

44.2.1 **Prayer opens spiritual communication** - When a couple prays together they learn about each other and they hear their spouses' hearts desires poured out to God. When a couple prays together they learn to mold their prayer lives together. The sooner flesh, spirits, hearts, and thoughts unify the better the marriage. Remember, nothing grows during an earthquake, not until the earth rejoins and the soil becomes fertile, does growth continue.

44.2.2 **Prayer quickens spirits** - God says He knows what we need before we even ask[91]. Knowing needs and meeting needs is not the same thing. When the Donaldsons pray, they get an answer. When I pray, and she prays for the same thing, it is not the same, because God receives two petitions from one house. When that happens, God is motivated to answer the person with best relationship to Him[92]. Why make Him choose? Why not let God flood our homes with His love and blessings? In prayer, one-size fits all is the best policy.

44.2.3 **Prayer builds power through unity** - Where any two touch and agree God promises to be there also. How wonderful a fact that we can invite God into sup with our family anytime we want to talk to Him. Like Abram in Genesis 18, we can offer God tea and bread and sit close to the One who meets every need. Prayer also forges a stronger bond between believers because humans tend to move and follow areas of success. Therefore, when God moves in a marriage the trusting couple moves in that direction because they know God only gives the best. The new direction from God therefore is the best approach to take, and the praying couple gets to see God working in and through their marriage.

The armor of God, like Christmas trees require power to shine. The only way to get the power to surge through our armor and give it life, light, and power is to pray, and stay in prayer with God. Only in praying does the power God wields itself though His gifts and His armor. A marriage without prayers is like a Christmas tree without lights; it has promise but lacks life.

According to Paul, the purpose of donning the whole armor of God is that we find ourselves able to stand against the devil. Jesus told us that some demons only come out with prayer and fasting. Jesus further taught prayer as the source of all His power. If we want our marriages to withstand the attacks of the enemy form within and without then pray as a couple. If we want to wield the power to deal with most demons fast and pray as a couple.

Although I will always teach that faith is the most important piece of the armor of God prayer is a part of the faith. Without faith, there is no power in our armor, and we will probably never put it on. However, without communication with God there will be little to no faith. Peter did not have little faith because of his weak prayer life it was because he did not know God. Jesus on the other hand knew God so He prayed. In His prayer life, He heard what God had to say and had for Him to do. In reading the Bible, we learn that faith comes by hearing and hear from the word(s) of God. There is no better place or way to hear form God than through prayer. This is another hidden application of the unceasing prayer life. In praying unceasingly, we hear from God constantly.

The unceasing prayer of the soulful couple maintains peace and tranquility in the marriage because they do not have to rely on each other's interpretation or interpolation they both get to hear the same thing from the same God at the same time. This process also maintains the equality of the yoke in the marriage.

45.0
Marriage as a Weapon

"Behold, thou [art] fair, my love; behold, thou [art] fair; thou [hast] doves' eyes within thy locks: thy hair [is] as a flock of goats, that appear from mount Gilead. Thy teeth [are] like a flock [of sheep that are even] shorn, which came up from the washing; whereof everyone bear twins, and none [is] barren among them. Thy lips [are] like a thread of scarlet, and thy speech [is] comely: thy temples [are] like a piece of a pomegranate within thy locks. Thy neck [is] like the tower of David builded for an Armory, whereon there hang a thousand bucklers, all shields of mighty men" - (Songs 4:1- 40).

Of the 10 commandments, 30% of the commandments deal with sexuality and human relations. It is not peculiar that of the ten God would take the time and effort to devote 30% of His laws to human sexuality. Jesus speaks of the problem with sexuality in Matthew 19:22, and says that we cannot control these urges without help. It makes sense that this must be an area issue of great significance.

Amazingly the church (until recently) does not consider sexuality worthy of congregational concern and discussion. Now we ordain openly gay marriages and ministers. We went from keeping the blessed union a secret to allowing the defiled to lead us.

There is a logical reason humans have control over their sex-drive. Biology is reason humans have control. The human sex drive does not start until puberty, is a necessary function to maintain the species. Every tree has to mature until such a time, as it is able to bear fruit. Despite our wretchedness, God designed sex to propagate His plan.

God's plans in the Bible include marital relations in the bedroom between the husband and wife, and bearing children is a result of that blessed union. Therefore, the immature body does not develop a sex drive until it is mature enough physically to bear children. Consequently, the world lies about pre-pubescent sexuality and homosexuality. Not only is this ignorant it begs the question…to what avail? Not only is the prepubescent unable to produce the hormones necessary to further and enjoy sex, the prepubescent will also lack any theoretical necessities (sexual arousal and fulfillment are bio-chemical in nature this is why the hormones come on line during puberty) to further a homosexual relationship.

Because God is merciful and understanding, He created a righteous manner to combat sexual impulses. Satan knows that there is a 30% certainty that we will sin sexually. If an army general determined that, his enemy had a plan which 30% guaranteed chance of failure, that General would rejoice. Not only is 30% a good margin for success. This gives the General a target, and 30% of his resources he can reallocate.

God created a perfect weapon to conquer lust, fornication, adultery, and loneliness. The weapon created by God to offset these sins is **MARRIAGE**. The way in which marriage counteracts this 30% deficiency is that it affords a righteous manner to placate the flesh. Marriage is probably the only institution God created and ordains which allows our sinful nature a legitimate avenue to express itself. There is no difference in sex in and out of marriage except God allows one. I drive a company car, and the company provides the gas. If I drove the same car filled with gas and did not work for the company, I would be a thief and have to avoid the police. The fact that I am an employee makes all the difference in the world.

No matter what type of normal sexual behavior spouses engage in consensually, God says it is ok in marriage--what an understanding God we serve. Paul says it best in 1 Corinthians 7:5, "**Defraud ye not one the other, except [it be] with consent for a time, that ye may give ourselves to fasting and prayer; and come together again, that Satan tempt you not for our incontinency**." Hebrews 13:4 tells us that the marriage bed is undefiled[93], and Solomon suggests that we let our wives breast satisfy us at all times. What this all means to believers is that God gave us a way to be righteous yet not go through life horny. Marriage: a sexually healthy marriage alleviates 30% of the sin in a human life. A righteous marriage is a powerful weapon in any arsenal.

Spiritual warfare has many enemies, which manifest themselves in the form of weapons against marriage. *Marital weapons are not offensive weapons*; marital weapons are flanking maneuvers designed to stop satanic attacks. The weapons and armaments geared towards *Guerrilla Evangelism* are not the same as marital weapons because they serve an offensive purpose. The way marital weapons work is that they assist couples stay in the fight with minimal damage. Perhaps a better explanation of the difference between Guerrilla Evangelism and marital warfare exists in the human body. When I participate in martial arts, I always sustain damage. No matter the safety precautions, every combative interaction involving flesh results in damage. If I punch you in the stomach, the damage to my hand is negligible (tiny blood vessels rupture during impact), but it does exist. To repair the damaged cells, the body uses white blood cells and lymph nodes. The lymph nodes take no active role in the physical combat, but they are integral to the warrior to keep the warrior in the fight. Spiritual warfare takes its toll on the flesh as well. Marriage like the lymph nodes contain those things necessary to repair damage sustained during the fight. With damage repaired, we can return or remain in the fight to keep the faith.

Marriage also aids in spiritual repair. The ability to rest allows the flesh to heal, but it also allows the spirit to find peace. In that peace, we find and hear from God. Had Jesus been married he would have found Satan's temptations less troublesome. Temptation only finds root in desire. With desire removed, there is no temptation. Jesus had to subdue His flesh because there was no safe fleshly port in which to hide. Yes, I used the word hide. I take refuge in my wife's arms and in bed. Rather than run from Jezebel I run to my wife. I have less to fear for my wife is kind and gentle. In times where I may fall, she goes with me--to keep my flesh safe. Like Elijah, Sampson, David, or most other men I too have weaknesses, and beautiful women fall near the top of the list of weaknesses. I therefore thank God that He gave me a beautiful woman of my very own to hold whenever we want. I do not have to borrow or share He made her to meet ALL my needs.

The benefits of marriage are mostly fleshly. Marriage gives us sex, children, companionship. God designed marriage to compensate for the fact that there is a void in fleshly life. The void in the flesh exists because God put a spirit inside the body that can only interact with spirits. The reason marriage is an effective weapon because it is a lifestyle. The lifestyle of good traits lends themselves to righteousness. As the Bible describes Job, we should all be, righteous in all our ways. How do we become righteous in all our ways? Marriage--flesh fulfilled. With lust gone and adultery gone it becomes easier to love the Lord with all our hearts and minds and souls. A by-product of absolute surrender is obedience. In obedience, we comply with all 10 of God's laws. The final mark of our maturity is love, in this we also obey. Now we see that marriage is the door to righteousness through satisfying the flesh not subverting it.

In God's design, He factored in armaments capable of sustaining marriage. Without armaments, chinks in the marriage grow uncontrollably and spread.

46.0
Week 7 - Work Area

46.1 How does truth develop trust?

46.2 How does truth support the integrity of a marriage?

46.3 What does the breastplate protect in marriage?

46.4 How does peace help deal with fear?

46.5 Explains how faith strengthens marriage and our relationship with God?
_____
_____
_____
_____
_____

46.6 Explain how salvation keeps our words chaste?
_____
_____
_____
_____
_____

46.7 How does the truth help maintain respect?
_____
_____
_____
_____
_____

46.8 How does prayer guide our future?
_____
_____
_____
_____

46.9 How alertness keep unity?
_____
_____
_____
_____
_____

Week 8

Marital Weapons

"And Abimelech called Isaac, and said, 'Behold, of a surety she [is] thy wife: and how saidst thou, she [is] my sister?' And Isaac said unto him, 'Because I said, Lest I die for her.' And Abimelech said, 'What [is] this thou hast done unto us? One of the people might lightly have lien with thy wife, and thou shouldest have brought guiltiness upon us.' And Abimelech charged all [his] people, saying, He that toucheth this man or his wife shall surely be put to death." – (Genesis 26:11).

47.0 - The eyes as weapons as a weapon against marriage
48.0 - The flesh as a marital weapon as a weapon against marriage
49.0 - Marital Sex as a weapon as a weapon against marriage
50.0 - Thoughts as weapons as a weapon against marriage
51.0 - The heart as a weapon as a weapon against marriage
52.0 - The tongue as a weapon as a weapon against marriage
53.0 - Week 9 - Work Area

47.0
The Eyes as Marital Weapons

"And Jesus knowing their thoughts said, 'WHEREFORE THINK YE EVIL IN YOUR HEARTS?" - (Matthew 9:4).

47.1 Short reasons
    47.1.1 **Eyes helps discern spirits - friends and foes**
    47.1.2 **Eyes protects kids**
    47.1.3 **Eyes learn to enjoy our wife**
    47.1.4 **Eyes discernment**

47.2 The eyes as weapons

    47.2.1 **Discerns Satan's tricks** - The eyes are indispensable. The eyes do not have to work for evil. The eyes guide us in the spirit and the flesh. Those that have eyes are supposed to see[94]. The problem is that men do not teach other men to see spiritual things. The fact is that men cannot see into the spirit kingdom. What men should teach each other is how to get close to God so that He can make us see[95]. Once we learn to see in the spirit, our Teacher will also teach us what to see. Discernment of spirits is a spiritual gift[96]. As with all good and perfect gifts, discernment comes from Heaven. Once God shows us, friend from foe, we learn to see what to pray for, and what to pray against. We also learn to see which spirits are against us, and those that are for Christ. There are many pitfalls in battle, which Satan camouflages and makes hard to discern. Once we learn to see the enemy in his many forms, we can begin to plan attacks or encroachments into Satan's kingdom.

    47.2.2 **Godly ability to see the truth** - The other benefit of seeing in the spirit is discerning the truth. The ability to discern the truth is important because His sheep know His voice. Discernment is nothing other than knowing the voice of our Father in heaven. The only way to recognize the speaker is to spend enough time to develop familiarity with His voice, ways, and words. There is only one lie in the universe, from this all lies stem. The real lie is that God does not and cannot do the things that He says. It is from this root of falsehood that Satan plants seeds of deception.

In a family, the truth is imperative. Whether we opt to believe God He is truth. Whether people acknowledge the heat of the sun, if they stay exposed to the Son too long they die. How peculiar and inexplicable to die from something we deny exists. God operates in the same manner, deny Him if we will, we still live and die by Him.

48.0
The Flesh as a Marital Weapon

"**Therefore, shall a man leave his father and his mother, and shall cleave unto his wife: and they shall be one flesh**" - (Genesis 2:24).

48.1 **Short reasons**
    48.1.1 **Cleaving to our wives makes infidelity more difficult**
    48.1.2 **Creates unity and singleness of heart**
    48.1.3 **Teaches what the relationship with God yields**
    48.1.4 **Marital-sexual fulfillment**

48.2 **The way flesh works as a weapon**

48.2.1 **Keeps Satan out** - *The greatest weapon against sins of the flesh is righteously satisfied flesh.* The one thing we know is that the sexually satisfied couple has fewer issues with lust, adultery, and idolatry. The way sex works for married people is that God says it is ok to lust after, engage in sexual activity, or adore [97] our spouses. God gave us this allowance to make righteous living within a marriage an easier route to Him.

    There are few entry points for Satan into a happy home. The two ways into a home are covertly or through an open route. The Prince of the Power of the Air understands the power of the media more than we understand. Television has opened more chinks in marital armor than any other single vehicle. I routinely stay up late to watch Star Trek or Miami Vice. The later the hour the more the programs seemed geared towards men. Media inundates men with infomercials about male enhancement and sexual enhancement. If that is not enough, the media adds the infamous Girls Gone Wild to the game.

    It is amazing to me how many young girls race to turn 18 just so they can act like, be like and get recognized as tramps. There is no honor in trampishness, but there at least used to be dishonor. The media has successfully removed the sting and humiliation of smuttiness. I saw a bumper sticker once which said, '*History does not remember good girls*,' rest assured God does.

48.2.2 **Healthy affection diminishes lust and covetousness** - I have seen many Victoria's Secret commercials. At first, the girls looked good. After a while, I looked at the lingerie more than the women did. I looked at the lingerie to find something that I would like to see my wife wear. I learned not to want the women in the commercials, but to want pretty things for my wife.

A healthy, aggressive, progressive sex life is essential to a happy marriage and it helps forge lasting bonds. The complete submission of our sexuality and yielding to our spouses engenders a level of trust unmarried people never achieve. I Corinthians 7:2-5". This passage was to be a footnote, but it is important to see that the Bible gives married people *carte blanche* to each other. **"Nevertheless, [to avoid] fornication, let every man have his own wife, and let every woman have her own husband. Let the husband render unto the wife due benevolence: and likewise also the wife unto the husband. The wife hath not power of her own body, but the husband: and likewise also the husband hath not power of his own body, but the wife. Defraud ye not one the other, except [it be] with consent for a time, that ye may give yourselves to fasting and prayer; and come together again, that Satan tempt you not for your incontinency** - Also in this passage, we see the easiest resolution to sin in the Bible. Unlike most biblical remedies to sin, which require sacrifice, God pours out a marital solution to sin that <u>requires</u> indulgence (frequent interaction).

In relationships, vulnerability breeds trust. The passionate, undefiled bedroom, filled with secrets, leads to passion and fond memories and minimizes sexual tension and temptation. Sexual tension in marriage arises from unfamiliarity, and selfishness. It is selfish not to want our spouses to enjoy sex. What this means is that the male that wants his partner to participate in sex games they dislike is selfish. The converse is also true; it is selfish not to try to meet our spouse somewhere in the middle. Once we find common ground, sex not only becomes more enjoyable, it becomes more fun for both parties. As a marital rule, the Bible agrees: that in lieu of variety, frequency and intimacy are viable substitutes.

48.2.3 Unified front - A happy couple is automatically immune to certain attacks from the enemy. A unified front is difficult for kids to breach from within the house. Imagine how much harder Satan has to work to breach it from outside that marriage. Once two spouses become one flesh the challenges against marriage become easier to manage. Wado-Ryu karate includes *Tai-Sabaki*, which in Japanese means *oneness of movement*. Oneness makes the decision-making process more efficient, the ideal marriage MUST include Tai *Sabaki*.

If we have ever seen drunks stumble, we understand the need for marital unity. If half of the union falls, it invariably drags the other side down. How can we fight if our bodies will not respond to commands? In marriage, discipline is imperative. Where the warrior once moved as one, he now meshes two into one. The warrior therefore fights two wars simultaneously, the one outside (enemy) and the one inside (inner me).

As part of spiritual warfare-training regime for ministers, we spend time in the wilderness as a group. On one such occasion, we travelled through the wilderness. As we prayed, a man approached. We were in the middle of a parking lot and the man just came out of nowhere. My back was facing the man, the Holy Spirit whispered in that ear, "Behind you!" As I turned the man stood there. He began to speak to one of the juniors in the group, but I interposed my body spoke to him. He asked for money we offered food. He then asked for prayer and we gathered around him and prayed. After the prayer he walked a few feet away and then began shouting at us, "I am Jesus Christ!" To which I replied *good then you should recognize me.* The man walked away. A few weeks later in that same area, we encountered the man again. This time as he got close, he looked and said, "I know you last time I saw you, you told me about Jesus and prayed for me." He turned and walked away.

    This is how we must use our flesh for kingdom work, as shields for the lost and as pillars of strength against evil. Be prepared to stand before the dragon and protect our families. That is easy. Matthew 5 requires us to stand exposed to the Dragon's breath for strangers, for leapers, for the deaf and mute, and for those who despitefully use us. Use the traits we develop to get or selfish desires like hard work, resourcefulness, patience, and begging to uplift Christ. When we lift Him, He promises to draw all men unto Him. Hands lifting Christ are often too busy to sin or commit adultery. The spouses lifting Christ will find their troubles too busy to bother them.

49.0
The Marital Bed as a Weapon

"**And she put her widow's garments off from her, and covered her with a vail, and wrapped herself, and sat in an open place, which [is] by the way to Timnath; for she saw that Shelah was grown, and she was not given unto him to wife. When Judah saw her, he thought her [to be] a harlot; because she had covered her face. And he turned unto her by the way, and said, 'Go to, I pray thee, let me come in unto thee;' (for he knew not that she [was] his daughter in law.) And she said, 'What wilt thou give me, that thou mayest come in unto me?' And he said, 'I will send [thee] a kid from the flock.' And she said, 'Wilt thou give [me] a pledge, till thou send [it]?' And he said, 'What pledge shall I give thee?' And she said, 'Thy signet, and thy bracelets, and thy staff that [is] in thine hand.' And he gave [it] her, and came in unto her, and she conceived by him**." - (Genesis 38:14-19).

49.1 **Short reasons**
    49.1.1 **Marital sex protects revelation**
    49.1.2 **Marital sex minimizes lust**
    49.1.3 **Marital sex maintains purity**
    49.1.4 **Marital sex supports submission**
    49.1.5 **Marital sex teaches communication**

49.2 **How sex work as a weapon**
    49.2.1 **Marital sex protects revelation** - There are few things as important to a life of flesh as sex. The problem: like seeing fat people at a buffet, human's always get the wrong idea. Sex is for Godly purposes and the main purpose is to combat sin. How much crime, greed, disappointment, and anger is centered around obtaining or maintaining sex? No matter the level of relationship, we participate in sexuality, as the ultimate expression of our feelings is sex. Women pretend as though sex is more important to men than to women, but the numbers are in--takes two to tango. For every whoremonger there must be a whore, all deadbeat dads had to *dad* with someone.

    Marital sex allows people to waste less time on the lusts of the flesh and concentrate on hearing from God. Horny, lonely people hear from God;

they just do not usually listen or care, because they are hungry. Jesus told the disciples He would not force the people to fast at the Sermon on the Mount. Jesus knew the secret, 'hungry people fall prey to *food.*' God also knows the same is true for sex, so He told us to marry and admonishes us to have all the sex we can stand--so we will not be hungry.

49.2.2 **Marital sex minimizes lust -** People frequently ask if watching porn is wrong and I always tell them yes, because people watch porn to satisfy lust. This is the easy answer and more oft than not true, but what about couples? If married couples watch adult movies and take notes from the movies as to positions, lubricants, etc., the marriage bed remains undefiled. Caution however sisters; do not expect the average man; Christian or not to ignore the women in adult movies. I wager wives will find that same man trying to watch those movies to '*learn positions*' even when they are not at home.

What I encourage married people to do with lust is turn it into a healthy sex life. When we have lustful thoughts pause the mental tape, change the woman or man we lust after or daydream about into our spouse then press play. A sexually active couple has fewer inroads for problems than couples that pretend sex is not important. If we ignore food, (which is what a fast is) does it not make our flesh weaker? If we deprive a marriage of the primary fleshly bonding exercise, how can that not weaken the marriage?

49.2.3 **Marital sex maintains purity -** Ironic is it not, the most popular sin in the world, practiced in marriage maintains purity. The beauty in God's plan constantly astounds. Who but God would allow His children to bask in their weakness, frailty, and decadence, yet call it undefiled--within the bounds of marriage? God does not expect our flesh to remain clean, so He gave us an approved playground, a fleshly pigpen inside which to wallow. This is why so many sexless marriages fail; flesh in marriage needs expression but it has no healthy means to express itself. The Bible says many fools call themselves wise and admonishes us to avoid people that preach abstinence[98]. Do not avoid them because abstinence is not Godly; avoid them because abstinence is not realistic[99].

God created us to have a sex drive, how do we think we can override His design. God designed the human sex drive to come on line when we are able to reproduce and of marrying age. It is not that abstinence is not possible[100]; it is not probable, nor profitable. Why deny self the one pleasure God granted. People: GET MARRIED; **MAKE LOVE, STAY SAVED**. Tacky, but it is gospel. I find the ability to be sexual, and sin free remarkable and one of the greater blessings because this is one area in which believers do not have to fail.

Marital sex supports submission - One important lesson married people learn is to suborn their personnel desires and share. During sex, both people enjoy the experience, but one is always doing more work than the other. In this equation, we learn how to share jobs and retain our authority. If a man prolongs foreplay to please the woman who is in charge? If the woman makes more money than the man makes but brings it all home and puts it in his hands who is in charge? What we learn is that a man who can run the house yet be in touch enough to make sure his wife is pleased in and out of bed is a man that knows how to rule his home well.

Marital sex teaches communication - Any husband that is a good lover knows how to communicate. What sexually happy couples do not tell us is how long it took them to become *sexually happy*. It takes a man a long time to learn what pleases a woman. Women learn very quickly that it does not take very much to please a man. Herein lays the problem, when it comes to the flesh women are gourmet chefs and men microwave cooks. It is difficult to change cooking styles for each other, but women have a lot more skill than men do. Women therefore should teach men to microwave; then, to use the toaster oven. The next step is stovetop and then baking. Baking requires a lot of preparation time and men learn to be patient. In doing this, in prepping before cooking, men learn to communicate to the woman and give them what they need.

49.3 Man cannot serve two masters

Matthew 6:24 dictates that men cannot serve two masters, I assumed God; the jealous God we serve simply eliminated His competition. Only after several years of marriage did God give the application for this passage.

Most militaries have a chain of command. Delegated authority gives the appearance and effect of subservience to more than one master. Man cannot serve two conflicting masters. It is not so simple a thing; the concept Jesus describes. The human creature God made of flesh first and spirit second. Therefore, humans live in that order, fleshly pleasure first then God. However, this is the secret to this dichotomy, whichever controls must have its way.

- **Flesh** - The flesh has nothing Godly in it.
- **Spirit** - The spirit has nothing fleshly in it.

Here is wisdom, if our flesh controls us, IT WILL NOT ALLOW THE SPIRIT TO GROW. The flesh as master is selfish, greedy, insecure, and ungodly. If our spirit controls, IT WILL NOT ALLOW THE FLESH TO REIGN. Many people admonish us to live the happy life serving God. I do not quite understand how they derive this fantasy. Our God tells us in many ways that to follow Him is costly, lonely, sad, and empty[101]. This is why it is not good that man be alone (without God), because in solitude man's flesh reigns.

It is not mystery why God's resolution to man's *solitude* was a woman. In order that the men have a chance against the flesh God created a righteous manner in which to control the flesh. GOD DID NOT GIVE THE WOMAN TO MAN FOR HIS SPIRIT; GOD GAVE HER TO MAN FOR MAN'S FLESH[102]. This is why we must love our wives' flesh with our flesh and her spirit with spirit. Spiritual laws must apply to all spiritual creatures. If we cannot love God in the flesh, why do we think we can love another fleshly being in the spirit?

49.4 Sex in the balanced marriage

God meant all things in marriage to be equal. Unfortunately, we listen to simpletons for marital advice instead of the Creator of marriage. Let us see what God describes as balanced marital relationship;

49.4.1 **Tasks** - The command and blessing applied to both Adam and Eve, "**And God blessed them, saying, 'BE FRUITFUL, AND MULTIPLY, AND FILL THE WATERS IN THE SEAS, AND LET FOWL MULTIPLY IN THE EARTH'**" - (Genesis 1:22).

49.4.2 **Rewards** - The wife and all the promises of young love are our fleshly reward and salvation in this life, "**Live joyfully with the wife whom thou lovest all the days of the life of thy vanity, which he hath given thee under the sun, all the days of thy vanity: for that [is] thy portion in [this] life, and in thy labour which thou takest under the sun**" - (Ecclesiastes 9:9).

49.4.3 **Dedication** - He is dedicated, and she responds, "**How fair is thy love, my sister, [my] spouse! How much better is thy love than wine! And the smell of thine ointments than all spices! Thy lips, O [my] spouse, drop [as] the honeycomb: honey and milk [are] under thy tongue; and the smell of thy garments [is] like the smell of Lebanon.** (Songs 4:10&11), **I am come into my garden, my sister, [my] spouse: I have gathered my myrrh with my spice; I have eaten my honeycomb with my honey; I have drunk my wine with my milk: eat, O friends; drink, yea, drink abundantly, O beloved**" - (Songs 5:1).

49.4.5 **Unity** - The Bible warns that adultery (of some kind) is relatively certain in a sexually

Anyone that tells us that sex in marriage is unimportant, is not worth taking advice from. If, however, sex is important, it makes sense that fleshly attraction is necessary. To this end, the old adage of loving a person for their mind or heart is folly. Last time I checked, sex does not occur in the mind or the heart. SEX IS ALL ABOUT FLESH. A balanced marriage MUST have a balanced sex life. Paul the Epistle writer; at the direction of God, tells us to not only pray unceasingly but to have sex as often as possible. Sex is integral to a balanced marriage because it allows the normally unrighteous nature of the flesh to stay controlled. Actually, the beauty of God's plan is that there do not have to be restrictions within the bounds of marriage. The lack of controls in marriage is actually another of God's mysteries for controlling the flesh of married people.

Adultery is always fleshly, no matter the justification given for adultery. The attention excuse only makes sense if the other person gave our flesh attention. This does not have to mean sex, but we are creatures made of flesh, the way interaction makes us feel is our desired result. Where does this interaction manifest? It manifests in the flesh. What God put together let no man put asunder the scriptures say. Regarding sexuality, what two fleshes God joins let them remain joined.

decrepit marriage. The command and warning are for both spouses, "**Defraud ye not one the other, except [it be] with consent for a time, that ye may give yourselves to fasting and prayer; and come together again, that Satan tempt you not for your incontinency**" - (1 Corinthians 7:5).

).4.6 <u>**Parameters**</u> - The command and warning are for spouses, "**Marriage [is] honourable in all, and the bed undefiled: but whoremongers and adulterers God will judge**" - (Hebrews 13:4).

49.5 But, I am not a missionary!

At some point, backwards Christians convinced themselves that sex was impure. Some went to so far as to believe sex was the original sin citing Adam's nakedness. One school of thought teaches that the *fruit* Satan shared with Eve was sex. However, through careful study of the episode in the garden we see that this is not the case. The nakedness referred to the condition of Adam's soul not his body[103]. We also learned that although men and angels copulated early in the Bible never alludes to this[104] as the cause of expulsion from the garden. Sex between species was not important in the garden because at that time there was no promise of the Son of man destroying Satan's kingdom. Not until God cursed Satan, was it important for Satan to ruin sexuality for humans. Because so many *children of hell*[105] disguise themselves as clergy men have for centuries used Christians as their own playmates. No one has done more to damage Christian sexuality than the church.

The missionary position developed because this position seemed to be the best way to conceive children. Since ignorant people believed propagation was the only reason for sex, this utilitarian position sexual mannerism approved by the church. Ironically, those who approved of this posture themselves engaged in all manner of sexuality and experimentation[106]. The celibate lifestyle is against Christian teaching[107]. Nunnery, and monastery living have not produced spiritual giants it produced spiritual deviants and tyrants. Sadly, people care more about sinful living than they do sinful Christians. Why would the church fight against abortion harder than it fights against pedophilia? Why would the church support openly gay marriages and clergy knowing they can NEVER be fruitful and multiply Godly seeds? Why would the church support homosexuality and pedophilia when the marriage bed is supposed to remain undefiled? Those who preach against fornication and adultery by default have to be against homosexuality.

The answer to the question is simple, yet sinister. As a child, I was taken advantage of (*touched*). The result of this *touch* marinated until such a time, as sex was important. Before I knew how to enjoy one of the best parts of life, it was tainted. When I learned about sex, it was as though I was deaf. I could see, and feel, but there was no sound, something was missing. It took years to realize what was missing. Intimacy requires self-esteem, what was lost as a child we call *innocence,* but it is actually self-worth. If we do not feel valuable, we can never feel sexy. If we have no self-worth, how can we ever feel desirable? Currently, older women and medical science have found a way to surgically reapply hymens in an effort to regain what was lost, what they gave away rather. It is impossible to go back to innocence once lost. The flesh and the imagination do not forget pleasure or horror. Even if we do not delve into fleshly pleasures, becoming indifferent has the same effect. The more impotent Christians Satan creates the fewer marital warriors there are.

This is another reason waiting until marriage for sex is imperative, we cannot undo sexual experiences. Once we venture out into a place that we find pleasurable we are not going to be able to satisfy our flesh with less. Adam and Eve show us this lesson in living color. Once we allow the defilement to enter, only the renewing of our minds by the Holy Spirit can control its influence. This is why fasting and dieting are so difficult. It is not the food value that the body craves the body craves the pleasure value sugars and fats have in them. It is this way with sex, once we taste of the wild side we cannot go back to the tame side without losing that which brought us pleasure. During marriage: before marriage, discuss what we want and need in the bedroom. This will change as we age, but there is a base line.

The rash of teen porn stars, and teen adolescent sexual behavior is a direct result of allowing people to devalue sex in the name of openness and partying. The toll on marriage is incalculable, across the ages. Throughout time, more wombs ended up wasted than torn. Marriages that produce useless children, and do not promote spiritual growth in the spouses are seeds that have fallen on the road eventually devoured by crows Satan is winning the war of the flesh, and he does not even have flesh.

50.0
Thoughts as Marital Weapons

"Casting down imaginations, and every high thing that exalteth itself against the knowledge of God and bringing into captivity every thought to the obedience of Christ" - (2 Chronicles 10:5).

50.1 **Short reasons**
    50.1.1 **Thoughts protect revelation knowledge**
    50.1.2 **Thoughts minimize lust**
    50.1.3 **Thoughts foster altruism**

50.2 **How thoughts work as a weapon**

    50.2.1 **Godly wisdom** - Truth, justice, love, virtue, and praise are things the Bible admonishes people to think about. Imagine if we spent the lustful hours of the day thinking of ways to make love to our wives instead of dreaming about Victoria's Secret models, or Hugh Heffner's rejects. The wisdom of the ages comes from the Bosom of the ages. There is no wisdom unless it comes from the bosom of the God that placed all things in order. As it was with Solomon, when we learn to think highly of the things of God, then and only then will He pour out His wisdom into the ruling of His people.

    50.2.2 **Thinking upon His thoughts** - God's thoughts are not our thoughts. Our vile thoughts are of no use to God. This also means that human plans to please Him, build His kingdom, and Lord over His people do not interest Him. The reason there is so little power, mercy, and justice in the world and in the church is that power, mercy, and justice are not creations of men. Therefore, the wretchedness we see each day in the church and the world is evidence of what men want. The way to make our thoughts function as weapons against Satan begins in the 56th Psalm. In this psalm, we learn that we must learn not to fear what the flesh can do to us.

    As we learn to trust God and to hear His thoughts, we learn to see the mysteries of His kingdom. The mysteries of God's kingdom are mysterious to us because we do not know how to pray we do not know how to think. The lack of Godly thought (Godly secrets) is the reason His people perish. **"Finally, brethren, whatsoever things are true, whatsoever things [are] honest, whatsoever things [are] just, whatsoever things [are] pure, whatsoever things [are] lovely, whatsoever things [are] of good report; if [there be] any virtue, and if [there be] any praise, think on these things"**[108]. The Bible tells us how to maintain balance and Godly power using out thoughts.

    50.2.3 **Thoughts make us creative** - As we learned from Genesis 6:5-6 the imaginations of men DO NOT SERVE GOD. History is full of designs of men that do not glorify God. What men conceive to do they achieve. Only the mercy of God caused Him to intervene at the tower of Babel. People teach that God wanted to withhold knowledge from humanity that is the philosophy of the foolish[109]. God did not withhold knowledge from humanity He withheld destruction.

The same men that make weapons of mass destruction could more easily make methods to feed the hungry and medicate the sick. The power of goodness is not gone; we stopped thinking about benevolence. The worse part of the prosperity doctrine is that it took the church's mind off helping and spreading the good news to lining our pocket.

51.0
The Heart as a Marital Weapon

"**BLESSED [ARE] THE PURE IN HEART: FOR THEY SHALL SEE GOD.**"
- (Matthew 5:8).

51.1 **Short reasons**
    51.1.1 **The heart is the center of life**
    51.1.2 **The heart is the center of love**
    51.1.3 **The heart is the center of problems**

51.2 **The heart as a weapon**
    51.2.1 **A pure heart is peaceful** - The things that defile men come from their hearts. The pure heart therefore does not have in it, murder, strife, lust, and envy. The pure heart does not grow weary in well doing, nor does it give into despair. The pure heart loves, shares, and above all the pure heart longs to see God. The pure heart is a place not even Satan can access. This longing was what Jesus spoke of in Luke 2 when He asked why Mary and Joseph looked for Him to be anywhere else. To do the will of the Father fills the pure heart and makes it a place devoid of a perch for Satan. Matthew 5:8 speaks of the outcome of purity, not just as a reward but also as an admonition against the impurity currently in our hearts. Those that are pure in heart will see God; this must mean that those with impure hearts will not see God.

    51.2.2 **Faith works in the heart** - Faith without works is just dead, as love without works is dead. Faith is an act of love; we just never recognized it is an act of love. Our faith in God grows it grows as our love for God grows, not with evidence and proof. ***The reason it is impossible to please God without faith is that it is impossible to please God without love.***

        John 14:15 says if we love God obey His commandments. When Jesus ordered Peter out on the water, the failing in Peter was not in faith, it was relationship/love with God. Peter knew of God but he neither knew nor loved Him. The reason the Bible calls John the beloved disciple was not his faith it was that he loved and was not afraid of love. The reason faith must work interchangeably with love is because it is through love that our faith hopes all things, suffers all things, and endures all things.

- **Teaches how to love despite problems** - We look upon *patience* as an act of discipline; it is not; it is a move of a disciplined heart. Patience is an act of the heart. As with our patience, in our love we possess our souls. The heart that learns to love learns patience, because there is no way to love and be impatient. There is no way to achieve love without attaining a by-product called patience.

Again, we turn to the wisdom of King David and we see that the strength in the righteous heart also comes from God. In Psalms 73:26, David says a thing wise beyond most men, "**My flesh and my heart faileth: [but] God [is] the strength of my heart, and my portion forever**." A heart filled with God has peace and it has power. The peace and power of God flowing from one spouses' heart into another makes marriage a paradise of heavenly portions.

52.0
The Tongue as a Marital Weapon

"But now ye also put off all these; anger, wrath, malice, blasphemy, filthy communication out of our mouth" - (Colossians 3: 8).

52.1 Short reasons
    52.1.1 **The tongue uplifts and exhorts**
    52.1.2 **The tongue reveals the heart's contents**
    52.1.3 **The tongue is for chaste conversation**

52.2 The tongue as a weapon

52.1   **The tongue uplifts and exhorts** - Speaking in tongues edifies us, but prophecy, (the superior gift) edifies the church. Sweetness and bitterness should not spring forth from the same river, however they always will when the river is the human heart. Bifurcation in the human heart exists because the sweetness comes from the spiritual side and the bitterness the fleshly side of our hearts. Darkness manifests itself through our dark thoughts and words. Prophecy is difficult for most because God requires a minimum of a subjected heart for prophecy.

52.2   **The tongue reveals the heart's contents** - Those that believe in the gospel of truth have to spread the gospel with truth. The tongue has directives not only to spread the gospel but also to maintain the truth of the gospel. The evidence of the tongue should mimic the evidence in the lives of the people spreading the good news. We must be aware of the fact that what we do almost always overshadows what we say.

    Therefore, we must create an over lapping in our lives to maintain consistency. This consistency should be reciprocal in our lives at home as well as in the gospel. Our spouses should never have to guess or doubt our love. Our tongues should give sweetness to our spouses as well as the truth of the Gospel.

52.3   **The tongue is for chaste conversation** - We must tell our spouses we love them. As unnecessary as it seems, this is an integral part to a happy relationship. We find that the Lord even thrives on this type of commitment. Reassurance works for both parties. One person saying *I love* resonates through the other person. The other person receives constant kindness and assurance. The security this breeds in both parties makes nauseating, intrusive, nagging behavior unnecessary.

Perfection in Biblical terms stems from the ability to control our tongues. Twix advertises their chocolate bar as a method to avoid saying stupid things. The Bible used this method first, it tells us to exhort of edify people otherwise keep quiet. Spouses have another remedy, instead of saying something stupid kiss our spouses and let tenderness have its way.

53.0
Week 8 - Work Area

53.1 How does alertness protects our kids?

___

___

___

___

___

53.2 Cite a scripture that implies that lesson produces more How alertness maintain

___

___

___

___

___

___

___

53.3 Why do children that are love feels more balanced?

___

___

___

___

53.4 How does Sacrifice keep material things in balance?

___

___

___

___

53.5 Why does Fidelity in marriage depend heavily on self-love?

53.6 How does unity increase power?

53.7 Why does forgiveness enable healing, for yours and God's perspective?

53.8 How does maturity make wilderness trails less difficult?

53.9 Why is revelation import to marriage and the church?

Week 9
Weaknesses in our Armor

       54.0 - Un-forgiveness as a weapon against marriage
       55.0 - The mystery of the lonely union
       56.0 - Common problems in marriage
       57.0 - The mystery the marriage's ultimate foe
       58.0 - Week 9 - Work Area

54.0
Un-Forgiveness as a Weapon

"And Sarai Abram's wife took Hagar her maid the Egyptian, after Abram had dwelt ten years in the land of Canaan, and gave her to her husband Abram to be his wife. And he went in unto Hagar, and she conceived: and when she saw that she had conceived, her mistress was despised in her eyes. And Sarai said unto Abram, 'My wrong [be] upon thee: I have given my maid into thy bosom; and when she saw that she had conceived, I was despised in her eyes: the Lord judge between me and thee.' But Abram said unto Sarai, 'Behold, thy maid [is] in thy hand; do to her as it pleaseth thee. And when Sarai dealt hardly with her, she fled from her face.'" - (Genesis 16:4-6).

54.1 Short reasons
  54.1.1 **Un-forgiveness makes loving difficult**
  54.1.2 **Un-forgiveness clouds heart condition**
  54.1.3 **Un-forgiveness creates other problems**

54.2 Un-forgiveness as a weapon

  54.2.1 **Do not overlook the abuse of sheep** - Anger can be useful if handled correctly[110]. The Bible says that judgment begins at the church[111]. *God does NOT forgive the abuse of His sheep, and neither should we.* Shepherds and believers alike should welcome all people into repentance. However, we should never allow or overlook the abuse of the sheep. There is a difference between personal sin and abusive sin. What we do to self, God punishes at judgment. What we share with others in the form of sin, God neither forgives nor casts asunder. God does not tolerate or overlook the abuse of people. God never forgave David for Uriah's murder--even though Uriah was a non-believer. James chapter 3 reminds us that teachers come under harsher judgment; Jesus reminds us repeatedly that the abuse of the sheep has not gone unnoticed nor will it be un-avenged.

  54.2.2 **Do not tolerate or overlook the misuse of sheep** - The Jews asked God for a fleshly king like the other nations. The equivalent of this is that Christians want to serve secular kings. God obliged His people by giving them the curse of a fleshly king. This accursed king abused and misused the sheep. Saul took their best and gave them nothing in return. God uses people for the uplifting of the Kingdom and guarantees their reward. However, humans, even Christian humans, seek to serve their flesh. Believers absolutely cannot be in spirit and in truth yet watch, allow, participate, or condone the misuse of the sheep. The church is the collective body of God's servants. **GOD'S SHEEP SERVE GOD IN HIS CHURCH; GOD'S SHEEP DO NOT SERVE THE CHURCH.**

  54.2.3 **Do not forgive Satan** - Never forgive Satan for his part in the fall of man. Although Satan only helped man to fall, he seems to find pleasure in continuing this enterprise. No matter how pleasing this life is, Satan and his minions are the rulers of this age. Beware the rewards of this life and this age, look to them, and see from whence they come.

Righteous indignation drove men from the temple, but it also caused a follower of Christ to cut off the ear of another man. Injustice is what we should not forgive. However, injustice committed by a believer is still injustice; we therefore must handle indignation with care so that we do not use it as a tool for legalism in our lives and our marriages. As Moses told Joshua God does not want an angry hateful nation, but He want those who will move when they need to and defend those who cannot help themselves. It was never God's plan for the church to prey on, attack, humiliate, or subvert the lost. The church in its unforgiving practices neglected the weightier matters of the law, things like justice forgiveness and mercy. We certainly remember the tithe but as Christ reminds us the weightier things, we should not have left undone.

55.0
The Mystery of the Lonely Union

"And the Lord God said, [IT IS] NOT GOOD THAT THE MAN SHOULD BE ALONE; I WILL MAKE HIM AN HELP MEET FOR HIM" - (Genesis 2:18).

There are few things God declared as '*not good*' or displeasing. One such thing was the solitude of man, this God declared not good. Man's solitude was half of the problem; the other part of the problem is that man's fleshly encasement makes it impossible to live in the spirit. The problem exacerbates by the fact that the flesh and the spirit have irreconcilable differences. God's solution presented itself in the righteous marriage. The righteous marriage represents a fleshly solution, a spiritual solution, and a Godly solution for the single man.

Sadly, through the power of the flesh and the weakness of men's spiritual lives the flesh overshadowed the power of the spirit in our lives. Now many married couples find that they are alone again. Unlike single people, lonely flesh in marriage only has one solution. We cannot pray away an empty bed, or sad heart. The result of a sexually decrepit marriage is loneliness.

Once we marry and the problems begin, the tendency to seek happiness elsewhere grows. We must resist believing the lie. One was born married; we made a conscience choice. If we wanted to marry another person so badly, we should have married them instead. No matter what problems arise in marriage, infidelity is the mother of them all.

Money comes and goes, scars fade, and broken plates we can replace. What of disease or the child from an outside source, these neither go away nor diminish they grow. If we learned nothing from history, no one can maintain too many kingdoms simultaneously; they all eventually weaken and fall. God only has one kingdom He is our guide. God only has one spouse He is our guide.

Like many diseases of the flesh, the effects of lust do not go away. Stay leery of people who pretend to have their flesh under control. If a person says they lust but do not sin; ask them how they maintain the righteous lifestyle. If; however, they say they do not lust, they lie. It is the nature of the flesh to lust. Women lye about lust more than men, because they do not actually always want the other man, they just want his stuff. Women lust for things and the reality of it is that there is a way to acquire these things. If we want to be the consort of the king or live in the king's palace at his will is the only way.

55.1 Marital Loneliness vs. Spiritual Isolation

We take a moment to contrast marital loneliness due to isolation with spiritual isolation due to living apart.

Marital Loneliness	Spiritual Isolation
"**Therefore shall a man leave his father and his mother, and shall cleave unto his wife: and they shall be one flesh**" - (Genesis 2:24)	"**But cleave unto the Lord your God, as ye have done unto this day**" - (Hosea 23:8)

In marriage, flesh must cleave together which means unity, pleasantry, and sexuality. Many of our pathetic lives have busy schedules. If we are too busy to make our spouses complete, then we are too busy to marry. Do not marry just to complete a list, because we often cause our spouses to do things they normally would have not done; just to fill the voids we create.

Our souls are our guides they have no direct power. An unfulfilling marriage not only wreaks havoc on our flesh it wreaks havoc on our soul. Unfulfilled flesh must devote spiritual energy to trying to maintain fleshly righteousness. We begin to see evidence of the loss of fleshly fulfillment in obesity, bad health, and poor hygiene. Many of these signs let us know the person's spirit is trying to fill fleshly voids weak spouses created. A spouse with fleshly voids finds spiritual warfare virtually impossible. **We need power to wage spiritual warfare successfully**. No one can wage an effective war with their arms and legs bound. The unfulfilled husband finds his flesh a challenge and most often falls for fleshly pleasures. The unfulfilled wife often finds distraction in material things or uses the children as a crutch.

Once Satan realizes a couple's deficiencies, he makes all manner of distraction available. Regardless of the temptation, Satan seeks to generate a covenant breaking interaction. In doings such, in breaking down the sanctity and security of marriage, Satan robs of us power and forestalls kingdom building. Eventually, if thwarted sufficiently, we cease attacking or completely fail at attacks: mission accomplished Satan neutralized another set of warriors. Neutralized married people are just a set of books ends, which make nice decorations for church, but they are of little value in the fight.

Physical contact is imperative in marriage[112]. Flesh craves flesh, without fleshly contact, adultery is just a matter of time[113]. Flesh craves caressing, tending to, and catering to, this does not mean sex, but sensual contact should comprise a large portion of marital contact. Strong sexual or sensual desires are normal, and in marriage righteous; therefore, married Christians should have the happiest flesh in the galaxy: all pleasure--no pain. God designed marriage to quell loneliness, in the Let the warmth of the undefiled bedroom make our lives in Christ truly joyful, and complete. Married bedroom there should be no room for solitude and indifference. It makes little sense for people to lay in bed at night lonely once married. Remember when we ran the streets as single people, sleeping around with anyone and getting NOTHING in return. Then we marry and get a house, cars, money, kids, and a future and to this person we give the cold shoulder, slothful affection, and apathetic sexuality. Is it a wonder so many men have affairs? If the one, we put our efforts into will not give the attention we deserve even the Bible predicts that we will go next door.

Although adultery is completely avoidable, it is only because spouses do not want to have affairs. The amount of pornography viewed, drugs used, alcohol consumed, divorce and even suicide among Christians proves that loneliness, especially avoidable loneliness is not going to be tolerated for too long. Perhaps that was why God said it was not good for man to be alone I the first place, because the methods he was going to use to abate this loneliness were not wholesome and rarely if ever led to righteousness. The flesh is not righteous, so its vices are probably not going to be righteous either.

In righteous manner, therefore let us render due benevolence unto our spouses, in tender, caring abundance

_____
_____
_____
_____
_____
_____
_____
_____

56.0
Common Problems in Marriage

56.1 How long do we hold the fake smile?

I walked the halls at work one day and ran across a supervisor that I did not care for. As he passed, I flashed him a smile. I held the pleasantry until he passed and then cut it immediately. When I looked behind to ensure that he was gone, he looked back. When he did, it was obvious that the smile was false. Not only was the smile fake everything it stood for and the sentiment behind it was fake too. The honeymoon begs the ultimate question however, how long do I hold the fake smile? Let us take a moment to look at some chinks in the armor of many marriages these chinks allow Satan unfettered access.

The reason things change after the honeymoon is because the remorse period expires the morning after the honeymoon. God's plan is peculiar, but in every way, marriage's mystery mimics the faith walk. We start both adventures by losing our freedom. Losing freedom is a frightening concept to most people. The sad reality is that most people do absolutely nothing of Godly value with their freedom. Make no mistake; when it comes to salvation, *losing our freedom* is akin to having a tumor removed. Many people with tumors do not realize how sick they really are, but they are sick. Most people do not realize they are useless, not until we become responsible for a family, and the care and nurturing of our spouses do we realize how much time righteousness takes.

Not long after my wedding, reality kicked in. Under the law we have three days to withdraw from major purchases, this process is buyer's remorse. Under the law, an unconsummated marriage has the same opportunity for annulment. The problems in most marriages fall into three major categories. In today's culture, those that do not consummate the marriage before the wedding most certainly do so on the honeymoon.

_____
_____
_____
_____
_____

56.2 Bait and switch

A common complaint voiced in marital counseling is the *bait and switch*. The bait and switch is where a person markets one personality before the wedding and soon after the honeymoon, another creature emerges. Albeit in many marriages, this actually occurs often due to maturation and marital influences. Most honest people do not want their spouses to see the ugly, dark side of their personality. The problem is that if these same people cared about themselves as much as they pretend they would not spend as much of their lives generating darkness and ugliness. As we discovered in the book The lights in Patmos, the flesh and the soul never agree. The most common cause of the *bait and switch* occurs because people marry in the flesh not in the spirit.

Obviously, this does not mean marry and angel, it means that when we marry based solely on fleshly criteria there is an inevitable conflict because marriage is a spiritual journey.

For both prevention and the method to resolve the bait and switch, we look again to the book of Songs. This time the wisdom comes from the woman not Solomon; it appears, the helpmeet has insight the man lacks. In Songs 3:1, we see that the woman adds a level to marriage most people never achieve, "**By night on my bed, I sought him whom my soul loves**."

    56.2.1   The woman uses her flesh in an effort to attain righteousness, not to further her sin. The manner in which she offsets the natural darkness of our flesh is through marriage.

    56.2.2   The second manner in which she makes the journey through the marriage mystery is that she loves with her soul. In reaching out to her lover with her soul, she plants seeds of unity in the marriage, which will produce peace early in the relationship.

56.3 **Peek-a-boo**

Peek-a-boo is a cousin to the bait and switch. Peek-a-boo is where we hide ourselves from everybody for fear of rejection. I watch children play peek-a-boo, and amusingly enough kids hide their eyes instead of their bodies when they play. They believe that if they cannot see us we cannot see them. We play this idiotic game with God and our spouses. We mask our sin and unrighteousness in money, wealth, tan oil, breast augmentation, and a host of other inane covers. The problem is that both God and our spouses see the true person behind the eyes. Nevertheless, this is the mystery of love; the love God ordained in marriage. Our deeds; forgiven. Our darkness; overlooked. In marriage, we find peace and absolution. In marriage, we find the love of God.

56.4 MILFs (Mates I'd like to fight)

The world has its definition of MILF. In the majority of marriages, I counseled, the definition of MILF is *Mates I'd like to fight*. Under Mosaic Law, the Bible advised a bill of divorcement in circumstances where spouses found no favor in their marriage they were to divorce (Deuteronomy 24:1.) However, in Matthew Jesus addresses the false practice stating that men did this because they were too immature to resolve their differences (Matthew 19:9).

Later in the Bible, we find teaching that clearly defines many of the marriages I counseled. Proverbs 21:19 and 27:15 assert how problematic living with a contentious woman is for marriage. Although there may be many contentious influences, which affect the marriage from outside, there are only two sources of contention in a marriage. Within the marriage, the contention comes from either the husband or the wife. I have met some pathetic men in my counsels, I am sad to say that many of the women I counseled were contentious.

Like Eve, the mother of all things many of these MILFs developed contention due to pathetic husbands, but that paradigm goes both ways. A man that marries a petite woman has every expectation of his wife putting effort into maintaining her weight. Of course, if one marries a bountiful woman it is unreasonable to expect her to go down to 125lbs. A woman that marries a man with nothing should expect nothing. Without land, property, or holdings the male of the species is not a *man*.

I dated a young woman who enjoyed every opportunity to make me miserable. When she finished her self-imposed mission, she informed me that her rationale was to make me deal with her brand of reality. This is not love, nor is it healthy. This type or *realism* is nothing but selfish, immature pettiness and a route to unhappiness for all involved.

56.5 A Mephibosheth styled marriage[114]

In the Mephibosheth style marriage, we choose certain traits in our mates that God cannot alter. The Mephibosheth style marriage has at its core some crippling attribute, which like Mephibosheth prevent the marriage from growing, moving, and becoming stronger. Fortunately, Mephibosheth issues were the result of an accident not hereditary. Therefore, the cycle can be broken, and our children do not have to be crippled.

Three components make a Mephibosheth style marriage:

56.5.1 People will not change – like paraplegics, many people in Mephibosheth styled marriages cannot alter their physical abilities they therefore stay disabled.

56.5.2 Baggage- baggage and scars from previous relationships often cause atrophy.

56.5.3 Unrighteousness always causes disease and encumbrances.

Remember believers, God honor *choice* that is why He wars against Satan for our freedom to choose. The reason God makes recommendations for marriage and not commandments is that once we marry persons and choose them with their faults those faults remain in them until they choose to change. God tells us that when we marry we should not marry outside the faith, or in an unequal relationship. Proverbs 6:27 reminds us that the person who marries the fool creates a problem that even God cannot reconcile.

It is reasonable to expect our mates to make an effort to maintain some semblance of the traits they possessed when we married. Be wary however that we do not cling to traits in our mates that though pleasing to our flesh our antithetical to righteousness. Your wife may have been quite the partier; quite the girl gone wild, however moms gone wild tend to lead to daughters gone wild. We may have been a player but teach our sons to be gentle and sensitive, so they can be better husbands not Don Juans.

Personality traits God helps to modify are traits that make us righteous. If your husband watches, more football than reads poetry that is not an area of God's responsibility. If, however your husband gambles on the games and loses great deals of money or cause the family to go without this is an area in which God will intercede. However, saints do not be deceived; God is not resolving his gambling to please you, but to honor His word[115].

Ecclesiastes 9:9 admonishes us to enjoy the spouses of our youth. Therefore, DO NOT MARRY A PERSON YOU DO NOT OR CANNOT ENJOY. We should not waste our youth trying to make circles into squares; MARRY A SQUARE or learn to live happily with the circle. In God's kingdom, people have the right to be whatever they want to be, He does not change people arbitrarily to make other people happy. What God says about those that choose to be losers is, "**I call heaven and earth to record this day against you, [that] I have set before you life and death, blessing and cursing: therefore *choose* life, that both thou and thy seed may live**" - (Deuteronomy 30:9).

If the husband; especially a Christian husband, decides to be contrary to the will of God and is a sorry husband, God corrects the issues of unrighteousness. In correcting the righteousness of our husband, the other issues should also come on line because part of righteousness comes out of Ephesians 5 and Colossians 3:19, which includes loving our wives in a manner that makes our marriage thrive. To this end, we should not pray for change in our spouses but pray for righteousness in our marriages.

_____
_____
_____
_____
_____
_____
_____

57.0
The Mystery the Marriage's Ultimate Foe

"**I said in my heart, 'Come now, I will test you with mirth: therefore, enjoy pleasure;' and behold, this also was vanity. I said of laughter, 'It is foolishness;' and of mirth, 'What does it accomplish?' I searched in my heart how to cheer my flesh with wine, my heart yet guiding me with wisdom, and how to lay hold of folly, until I might see what it was good for the sons of men that they should do under heaven all the days of their lives. I made myself great works. I built myself houses**" - (Ecclesiastes 2:1-3).

All marriages have problems because they consist of two problematic people. Christian marriages are not immune from strife; we simply have one great alternative to the unsaved--a God that desires to assist. I am sure that God would help the unsaved too, but they opt not to enlist His aid.

In the marital counseling I attended, and have provided, the underlying problems in most are dissatisfaction or unhappiness. Solomon writes in Ecclesiastes 2 that with all he had he was bored and unfulfilled. What Solomon goes on to explain is another marriage and ministry mystery. Through Ecclesiastes 1:16-17 we uncover more tiers, which cause Christian failure in marriage and ministry, "**I communed with mine own heart, saying, Lo, I am come to great estate, and have gotten more wisdom than all [they] that have been before me in Jerusalem: yea, my heart had great experience of wisdom and knowledge. And I gave my heart to know wisdom, and to know madness and folly: I perceived that this also is vexation of spirit.**"

57.1 The two-tiered mystery of why so many marriages fail
    57.1.1 Discontentment
    57.1.2 Creating our own wisdom

Marriage and ministry both have rules imposed by a sovereign God. To succeed at marriage and ministry Godly standards requires input and direction from God. Paul states unequivocally that he *learned* to count hardship and grief as joy. However, Solomon tells us the true emotional effect of maturing in Christ, in Ecclesiastes 1:18, "**For in much wisdom [is] much grief: and he that in increaseth knowledge increaseth sorrow.**" There is no way to avoid this, for the truth of God unveils the evil, hurt, and sadness both in our hearts and in the hearts of His people.

This brings us to one of the greatest questions ever posed to me. *How do we spread hope when we have none*? This question is beautiful in its artisanship. In this question, we see query, despair, and resolution. This is what Solomon spoke of in verse #16. This person, while trying to keep the faith has no trust in the faith. In other words, we cannot motivate ourselves to preach, follow, and serve a God we no longer trust. Like this young woman who in her question makes her admission *I lost faith*. Solomon also gave up relying on God's wisdom and created his own. The policy of creating our own wisdom brings about the unrelenting misery Christians experience before they finally divorce, commit adultery, leave the faith, or worse commit suicide.

Believers, 2 Peter warns us, as does Jesus in Matthew 12:43-45 and Paul in Romans 1:28, that when we commune with our own hearts and create our own wisdom we go places we did not even go when we were unsaved. The knowledge we possess and use for evil exceeds the wisdom we use to do good things. The flesh does not have any traits in it worth saving. God said all the creativity and resourcefulness men possess they continually use for evil[116]. Consequently, we see men and women of

God walk into the clutches of sin and submerse themselves. Like Eve, we know the cost; we calculate the cost, and decide if the cost is worthwhile.

Let us look at Song of Solomon to uncover several Biblically acceptable methods to keep our marriages vital and growing. There are many commentaries on Songs espousing metaphor and prophetic usage; here we are looking at marital issues related to intimacy and longevity. The passages contained herein entail sexual allegory, which we will tastefully explore. We learn as we read that the secret to righteous flesh is marriage. Marriage satisfies our wanton desires.

57.1.2.1 **"Beloved let him kiss me with the kisses of his mouth; for your love is better than wine"** - (Songs 1:1-2). Solomon's wife refers to the intoxicating affect her man has on her. The term *love* applied here refers to the total package although later use directly implies lovemaking.

57.1.2.2 **"Your oils have a pleasing fragrance"** - (Songs 1:3). This phrase describes the scent of their lover's body and the pleasant fragrance of their passion.

57.1.2.3 **"Tell me, you whom my soul loves, where you graze your flock, where you rest them at noon; For why should I be as one who is veiled beside the flocks of your companions"** - (Songs 1:7). Here the message is twofold. The lover identifies Solomon as the one her soul loves. This level of intimacy elevates her from the typical consort to his intimate partner. Here the Queen of Sheba reminds him that it is her level of love for him sets her apart from his other women.

57.1.2.4 **"Beloved while the king sat at his table, my perfume spread its fragrance, my beloved is to me a sachet of myrrh, that lies between my breasts"** - (1:12-13). In these two stanzas, we see again the intoxicating effect Solomon has on his lover. She sat in wait, at the table making herself known to her lover through body language and gesture. She then likens his scent and presence to a fragrant amulet that sits just below her nostrils constantly filling them with a reminder of him.

57.1.2.5 **"Strengthen me with raisins, refresh me with apples; For I am faint with love. His left hand is under my head. His right hand embraces me"** – (Songs 2:5-6). In this tender embrace, the woman describes how weak Solomon makes her and how much power he wiled over her. His touch makes her weak, willing to give him her all. She needs his support to offset the vulnerability she feels, her openness before him scares her so she looks to him for strength.

57.1.2.6 **"By night on my bed, I sought him whom my soul loves. I sought him, but I did not find him"** - (Songs 3:1). In the late hours of darkness, she seeks the apple of her eye. She feels the loneliness her soul mate's absence causes. Her bed is lonely for the one that giver her strength and makes her feel whole.

57.1.2.7 **"I will get up now, and go about the city; in the streets and in the squares I will seek him whom my soul loves. When I found him whom my soul loves. I held him, and would not let him go, until I had brought him into my mother's house, into the room of her who conceived me"** - (Songs 3:2&4). Her desire for the man causes her to seek out his fragrance. She searches for him in places she knows him to go.

Her intention is to find him and captivate him with more of her delicate passion that he does not leave again this night. She is determined to exercise her feminine controls even if it means sneaking him into the master bedroom of her mother's house. Obviously, the reference to her mother's bedroom is not literal considering how far she is from home. What she implies is that the bond she wants to share with him, the marriage bond is undefiled and therefore no cause for shame to make love to him in her parents' home.

57.1.2.8 **"Lover behold, you are beautiful, my love. Behold, you are beautiful. Your eyes are doves behind your veil. Your hair is as a flock of goats, that descend from Mount Gilead. Your teeth are like a newly shorn flock, which have come up from the washing, where every one of them has twins. None is bereaved among them. Your lips are like scarlet thread. Your mouth is lovely. Your temples are like a piece of a pomegranate behind your veil. Your neck is like David's tower built for an armory, whereon a thousand shields hang, all the shields of the mighty men. Your two breasts are like two fawns. Until the day is cool, and the shadows flee away, I will go to the mountain of myrrh, to the hill of frankincense** - (Songs 4:1). Solomon takes great again to tell his bride how sensual and sexually pleasing she is to him. He reminds her of how beautiful he thinks she is.

57.1.2.9 **"You have ravished my heart, my sister, my bride. You have ravished my heart with one of your eyes, with one chain of your neck"** - (Songs 4:9). Sweet pillow talk goes a long way, for most women and many men. Sweetness is usually welcomed.

57.1.2.10 **"Your lips, my bride, drip like the honeycomb. Honey and milk are under your tongue"** - (Songs 4:11). These are simple references to the sweet speak lovers should share.

57.1.2.11 **"Awake, north wind; and come, you south! Blow on my garden, that its spices may flow out. Let my beloved come into his garden, and taste his precious fruits"** - (Songs 4:16). Here the man prays for a warm, soothing breeze that his lover may feel romantic and avail herself to him. Solomon describes his lover as a garden, something growing and vibrant that needs care (husbandry). The north in Biblical terms implies evil and cold, but with the winter comes endurance of the evergreen. Solomon is not preparing for a quickie; he lays the foundation for a night of torrid lovemaking.

57.1.2.12 **"Lover I have come into my garden, my sister, my bride. I have gathered my myrrh with my spice; I have eaten my honeycomb with my honey; I have drunk my wine with my milk"** - (Songs 5:1). Like most men, Solomon has a problem expressing deep feelings. He cannot liken his love for the woman to any other woman. Therefore, he likens his love for her unto his love for a sister--a deep, patient blood bond. Solomon continues to describe the tender loving they shared and that he has eaten his fill of all she has to offer.

57.1.2.13 **"I was asleep, but my heart was awake. It is the voice of my beloved who knocks: 'Open to me, my sister, my love, my dove, my undefiled; for my head is filled with dew, and my hair with the dampness of the night'"** - (Songs 5:1).

Solomon describes the woman as undefiled, meaning he has married her, so their lovemaking does not defile his wife. His wife even dreams of his voice beckoning at her heart, reminding her of the time they shared a night in the warm breeze *submitting* to each other.

57.1.2.14 "**I have taken off my robe. Indeed, must I put it on? I have washed my feet. Indeed, must I soil them? My beloved thrust his hand in through the latch opening. My heart pounded for him. I rose up to open for my beloved. My hands dripped with myrrh, my fingers with liquid myrrh, on the handles of the lock. I opened to my beloved; but my beloved left; and had gone away**" - (Songs 5:3-6). The woman rises with passion for him; so much so that she awakes ready for is hands to caress her and to explore her body. However, we begin to see the ending of the honeymoon phase. Here her man arouses her and then leaves her at home wanton. He probably had to go to some stupid armor bearer's meeting or trustee function. Never leave our women uncovered; else, someone else will cover their bodies and hearts.

57.1.2.15 "**This, your stature, is like a palm tree, your breasts like its fruit. I said, 'I will climb up into the palm tree. I will take hold of its fruit." Let your breasts be like clusters of the vine, the smell of your breath like apples'**" - (Songs 7:7-8). Solomon likens his woman to a palm tree, a dessert oasis to a lonely heart. Solomon longs to take sweet drinks from her breasts, as a king would sup wine from skins. Solomon also in this metaphor lets us know that her breasts as young and ripe, he finds them captivating and rich.

_____
_____
_____
_____
_____
_____
_____
_____
_____
_____
_____
_____

This is a peek into the happy goings on in a marriage. With the time they spent pleasuring each other, dreaming about each other and intimately talking, the marriage only seems to have one weak spot; the woman has to go looking for her husband. Beware men; do not leave our women at the door dripping myrrh. There are many wolves in sheep's clothing waiting to comfort them.

_____
_____

58.0
Week 9 - Work Area

58.1 Mutual respect aids longevity, how does this work?

_____
_____
_____
_____
_____
_____
_____
_____

58.2 Prayer works within the marriage to increase power how does this work?

_____
_____
_____
_____
_____
_____
_____
_____

58.3 How does a husband's sacrifice fortify marriage?

_____
_____
_____
_____
_____
_____
_____
_____
_____
_____

58.4 Why is it hard to be the head of the house without self-love?

_____
_____
_____
_____
_____
_____
_____
_____

58.5 Why does unity make decision making easier?

_____
_____
_____
_____
_____
_____
_____
_____

58.6 How does forgiveness keep the marriage moving forward?

_____
_____
_____
_____
_____
_____
_____
_____
_____
_____

58.7 How does maturity make marriage easier?

58.8 What is revelation?

58.9 How does revelation work?

Week 10

Weapons of the Enemy Against Marriage

59.0 - The weapons of the enemy against marriage
60.0 - Civil war as a weapon against marriage
61.0 - The eyes as a weapon against marriage
62.0 - The flesh as a weapon against marriage
63.0 - Fornication as a weapon against marriage
64.0 - Week 10 - Work Area

59.0
The Weapons of the Enemy Against Marriage

"**BUT I SAY UNTO YOU, THAT WHOSOEVER LOOKETH ON A WOMAN TO LUST AFTER HER HATH COMMITTED ADULTERY WITH HER ALREADY IN HIS HEART**" - (Matthew 5:28).

Many successful attacks by Satan cause harm and crises of faith. No attack has caused as much damage and cost Satan as little as the attack against the family. Satan is not against sex, children, or good health, as long as we serve Satan with them. To this end, Satan promotes sex, children, or good health because he successfully uses them to grow his dark territory.

Satan is not interested in destroying marriages he is interested in destroying Godly seed producing trees[117]. Remember, Genesis states that God plants seed bearing trees that produce after its own kind. Non-Christian marriages also produce good products; the only difference is that children in Christian marriages are born enemies of Satan. The attack on marriages is not about us, it is about the Godly tree bearing potential of Godly people.

Genesis 3:15 spells out why there is enmity between Satan and the seeds of married people. "**AND I WILL PUT ENMITY BETWEEN THEE AND THE WOMAN, AND BETWEEN THY SEED AND HER SEED; IT SHALL BRUISE THY HEAD, AND THOU SHALT BRUISE HIS HEEL.**" Couple Genesis 3:15 that with Genesis 1:11 "**And God said, 'LET THE EARTH BRING FORTH GRASS, THE HERB YIELDING SEED, [AND] THE FRUIT TREE YIELDING FRUIT AFTER HIS KIND, WHOSE SEED [IS] IN ITSELF, UPON THE EARTH: AND IT WAS SO**," and Matthew 11:11 "**VERILY I SAY UNTO YOU, AMONG THEM THAT ARE BORN OF WOMEN THERE HATH NOT RISEN A GREATER THAN JOHN THE BAPTIST: NOTWITHSTANDING HE THAT IS LEAST IN THE KINGDOM OF HEAVEN IS GREATER THAN HE**." We find that Satan does not fear us, what he fears is the potential of another Jesus. The same God that made Jesus great would make others great, if they were willing to pay the price. The specialty of Satan is to do as he did with Adam and Eve, to convince us that the price of salvation is simply too high.

59.1 Ungodly Spiritual Influences

All spiritual influences come from God, for He made all things. It is what the spiritual influences do, which makes them evil, not from whence they came. All spirits came from the Holy Mountain of God (heaven Ezekiel 28:14)

- **That the sons of God saw the daughters of men that they were fair; and they took them wives of all which they chose** (Genesis 6:2).

- **There were giants in the earth in those days; and also after that, when the sons of God came in unto the daughters of men, and they bare children to them, the same became mighty men which were of old, men of renown** (Genesis 6:4).

- **Again, there was a day when the sons of God came to present themselves before the Lord, and Satan came among them to present himself before the Lord** (Job 2:1).

- **When the morning stars sang together, and all the sons of God shouted for joy?** (Job 38:7).

However, since the civil a war in heaven, some of these influences (all 9 kinds included; Seraphim, Cherubim, Thrones, Dominions, Virtues, Powers, Archangels, Principalities, Angels) were exiled in Ezekiel 31 and therefore comprise the cadre of ungodly (Traitors who no longer follow the lead of the King) spiritual influences[118].

59.1.1 **The Familiar Spirit -** The familiar spirit is probably the most common spiritual influence we encounter. This entity like a mattress, by itself is not evil. Just as the marriage, bed is undefiled, and the bodies of dead young men line the way to the prostitute's bed. The familiar spirit makes itself available to pleasure; this spirit unlike the others entices pleasurable pursuits rather that vile, self-destructive, and morose. The familiar spirit has an inviting disposition, much like the spirit of divination. Like Cleo, the *psychic* the familiar spirit is friendly and eager please. The familiar spirit is not eager to please us, but instead the dragon. No matter how friendly the familiar spirit, it serves the dragon. It is friendly to us so that they can steal our souls. **"Then said Saul unto his servants, seek me a woman that hath a familiar spirit that I may go to her, and enquire of her. And his servants said to him, Behold, [there is] a woman that hath a familiar spirit at Endor"** - (1 Samuel 28:7, 1 Chronicles 10:13).

59.1.2 **The Spirit of Whoredoms** - The spirit of whoredoms is a spirit of excess, sexual excess and immorality. Unlike lustful eyes that crave everything, the spirit of whoredoms is sexual in nature. **"My people ask counsel at their stocks, and their staff declareth unto them: for the spirit of whoredoms hath caused [them] to err, and they have gone a whoring from under their God"** - (Hosea 4:12).

59.1.3 **The Spirit of an Uncleanliness** - The unclean devil is another way of calling the spirit a demon. The word Devil seems to be of Eastern origin and pronounced *Devi*, which means spirit. The clarification here is the word unclean, which informs the reader that this spirit is not from God. Also, the term 'An' indicates that this demon can manifest itself in different ways. Many times, the name or clear intention of the spirit is not clear, but by its words or actions, one can determine whether it is clean or unclean. **"And in the synagogue, there was a man, which had a spirit of an unclean devil, and cried out with a loud voice,"** - (Luke 4:33, Luke 11:24, Mark 1:26, Mark 5:2, Mark 7:25).

59.1.4 **The Spirit of Infirmity** - Sin and demons caused Infirmity and diseases. This woman could not heal because a demon possessed her. As long as the demon inhabited the woman not medicine would work. When Jesus healed the woman, He said she was free from her infirmity, free of the spirit. As proof that Jesus had the power to forgive sins, He *forgave* this woman and freed her from demonic bondage. **"And, behold, there was a woman which had a spirit of infirmity eighteen years, and was bowed together, and could in no wise lift up [herself]"** - (Luke 13:11).

59.1.5 **The Spirit of Divination** - The spirit of divination (I like to call it the Cleo spirit) is the spirit involved in fortune telling and tarot cards. People like Nostradamus, wizards, witches, and fortunetellers tie into the spirit world via the spirit of Divination. What this spirit does is give the person tapping in access to the spiritual realm. Remember all spiritual laws God set in place. Whether or not the *sons of god* still live in heaven, they still are spirits. Just as God used the lying spirit in Kings Satan's unclean spirits also speak to people. This relationship is how the Antichrist and the first Beast get their power. **"And it came to pass, as we went to prayer, a certain damsel possessed with a spirit of divination met us, which brought her masters much gain by soothsaying"** - (Acts 16:16).

59.1.6 **The Dumb Spirit** - The dumb spirit controls the speech center. Just like John the Baptists father could not speak until the Lord allowed him to speak, the dumb spirit prevents the possessed person's talking. The purpose of the dumb spirit is to create misery and despair in both the victim and the people trying to help the victim. **"And one of the multitude answered and said, Master, I have brought unto thee my son, which hath a dumb spirit"**; - (Mark 9:17)."

59.1.7 **Spirit of Anti-Christ** - Spirit of the anti-Christ represents any high-level spiritual movement against Christ. This 'spirit' is therefore not any singular angel; it is the intention of the angel. This is another reason we must try the spirit by the Spirit. If the two spirts do not jibe it is because there is enmity between them. **"And every spirit that confesseth not that Jesus Christ is come in the flesh is not of God: and this is that spirit of Antichrist, whereof ye have heard that it should come; and even now already is it in the world,"** - (1 John 4:3).

59.1.8 **Spirit of Error** - This is also another name of Satan or satanic influence. Remember Lucifer is the king of the fallen army. All evil he oversees. Like the good angels, whose names appear rarely, it appears that names for the angels are only important to the ones that interact directly with humans. **"We are of God: he that knoweth God heareth us; he that is not of God heareth not us. Hereby know we the spirit of truth, and the spirit of error,"** - (1 John 4:6).

59.1.9 **Spirit of Disobedience** - This is just another name of for Satan, it is a reference to and an explanation for the behavior of ungodly people. **"Wherein in time past ye walked according to the course of this world, according to the prince of the power of the air, the spirit that now worketh in the children of disobedience,"** - (Ephesians 2:2).

59.1.10 **Spirit of Fear** - Fear in Christians stems from a spiritual influence. The Bible says that this spirit does not operate from God. Therefore, this is an actual Spirit who operates both by enhancing pre-existing and introducing fear in the lives of Christians. **"For God hath not given us the spirit of fear; but of power, and of love, and of a sound mind,"** - (2 Timothy 1:7).

59.1.11 **Seducing (deceiving) Spirit** - Seducing spirits is a collective name given to spirits that utilized their influence humans to entice him to do things that they normally would not do it is not specific to an action it is protection in specific more to the relationship between the spirit and the human. **"Now the Spirit speaketh expressly, that in the latter times some shall depart from the faith, giving heed to seducing spirits, and doctrines of devils,"** - (1 Timothy 4:1).

59.2 How spirits gain entrance

According to Satan, men gave him ALL the earthly authority he possesses (Luke 4:6). This statement by the deceiver of humankind is the ultimate statement of demon possession. This statement sets all demon possession in place. The Dark Lord clearly states that all his power derives from HUMAN *CHOICE*, not from his own power. I pointed out that the Bible **never** calls Satan our ruler. Jesus calls Satan our father because of our actions, not because of Stan's authority.

Choice is the unwitting focus of this book and now we see why. In Genesis what repented God was what human *chose*. We see all through the Bible bad *choices* displease God. We see in John 14:15 that God gauges *choice* to determine human love. The same ungodly choice gives Satan power over our lives.

In the adversarial game of chess, there are two pivotal moves: check and checkmate. When Christ was born, Satan was as they say in Chess '*in check.*' Jesus' death '*check-mated*' Satan. Jesus informs all interested parties that God gave Him ALL power (in heaven and in earth). All the power returned to God's throne via the house of David. The reinstitution of power means that ALL demon possession post--Christ is a result of human *choice*.

This concept may shock us, but it is the truth. There are many ways to leave our houses untended, thus inviting demons. Demons can enter our houses through the strong man, through weaker vessels, or through sinful vessels. This is why the Bible requires deacons and elders to rule their houses well.

I once had a friend tell me that God told him to pray for the doors in his house. He then went on to say that he walked the entire house praying for all the doors in the building. I asked him did he really think that God wanted him to pray for the closet and the bathroom doors? I asked him did he think it was more likely that God mean that he should pray for the people in his house. A door is a point of entry into a building. The people in our lives are the doors by which Satan and God enter. Many do not understand that is was the same principle Jesus spoke about when He said that no man goes to the Father but through Me. Jesus is the fleshly door that enabled the Spirit of the Lord into the house (Earth).

Believers, demons enter or respond to four states in our lives:

59.2.1 **The Sinful State** - Drives a wedge between us and the Lord allowing space for Satan to enter.

59.2.2 **The Unsaved State** - Has little to no protection from the wiles of the devil. All the wicked imaginations and lusts of the flesh and heart are fully exposed to the unsaved.

59.2.3 **The Rebellious State** - Is Satan's favorite state. Here we turn away from and refuse the guidance of the Master. It is in this state the Bible says we are practitioners of witchcraft[119].

59.2.4 **The Complacent State** - In this luke-warm state, we have some protection from Satan but are displeasing to God. This state we most commonly called backsliding. In this apostate state we often ignore, overlook, or simply do not address demonic influence. It is like having a *buzz or tipsiness.* We are not drunk, so we ignore the fact that we are physically and mentally impaired. In this state, we lay down one of our best weapons against Satan…Alertness. Alertness is on the list in Ephesians as a component of the 'whole' armor of God. This means that as a spiritual weapon it is no less important than the other components.

Does this list mean that demons do not attack the righteous? Not at all, demons attacked Jesus. Demons attacked Jesus, but they could not tempt Him. When the demons attacked Jesus they did not win, and they do not have to defeat us. What Satan could not do was convince Jesus to break fellowship with the Father.

Mark 5:12-23 ends this chapter. We discussed possession and indwelling in this chapter. Mark 5:12-23 shows that demons have no *choice* when it comes to Christ's authority. No matter what preachers teach, the scripture **must** be our standard for truth. Matthew 28:18 confirms that Christ rules in Heaven and on Earth. If Christians are Christ's people then their King provides for their spiritual safety, growth, and maturation. No one can pluck us from the hand of our King, but we can choose to leave at any time.

Anytime we see a believer backsliding, lost, sinning, or destroyed, they *choose* to be there. Nothing gets past Christ unless we allow it inside. Once demons enter our hearts, Christ is not responsible for controlling the amount of damage the evil ones do. If we purchase a Pit-bull despite the warnings against the breed and take it home, the dog is our responsibility. Can we then blame the pet-store? When our animal (the one we purchased and brought home) destroys our home, attacks and kills the children? A sad tale nonetheless, but we are responsible for the sin we allow in our life. Demons only add a variety of opportunities to fulfill the loathsome desires that fill that human heart, they do not create them.

59.3 <u>The Mark of the Beast</u>

The *mark of the* Beast is by far the most difficult part of the Beast with which we deal. This is a difficult part because we have so much tradition and so little understanding of the Beast. Believers adhere to the common inaccuracy of a 666 tattoo, brand, or Microchip as the *mark* of the Beast. Look with me to Revelations 19:20 and see that this is clearly not the case. "**And the beast was taken, and with him the false prophet that wrought miracles before him, with which he deceived them that had received the *mark* of the beast, and them that worshiped his image. These both were cast alive into a lake of fire burning with brimstone**." The confusion undoubtedly arises from the story of Cain and Able in Genesis 4:15 wherein God *mark*s Cain. "**And the Lord said unto him, THEREFORE WHOSOEVER SLAYETH CAIN, VENGEANCE SHALL BE TAKEN ON HIM SEVENFOLD. And the Lord set a *mark* upon Cain, lest any finding him should kill him**." Come, let us reason together, and read with understanding. There was only Cain, Able, Adam, and Eve near the garden. Who else would have known about Cain's deeds? The *mark* on Cain was not punishment it was an identifier. If God wanted to punish Cain, does it not make more sense to either kill him or let someone in Nod slay Cain? Moreover, why was there punishment set aside for whoever slew Cain?

To understand the punishment, we must remember that Cain murdered Able out of jealousy. Jealousy existed between Cain and Able because God rejected Cain's mediocre sacrifice and accepted Abel's first fruit. Cain's sin was covetousness like his father Satan; violence blossomed in Cain only after evil blossomed. Therefore, the *mark* of Cain is not a blemish or brand, but the product of Cain's deed. Cain after all is the first murderer on this planet. Cain introduced murder to humanity. Therefore, the one that murders a murderer is more wicked that the first. Cain was the first murderer, but the subsequent murders are evidence of Satan's continued influence.

God has an inhuman way of looking at humanity. God sees the hearts of men. God is more interested in the motive than a deed. When a man murders, God sees what was in his heart that caused the man to murder. All God needs to see is that what is in the murderer's heart is not of God. Although Cain committed the first murder, God waived judgment. After God set forth the law, anyone that murdered, God judged as a murderer.

I find it noteworthy at this point to bring to our attention that at no time does Genesis 4:11-15 specify the type of tattooing, brand, blemish, or discoloration on Cain. Genesis 4:11-15 certainly does not indicate any type of technology. Preachers and theologians not scripture sold the concept of Microchips and all other forms of fables.

_____
_____
_____
_____
_____
_____
_____

59.4 The Mark on the right hand

Why is the mark of the Beast placed in the right hand of those that follow the Beast? Psalms 109:5-6 - "**And they have rewarded me evil for good, and hatred for my love. Set thou a wicked man over him: and let Satan stand at his right hand.**" The purpose of using the right hand is that the right hand represents the authority, will, might, or *choice* of the person. The wedding band rides on the left hand in conventional marriages and the right in homosexual marriages. The mark on the right hand represents the same thing Nimrod's tower, the pyramids, and the sphinx represent-- rebellion against God. The throne room has two seats. In terms of power, the word seat means *post of* *authority*. The two seats are the throne and the lesser seat on the right. The seat on the right is only lesser because God sits on the throne[120].

Psalms 48:10 tells us the right hand is full of righteousness. Jesus sits at the right hand because He is full of righteousness. Satan never sat at the right hand; he sat in the seat of God. Lucifer sat in the seat because God only allowed him to keep the seat warm and do God's bidding. Like Potiphar, Lucifer was merely steward. Jesus is the prince, heir to the throne, a marker of the righteousness of God in men.

A person who receives the mark of the beast acknowledges their disdain for God and in the words of Isaiah the show of their countenance shows against them (Isaiah 3:9-10). The reason the penalty for *receiving the mark in their right hand or their forehead* (The receptacle for the imagination) is because this allegiance with God's enemy is unholy and in God's mind the bearer of the mark hates Him. To worship another god, and bear his mark, a right reserved for ownership is to align with that spirit chief against God. It is better to die for righteousness sake that to stand before the throne bearing the mark of another God. GOD MAKES NO ROOM IN HEAVEN FOR THE CHILDREN OF ANY OTHER GOD.

_____
_____
_____
_____
_____
_____
_____
_____
_____
_____
_____

There is only one reason the Bible gives the number of the 𝔅east. It is to indicate to us that the Anti-Christ is human. Therefore, the mark of this 𝔅east must be a human characteristic. There is a book in the New Testament that not only mentions the 𝔅east but also gives clear concise indicia of the *mark*s (characteristics) of the 𝔅east. The tri-numeric 666 links the 𝔅east to humanity. Conversely, 666 also links humanity to the 𝔅east. Starting with Romans 1:21, we look together to see what *mark*s God has given to use to discern the children of the 𝔅east.

I enumerate the traits so that we may see that the component parts comprise only one *mark* of the 𝔅east. The components are therefore traits or indicators of the spirit of the 𝔅east manifest in people. I point this out to illustrate that except for one of the listed traits the behavior indicates the influence of the 𝔅east--not possession by the 𝔅east.

Let us look now at the evidence of this 𝔅eastly nature found in the Book of Genesis. I will indicate via the '𝔅' trait found in the list. For example, if the people are unmerciful I will place '**Bw**' beside the scripture.

- (Ba) Full of all unrighteousness.
- (Bb) Full of sexual immorality[121]
- (Bc) Full of wickedness
- (Bd) Full of Covetousness
- (Be) Full of malice
- (Bf) Full of envy
- (Bg) Full of murder
- (Bh) Full of strife
- (Bi) Full of deceit
- (Bj) Full of evil habits
- (Bk) Secret slanderers
- (Bl) Backbiters
- (Bm) Hateful to God
- (Bn) Insolent
- (Bo) Haughty
- (Bp) Boastful
- (Bq) Inventors of evil things
- (Br) Disobedient to parents
- (Bs) Without understanding
- (Bt) Covenant breakers
- (Bu) Without natural affection
- (Bv) Unforgiving
- (Bw) Unmerciful

- Genesis 18:20-26 - "**The Lord said, "BECAUSE THE CRY OF SODOM AND GOMORRAH IS GREAT, AND BECAUSE THEIR SIN IS VERY GRIEVOUS**{Ba}, **I WILL GO DOWN NOW, AND SEE WHETHER THEIR DEEDS ARE AS BAD AS THE REPORTS WHICH HAVE COME TO ME. IF NOT, I WILL KNOW** {Bq}." **The men turned from there, and went toward Sodom, but Abraham stood yet before the Lord. Abraham drew near, and said, "Will you consume the righteous with the wicked** {Bt}." **What if there are fifty righteous within the city? Will you consume and not spare the place for the fifty righteous who are in it? Be it far from you to do things like that, to kill the righteous with the wicked, so that the righteous should be like the wicked. May that be far from You. Shouldn't the Judge of all the earth do right**?" **The Lord said, "IF I FIND IN SODOM FIFTY RIGHTEOUS WITHIN THE CITY, THEN I WILL SPARE ALL THE PLACE FOR THEIR SAKE**."

Let us look further at the evidence of this 𝕭𝖊𝖆𝖘𝖙𝖑𝖞 nature found in the Book of Genesis. Genesis 19:19:1-17 - "**The two angels came to Sodom at evening. Lot sat in the gate of Sodom. Lot saw them, and rose up to meet them. He bowed himself with his face to the earth, and he said, "See now, my Lord s, please turn aside into your servant's house, stay all night, wash your feet, and you can rise up early, and go on your way." They said, "No, but we will stay in the street all night." He urged them greatly, and they came in with him, and entered into his house. He made them a feast, and baked unleavened bread, and they ate.**

But before they lay down, the men of the city, the men of Sodom, surrounded the house, both young and old, all the people from every quarter {Bb}." They called to Lot, and said to him, "Where are the men who came in to you this night? Bring them out to us, that we may that we may know them {Bb}." Lot went out to them to the door and shut the door after him. He said, "Please, my brothers, don't act so wickedly {Bu}. Behold now, I have two daughters which have not known man; let me, I pray you, bring them out unto you, and do ye to them as [is] good in your eyes: only unto these men do nothing; for therefore came they under the shadow of my roof {Bn}. And they said, Stand back. And they said [again], this one [fellow] came in to sojourn, and he will needs be a judge: now will we deal worse with thee, than with them. And they pressed sore upon the man, [even] Lot, and came near to break the door {Bp}. But the men put forth their hand, and brought Lot into the house to them, and shut the door {Be}. And they smote the men that [were] at the door of the house with blindness, both small and great: so that they wearied themselves to find the door. And the men said unto Lot, Hast thou here any besides? son in law, and thy sons, and thy daughters, and whatsoever thou hast in the city, bring [them] out of this place: For we will destroy this place, because the cry of them is waxen great before the face of the Lord; and the Lord hath sent us to destroy it {Bm}. Lot went out, and spoke to his sons-in-law, who were pledged to marry his daughters, and said, "Get up! Get out of this place, for the Lord will destroy the city." But he seemed to his sons-in-law to be joking. When the morning came, then the angels hurried Lot, saying, "Get up! Take your wife, and your two daughters who are here, lest you be consumed in the iniquity of the city {Ba}." I include the last part of Lot's story to show that unrighteousness can exist in those we love, but only at a lower level. What happens to pre-existing evil in our hearts is like any other fertilized seed it GROWS. Although God found Lot to be righteous, there was a lingering desire for the old ways in Lot's wife and in his daughter's.

- Genesis 19:19:26 - **"But his wife looked back from behind him, and she became a pillar of salt** {Babcfijs}.**"**

- Genesis 19:19:30-38 - **"Lot went up out of Zoar, and lived in the mountain and his two daughters with him; for he was afraid to live in Zoar. He lived in a cave with his two daughters. And the firstborn said unto the younger, Our father [is] old, and [there is] not a man in the earth to come in unto us after the manner of all the earth** {Bbijqrsu}.**" Come, let's make our father drink wine, and we will lie with him, that we may preserve our father's seed** {Bbijqrsu}.**" They made their father drink wine that night: and the firstborn went in and lay with her father. He didn't know when she lay down, or when she arose** {Bbijqrsu}. **It came to pass on the next day, that the firstborn said to the younger, "Behold, I lay last night with my father. Let us make him drink wine again, tonight. You go in, and lie with him, that we may preserve our father's seed** {Bbijqrsu}.**" They made their father drink wine that night also. The younger went and lay with him. He didn't know when she lay down, nor when she got up** {Bbijqrsu}.**" Thus, both of Lot's daughters were with child by their father** {Bm}.**"**

_____
_____
_____
_____
_____
_____
_____
_____
_____
_____
_____
_____
_____
_____
_____
_____

 The purpose of all the above information is to remind us that the 𝕭𝖊𝖆𝖘𝖙 has no power over us. Here we see in Genesis 19:30-38 the actual power the 𝕭𝖊𝖆𝖘𝖙 has in our lives. In Luke 4:6, we see that Satan had all power over all the kingdoms of the world. Satan asserts that all the power he had humans delivered to him[122]. Consequently, God sent His Son and that Son rose high enough in the sky to conquer Satan and crush his head. Since the power Satan once had God returned to humanity Satan is powerless to do anything other than deceive.

 In the Story of Lot, we find a vivid example of the traits of the 𝕭𝖊𝖆𝖘𝖙. In this story, we missed something vitally important in our dealing with homosexuality. Homosexuality was not and is not a curse; it is a sign of how far we are from God. Homosexuality is a physical manifestation of unrighteousness. Remember, the scriptures say that the sin in Sodom waxed great before God. God did not specify that the sin He referred to was Homosexuality. God did not destroy the city because of fornication or sexual immorality but because of the grievous level, and variety of sin in the city[123]. We do not see what the scriptures point out clearly about sexual immorality. To understand we must look again to Romans and then to I Corinthians 6:18-20.

  Yes, there is a beginning to homosexuality as there is with all sin. There is no such thing as gay at birth. By sheer definition, homosexual behavior involves sex; sex with a person of the same sex. It is impossible to be a homosexual, and not be sexually active. Devoid of secondary sexual characteristics[124], there is no natural sexual activity in the human kingdom. The human creature is not truly sexual until it has the ability to reproduce. Sex in humans serves a variety of purposes. Some of the sexual purposes are good while others are bad. God however, only ordained a few purposes for sex, marital sex. The simple fact is God ordained sex for four purposes in humanity. The scriptures indicate that God ordained sex for the purposes of:

      59.4.1 Enjoying the marital state, which includes sexual satisfaction, companionship, and nullifying adultery - Ecclesiastes 9:9.
      59.4.2 Reproduction - Genesis 1:28.
      59.4.3 A pleasurable incentive for reproduction - Genesis 3:16.
      59.4.4 A bond developing relationship between a man and a woman - Genesis 2:24.

    The normal state for female animals is to desire sex when they are able to produce children. The unhealthy sex drive in mankind like all the other sin came from the father of sin and evil. The fallen angels brought sexual perversion to the earth. 2 Peter 2:4 and Genesis 6:1-2 shed light on the origin of deviant sexual behavior in humans. The other part of this unnatural use involves things like sado-masochism, bestiality, bondage, torture, and humiliation.

    No naturally occurring species is born with the inability to reproduce. Mules are hybrids bred for farming. A by-product of the mutation is that they are all male. If humans stop the crossbreeding mules and horses, the Mule species will cease to exist. Albinism is similar. A Bengal Tiger is orange and black. If one of the litters is Albino, it is considered rare; but the albino tiger is also an anomaly.

    Homosexuality, which is by no means rare, is of the same candor. Homosexuals can neither reproduce nor maintain their species; a consequence of a lifestyle that is not natural. For this reason, recruitment and secretive bi-sexuality is important. Homosexuals must increase their flock the same way drug dealers do. For this reason, both groups offer a product that appeals to a certain population of people inclined in that direction. In other words, if we are not inclined to use drugs there is no temptation for us. However, if we are already hypersexual, experimental, (like the people in Sodom and Gomorrah, and Romans chapter one) or an extremely curious person, homosexuals only have to get our inhibitions low enough to get us to 'experiment.'

    All the people on the list of Beastly behavior are the same. The act of homosexuality <u>does not define</u> the person. On the contrary, the wretched, Godless, God hating heart creates homosexuality. This is what differentiates homosexuals from fornicators. According to the Bible fornicators hate themselves and *homosexuals hate God.* This difference causes the response from God that resulted in Sodom and Gomorrah's destruction. God does not tolerate those that hate Him, no matter what they do, to how they act upon this hatred.

    Believers, God tells us He is both jealous and wrathful, why must we anger Him. It is not that God hates sex--God hates SIN. God conditionally allows all the sex we desire. Paul says it should occur virtually unceasingly--as long as it is with our wives. Remember, God said we would have Life more abundantly. Therefore, the same--sex marriage concept cannot reconcile itself with God's plan set forth in the book of Genesis 1:12. In this principle, the seeds God ordains reproduce seeds of like kind. This is why we call the process reproduction and not production. Sin produces homosexuals; conversely, copulation reproduces humans.

    The subtlety of the same sex marriage has nothing to do with sex. The object of Satan's war is to elevate his kingdom, or at least stalemate God's kingdom. The sin of adultery prohibits that lifestyle's acceptance by God, but what if adultery was legal? What if fornication and adultery became *marriage?* If this legalization occurred, then I Corinthians 6:9 would no longer apply to homosexuals. Here we see the latest attempt by Satan to regain a foothold in heaven. Another tower of Babel draws neigh, when completed man will not be restricted by God. If we can change the laws against this sinful behavior, then where do we stop…will murder eventually become legal?

The summation therefore is clear. The clearest evidence of the *mark* of the Beast comes from Genesis the 6th, 18, & 19 chapters. In these chapters, the Bible describes a lifestyle of sexual immorality. The issue is not the sex it is what desires the sex: the heart condition. In both cases, God was not attempting to destroy sex or sexuality but the wicked wretched hearts that *choose* to worship something other than God[125].

60.0
Civil War as a Weapon Against Marriage

"**For Herod himself had sent forth and laid hold upon John, and bound him in prison for Herodias' sake, his brother Philip's wife: for he had married her. For John had said unto Herod, 'It is not lawful for thee to have thy brother's wife.' Therefore, Herodias had a quarrel against him, and would have killed him; but she could not: For Herod feared John, knowing that he was a just man and an holy, and observed him; and when he heard him, he did many things, and heard him gladly,**" - (Mark 6:17).

60.1 **Short reasons**
    60.1.1 **Civil war dissolves unity**
    60.1.2 **Civil war makes decisions difficult**
    60.1.3 **Civil war leaves all four flanks unprotected**

60.2 **How civil war is used**

    60.2.1 **Civil war attacks authority from within** - The attack between spouses; putting each other at odds, is old but still works. Everyone, including our own children learn to use this approach. The simple fact is that civil war works because people are more concerned with being right than righteous. Godly peace in a marriage is always the right way. Does it matter who is right in a divorce? Does it matter who is correct when we stop sleeping together and one commits adultery? What is better to be right or to live right? If prayers are hindered everybody suffers. The prayers of the people in charge affect the present and future of the entire family. I wrote people in charge because a true family has a head and a neck. The man without support finds himself in the position God called *not good*. If God ordained for the man and woman to work together and live together does it not make sense that He ordained them to think together.

    60.2.2 **Civil war sets up spies in the camp** - The saddest thing about divorce or single parenting is that it invariably sets up favoritism and eventually makes the children take sides. How does a normal person choose between their left and right side; which is more important to completion? Which side do we need less, the feeling or the thinking side? The law decided that the mother was the best parent in cases where two people cannot get along. They based this decision on the emotional health of the child. The flaw in this concept is that an emotionally immature person:

- Does not have the ability to make a decision
- Is not balanced
- Develops slowly
- Has issues of enhanced selfishness
- Has anger management issues
- Has bonding issues
- Has issues accepting fault

    Emotional people are always good fodder for spies because emotional people feel and do not think. It is easy to think the wrong think when making decisions emotionally, without fact; using feeling alone the outcome cannot be in the best interest of all.

60.2.3 **Civil war creates permanent inlets into the fort** - When a spouse refuses to forgive an incident or continues to bring that incident up it creates permanent inroads for Satan to utilize. Paths of non-forgiveness and hard heartedness give Satan places to hide in and to attack from throughout the marriage. Continual strife eventually gives Satan access to the children. Continual strife forces the children to employ their own set of values to reconcile the issue in their minds that their parents refuse to let die. Simultaneously, the child invariably decides who is right and then tends to lean more towards that parents decision-making process. The child: if for no other reason than to use this favor to accomplish things, the other parent denies them access to.

___
___
___
___
___
___
___
___

60.3 <u>Sexless marriages and divorce</u>[126]

"Since around 20 percent of married couples have a sexless marriage and another 25 percent of them have sex less than once a week, considering that the overall divorce rate is around 40 percent, we may assume that most of the sexless marriages (at a total of around 45 percent of all marriages) will end in divorce."

There is no bigger fool than the married person that removes the physical from their marriage. If we do not even want to indulge in the basest, most pleasant form of fleshly indulgence, then what do we two enjoy. Companionship is the most common answer I get. Sadly, those who say such do not understand that companionship is not asexual it is higher sexuality. A one-night stand is sex. Marriage is taking that one physical act and deciding that we want to share that with this one person until we die.

Since everyone gets old, it makes sense that we understand that intercourse will fall off by default. So, what do we cling to? ONE FLESH. Send enough time making love and when we leave home the chemical bond still us hormones to bind us physically to our spouse. In other words, the results of allowing her breast to satisfy us all times, it that our brains maintain our pleasure when apart. God made the human design to respond to His ways (love, joy, peace, long-suffering, gentleness, goodness, faith, meekness, temperance).

Yes, our spirits may crave these things, but for our flesh, God said HE DID NOT ORDAIN US TO BE WITHOUT SEX[127]. Here is some information about sex, marriage, and divorce[128].

60.3.1 "A new study on Christian attitudes toward dating and marriage reveals a broad acceptance for cohabitation, premarital sex and a rejection of traditional gender roles. Experts believe that many Christians are following cultural. 'Christians are perhaps more influenced by the

culture than they are by the teachings of scripture or the church.' According to the "2014 State of Dating in America" report published by Christian Mingle and JDate;
- 61% of Christians said they would have sex before marriage.
- 56% of Christians that it is appropriate to move in with someone after dating for a time between six months and two years.
- 34% of Christians responded that while it would be nice to marry someone of the same faith, is not required.

60.3.2 In the same study one of the researchers remarked, '…she hears from religious patients: "I practice what the church teaches me, but this is something personal between me and my partner." The therapist commented that, in many ways, churches are "fighting an uphill battle because this is nature."

60.3.3 According to the study, many researchers have shown "that even though partners often cohabit as a trial marriage, couples who cohabit before marriage are more likely to divorce, not less likely." He noted that these couples "are not actually practicing marriage - they are practicing lack of commitment."

60.3.4 Further understanding of the importance of sexually contact within marriage comes from an article, #5 things couples get wrong with sex[129]. The authors contend, dismiss these fallacies, and enjoy a better relationship.
- *Sex is a hot date activity* - Sex is a not a game or just a casual thing to do.
- *Sex is not vital* - This steals power from marriage.
- *Sex is steamier if we use porn* - Porn has a counterproductive effect on marriage and has the potential to destroy libido and open our minds to explore things not previously considered or attempted.
- *Sex is impossible without a babysitter* - We did not need a sitter when we were dating? Why now find ways to sneak, creep, and freak!
- *Sex has to be spontaneous to be sizzling* - Few sexual encounters are truly spontaneous. Even the drive over, the gift purchase, the hours dressing etc. are part of the encounter, how then can it be spontaneous. Natural is more likely, it should be a natural response to send time in close proximity to the person we chose to send the rest of lives with.

60.3.5 Even the world has realized that sex is required to make a relationship work. Without sex the species devolves into lower life habits. Once there is no cohesion with the family, the society also begin s to break down. Once there is no relationship all interactions become based in flesh.

This is how it was in Sodom and Gomorrah. The flesh without love needs to be fed constantly. As it is with things that live on death, Satan, and the Children of Pride, hate God. Their hatred for God makes them not even care about themselves. Everything, even their own cubs are just flesh for the gobbling. The emptier they are the more they need to eat.

Remember it was not homosexuality that caused the downfall of the two cities; it was they loathsome nature in which they gobbled and traded flesh that angered the Creator. It was their worship of the creature (Golden Calf) rather than the Creator that waxed great in His sight[130].

60.3.6 According to studies carried out since 1972[131], 58% of married couples have sex on average 58 times per year, and couples under #30 years old #111 times per year. Approximately 15% of the people studied had not had sex with six months of the study. The three most important things determined during the study are;
- Sexless marriages are far more likely to end in divorce
- Sexless marriages are more difficult to rekindle
- Couples in sexless marriages are less happy

60.3.7 From Marriage Facts[132], we amass some additional facts about marriage.
- 75% of people who marry partners from an affair eventually divorce.
- 1 in every 5 couples has a sexless marriage, having less than 10 encounters a year.
- First marriages that end in a divorce usually last approximately 8 years.
- Couples who live together before engagement have a higher divorce rates than those who wait.
- There are 100 divorces every hour in the U.S.
- Couples who spend more money on their wedding have a higher divorce rate.
- In 1960, 59% of American adults aged 18-29 were married, today, only 20% are married.
- People in the most successful marriages spend an average of 5 more hours a week being together and talking.

Marriage is in trouble. No matter the lies we tell ourselves, God made sex desirable and an integral part of marriage for a reason. Bonds that go beyond words last longer. If all we must bind us to our spouses or to God are words…then the relationship is doomed.

We need to sure up our marriages. Now we can go on retreats, and couples' weekends, and read all the books we opt to. Solomon has the best advice, and the best solution for the weak marriage. GET NAKED, AND LET HER BREAST SATISFY US AT ALL TIMES. Our spouses will not mind gentle, caring, she has two breasts (just in case we get greedy). Spend more time naked together, talking, laughing, and loving. If we must argue, then commence the peace talks. Dress the part, dress appropriately, wear nothing to the peace talks, if we still opt to argue; your marriage is in trouble.

60.4 What to do when they cheat?

Infidelity is never ok with God. If a spouse commits adultery, under God's law the other is free. However, looking at the rules pertaining to marriage and forgiveness it appears that three laws pervade,

> 60.4.1 Matthew 6:14-15, "**FOR IF YE FORGIVE MEN THEIR TRESPASSES, YOUR HEAVENLY FATHER WILL ALSO FORGIVE YOU: BUT IF YE FORGIVE NOT MEN THEIR TRESPASSES, NEITHER WILL YOUR FATHER FORGIVE YOUR TRESPASSES.**"
>
> 60.4.2 Matthew 18:18, "**VERILY I SAY UNTO YOU, WHATSOEVER YE SHALL BIND ON EARTH SHALL BE BOUND IN HEAVEN: AND WHATSOEVER YE SHALL LOOSE ON EARTH SHALL BE LOOSED IN HEAVEN.**"
>
> 60.4.3 1 Corinthians 7:14, "**For the unbelieving husband is sanctified by the wife, and the unbelieving wife is sanctified by the husband: else were your children unclean; but now are they holy.**"

From these three rules we glean that the spouse who does not commit adultery is free to leave but if inclined to stay can forgive the act. Although there is no forgiveness found in God for this, we find forgiveness because of Him. God will always allow the faithful spouse to leave. This is what I mean when I say there is no forgiveness found in Him for adultery, one spouse cannot destroy another. However, in order that the bed become undefiled again, the clean spouse must intercede on behalf of the other removing from them the stain of sin by calling upon their undefiled covenant with God and putting it under the Blood. By forgiving the adulterous spouse and binding that issue, God withholds judgment. This is what the Bible refers to as presenting the spouse without spot or blemish. By this is the process we clean our spouses and maintain marriages. A failed marriage is not one with flaws but one in which there is no longer forgiveness.

60.5 Why divorce is bad

If we refer to (1.1.1, 1.1.10,1.1.11) we must again look to what husbandry is. Husbandry is gardening; therefore, they must have similarities. When planting into the earth the reason the plant grows is because it not only derives its nourishment from the earth it becomes one with the earth. The marriage of the two, allows the exchange of the nutrients needed to produce offspring while simultaneously ridding them both of waste products.

Divorce (putting away)[133]; is the tearing apart or replanting. Once a plant *marries* to the soil, they leant to live with whatever it has to offer. When we uproot plants, often times we cannot understand why the plants die. Common errors in replanting included[134];

- 60.5.1 Planting too deep - If planted too deeply, roots often cannot to get enough oxygen, so they suffocate.
- 60.5.2 Watering - Not enough water is just as bad as too much water, wither one can kill the plants
- 60.5.3 Improper Planting - Improperly choosing site, depth, soil, and sunlight will adversely affect the plant. It may thrive for a while, because it was healthy, but it will eventually die. Moreover, if planted improperly, the roots often cannot reach adequate water.
- 60.5.4 Root Damage - moving plants or tearing them out of the soil often results in root breakage or damage. Without a healthy root system, even the hardiest of plants die.

In the same manner, once married (planted) the two fleshes become one. The married couple forms a union that is supposed to benefit both. Whether they both grow in a positive manner, is not the issue; the fact is they do merge.

This why bad marriages are so disheartening, they actually hurt. It is because we cannot get the necessary nutrients, or worse, the marriage itself is choking our roots and killing the plants.

Sadly, children born to marriages are not just torn from the soil they were potted (born) within. They are torn in three different segments. The children are torn from the;

- Soil of the union (23 pair of chromosomes - one from each parent)
- Soil of the mother
- Soil of the father

How is a plant supposed to decide which life-giving nutrients it does not need? Why do so many children from broken homes lead unhappy lives? Because they are not healthy physically or spiritually.

The seed (marriage or children) grew from the soil, and in the soil. So, when we transplant them or simply uproot them they have trouble adapting the uprooted plant, simple spends the rest of its life trying to survive. It has no reason to produce fruit. The transplanted planted finds that no matter the it tries it cannot reproduce the new soil, because it does not carry the seed from the new life, but instead the old. This is why there are so many emotional special needs kids, both in and out of church.

Other than the obvious, there is biblical reason expressed as to why divorce is never the preferred methodology to resolve marital problems. The world will have us believe our God ordains, condones, and periodically suggests divorce--this is a lie. God tells us that Moses permitted divorce because men were too unrighteous to mend their marriages, but it was NEVER His will or way[135].

For those who believe that Malachi 3:10 holds both punishment and promise for the non-thither let us look with that same air of reverence to what the same writer says about divorce. If it is the same book, the same author, and the same God, it must be the same truth: if not the teaching is false. There is no way possible to misinterpret, rearrange, or modernize the meaning of God's words in Malachi 2:14-17. **"You cry out, '*Why has the Lord abandoned us?*' I'll tell you why! Because the Lord witnessed the vows you and your wife made to each other on your wedding day when you** were young. But you have been disloyal to her, though she remained your faithful companion, the wife of your marriage vows. Didn't the Lord make you one with your wife? In body and spirit, you are His. And what does He want? Godly children from your union. So, guard yourself; remain loyal to the wife of your youth. 'FOR I HATE DIVORCE!' says the Lord, the God of Israel. 'IT IS AS CRUEL AS PUTTING ON A VICTIM'S BLOODSTAINED COAT,' says the Lord Almighty. 'So, guard yourself; always remain loyal to your wife.' You have wearied the Lord with your words. 'Wearied Him?' you ask. 'How have we wearied Him?' You have wearied Him by suggesting that the Lord favors evildoers since He does not punish them. You have wearied Him by asking, "Where is the God of justice? - NLT[136]."

I make no judgment I relay the word. Do not waste time feeling anger towards the Word of God; they change not, neither does He. Bearing in mind the topic is spiritual warfare and marriage let us look at the many chinks in the divorce, or pre-divorce armor.

60.5.1 **"You cry out, "Why has the Lord abandoned us?"** - Our prayers go unanswered and needs fulfilled. If we find ourselves asking where God is then the gifts and anointing, we have we will find themselves lacking power. Although they are without repentance it does not mean He has to give them power. Aaron walked with Moses for 40 years, but the Bible contains nothing about his power. Like Saul the job maybe ours, but neither time nor God is on our side.

60.5.2 **I'll tell you why! Because the Lord witnessed the vows you and your wife made to each other on your wedding day when you were young. But you have been disloyal to her, though she remained your faithful companion, the wife of your marriage vows** - If the cause of divorce stems from adultery, God articulates that He was there on our wedding day and heard our vows. He points out that we broke our vows, which actually releases God from His obligation to our marriage and us. When we divorce, God sees us as He saw the wife of Uriah the Hittite, a permanent part of a failed team. However, His laws on adultery remain in effect.

60.5.3 **Didn't the Lord make you one with your wife? In body and spirit, you are His** - God is a God of covenant He prefers blood covenants. When He made our spouses and us one, it was unto death. Unlike the

60.5.4 **And what does He want? Godly children from your union** - The result of the failing of the Godly parents is that Godly children now come under permanent attack. Children of broken homes are more likely to lose spiritual battles because their armor is incomplete. In addition, regarding unmarried, or homosexual parenting--there can be no Godly children from an ungodly union. This does not mean children from these unions cannot be saved, it means they forge their armor with flawed metal, which, if not tempered, will not stand the test of time. Since parents in ungodly unions do not know the God of the forge, their children usually remain lost or indifferent.

60.5.5 **"FOR I HATE DIVORCE!" says the Lord, the God of Israel. "IT IS AS CRUEL AS PUTTING ON A VICTIM'S BLOODSTAINED COAT," says the Lord Almighty** - God makes His feelings clear and goes on to reference Joseph and his brothers. God makes His feelings about losing His children plain. As Jacob felt about Joseph's death, God feels about the death of our marriages. God finds the man, especially the spiritual warrior that pretends to be the victim in divorce disgusting. Like the brothers, the divorcee lies to God because they said they would never break their vows. The truth of their marriage is not dead; they have hidden it to get rewards they do not deserve.

60.5.6 **You have wearied the Lord with your words. "Wearied Him?" you ask. "How have we wearied Him?" You have wearied Him by suggesting that the Lord favors evildoers since He does not punish them** - Finally, it makes sense that the God we anger and disappoint with our treacherous ways is in no hurry to bless us, why should He, we cannot be trusted. Sadly, Malachi goes on to remind us that the lying witness is no witness of God. Those who cannot keep their own bride do not deserve the chance to defile God's bride.

60.5.7 **"And Jesus said unto him, 'NO MAN, HAVING PUT HIS HAND TO THE PLOUGH, AND LOOKING BACK, IS FIT FOR THE KINGDOM OF GOD'** - Luke 9:62." We may not understand the use of this passage in marriage, but remember God said divorce is treacherous. We see here that Christ takes a firm stand on the new life. If we choose the new life, a life of righteousness there will be failures; but to turn away from this makes us unworthy says the Lord. When we take a spouse, we make a great leap because we just made the longest, most intricate commitment of our life. As we discussed many times throughout this book the Christian marriage is an indicator to God of how we will treat His bride. What father would give his daughter to a man that will leave her at will? Those who walk away from troubled marriages fail to understand two things. Firstly, that there can be no resolution to problems we run from and the second is much more important. If we were half of the problem in the first marriage, we take that same problem with us into the next marriage.

60.6 Divorce tears relationships apart

Even more problematic for Christians than unworthiness is the simple fact that divorce tears relationships. Circumcision like marriage is a sign in the flesh of restraint and dedication. In both rituals, the flesh gives up a portion of itself, a sacrifice for the better life. As a reward for this life of fidelity, we find joy, safety, unity, and power. When spouses support each other, they excel in their lives past the disjointed counterparts. When saints live a life or righteousness, they wield power. Like material wealth, the power couples wield stems from unity. When we join to the Source of that power, we tie into all His nutrients. When God is the Tree in our lives, we become His fruit. As fruit of the Tree of Life, we wield all goodness and righteousness and truth, love, joy, peace, long-suffering, gentleness, goodness, and faith[137].

When I had problems in my marriage, I looked at the things I stood to lose if we divorced. I looked at my beautiful kids and often watched my beautiful wife as she slept (this way she was quiet). I realized one day that it would be worse without her that the worst days with her. To that end, I decided divorce is not a good thing. When I looked at all the things I stood to lose in the spirit realm, it made the decision even easier.

When we divorce, the Bible says we are treacherously dealing with our spouses. The treachery is not in our deeds; it is in the fact that we vowed to make the relationship work despite our sinful ways. When we choose Christ and go into apostasy, we have dealt with Him treacherously as well. We no longer risk damnation; we risk powerlessness and loneliness in this life. Perhaps when Olsten and Pearson speak of the *hell in this life* it is to this state they refer.

In all marriages, there are problems, some in the foundation, some in the walls, and others still in the roof. Consequently, all marriages have inroads for satanic encroachment. What Jesus says is that spouses should not add to their problems more issues and concerns about tomorrow for there are ample that occur naturally--we do not need to add problems for them to exist.

60.7 **Rope-a-dope**

The rope a dope method of fighting became popular under Muhammad Ali. Ali would allow the opponent to strike him until they were tired, and then when they became careless, he attacked. In marriage, we use this tactic when we ignore each other's needs, knowing the other spouse suffers loneliness, sadness, and anger. Since we are married however, we assume that the other person cannot leave so we continue to rope a dope. This tactic is extremely selfish and destructive when used on Christians. The rope a dope creates desperation and resentment, who likes being held against their will? It is a horrible feeling to wake every morning knowing that a person who could give a little and make a paradise like Milton would rather reign in Hell. Most marital strife is a childish battle of wills.

61.0
The Eyes as a Weapon Against Marriage

"And it came to pass, after the year was expired, at the time when kings go forth [to battle], that David sent Joab, and his servants with him, and all Israel; and they destroyed the children of Ammon, and besieged Rabbah. But David tarried still at Jerusalem. And it came to pass in an evening tide, that David arose from off his bed, and walked upon the roof of the king's house: and from the roof he saw a woman washing herself; and the woman [was] very beautiful to look upon," – (2 Samuel 11:1-2).

61.1 **Short reasons**
    61.1.1 **The eyes constantly infuse garbage**
    61.1.2 **The eyes increase covetousness**
    61.1.3 **The eyes absorb life**

61.2 **How the eyes work against marriage**

61.2.1 **Lustful opportunities** - Most temptations manifest themselves through the visual center. Even when we day dream or imagine it is always visual. Satan knows this; this is why he offered Jesus visible things. Even if the thing offered is power, it always manifests through the things we can access and control. The more we give in to our eyes, the more lustful opportunities Satan creates. This is why Hollywood makes so many R-Rated movies. G-rated movies make an average of 17 times the money their R-Rated counter parts earn. However, the prince of the power of the air realizes he can do more damage to marriages and to saints through R-Rated love scenes, sex scenes, and rape scenes, than he can with Bambi and Dumbo.

61.2.2 **Lustful eyes make heart's desires available** - The Bible tells us that whatever our heart dwells on long enough we will do, "**But every man is tempted, when he is drawn away of his own lust, and enticed. Then when lust hath conceived, it bringeth forth sin: and sin, when it is finished, bringeth forth death,**" – (James 1:14-15). If it is scripture, then it is true. The truth is for God's people, but Satan has

The eyes are not evil, but the see evil all day. It is impossible to see evil all day and it not have an affect us. Matthew 5:29 warns us to be aware of what information our eyes interpret. To see a beautiful woman, is normal. To acknowledge her beauty is acceptable, but to desire her sexually is a sin. To this end, Jesus tells us to pluck our eyes out rather than go to hell. I suggest we train our eyes to do our bidding rather than live in the hell of denial and constantly seeking forgiveness.

access to the truth also. Since Satan has access to the truth, he also knows the duration and determination of human flesh. Therefore, Satan specializes in providing opportunities for sin to flourish.

61.2.3 **Lustful eyes keep faith at unrest** - As long as there are other people getting ahead in areas we perceive we should, we will always have crises of faith. All Satan has to do is what he does well; remind us of what someone else has. The commandment against coveting, we see now is not aimed at theft (another commandment covers that) it is aimed at assisting our faith walk. If we do not covet, we do not lust, and we do not contrive sinful ways to obtain what we do not possess.

62.0
The Flesh as a Weapon Against Marriage

"*Now the works of the flesh are manifest, which are [these]; Adultery, fornication, uncleanness, lasciviousness,*" – (Galatians 5:19).

62.1 **Short reasons**
    62.1.1 **We are trapped in the flesh**
    62.1.2 **The flesh determines movements**
    62.1.3 **The flesh manifests thoughts**

62.2 **A dirty little secret**
According to New Testament usage of the Greek word, *sarkikos* has four definitions.
    62.1.4 Having the nature of flesh, i.e. (Under the control of the animal appetites)
    62.1.5 Governed by mere human nature not by the spirit of God
    62.1.6 Having its seat in the animal nature or aroused by the animal nature
    62.1.7 Human: with the included idea of depravity

All of these seem to point to one thing; the flesh is about flesh, not love. As I have grown older, I finds many answers to questions which once baffled me. One such question is why would a man cheat? The second question, why would a man cheat on his wife with a lesser creature (less attractive woman)? The answer is simple yet disgusting. Look at list 63.3, the flesh does not care. To flesh, all flesh is the same.

The spouse who cheats
- With attractive first choice
- Their emotional second choice
- The convenient third choice or the
- The catering fourth choice

I think definitions 3 and 4 give the explanation best. The flesh, like any cannibal, will eat anything. As long as it is meat. What this means to marriage is that ANY marriage that does not have a healthy dose of the anti-dote to this filthy nature (the undefiled wedding bed) is fooling themselves. The flesh is ALIVE! Just like in a Stephen King novel, without it you would not be married. Why then deny your nature?

Marriage is about forsaking all others, for the sole purpose of getting your own set of breast or strong arms to satisfy you at all times. This should help you understand why obese women wear scanty clothes, or super tight outfits, they have the dame flesh as a model, it is just a matter of which tier the man is on when they meet. Why sleep with a child, or a person of the same sex: it is flesh[138]! To this Romans 1 spoke of when it called people like these reprobates.

When we look at what out spouse has replaced us with and cannot understand the reason, try remembering what it was like when you were easily aroused and didn't care about where or when? Then look at here you are now, once a month, quarterly, dry, mechanical, and routine. No matter what we think about sex and how little we made need, the cheating spouse obviously needs something more. Either we give it, they have to do without, or they get it elsewhere.

62.3 How the flesh works against marriage

62.3.1 **Life keeps flesh satisfied** - Life offers a wide range of diverse temptations for the flesh. There is no time or place in the world (including the church) that there are not distractions for the flesh. Once the flesh finds a pleasing distraction, it finds difficulty in relinquishing temptation. The aim of Satan's distractions is to make us under-appreciate the things God actually gave us to please our flesh. The reason for naked women in underwear commercials is to please the flesh. Women see sexy women and dream of looking thusly, and their men dream of the woman in the underwear. There is no logical reason to market underwear via *supermodels*. I have been to the underwear stores with my wife, and (other than my wife) none of the women in the store look like the ones on television. Television markets dreams and lust to people; someone sees something their flesh likes. Look at the clothes and fashions for teenage girls--is it a wonder teenage pregnancy rates climbs, as well as teen rape and statutory rape increase? We market flesh to the flesh, and flesh responds.

62.3.2 **The flesh discourages denial and sacrifice** - Sadly enough, the Ad-council is about the only entity encouraging restraint and sacrifice. The government once encouraged parents to allow children their privacy. We now see that left untended the flesh makes few advances towards decency. Although certain stratums in life over look bad behavior, it is still bad behavior. Television, radio, movies, books, and media encourages skanky behavior, lewd clothes, and unrefined social lives. When society accepts low morality as a defining action: historically, the results are what we see now; a society raised and broached against marriage and decency.

3.3 **The flesh makes peace difficult** - How can any home have peace when all we see on TV is MTV Cribs, Atlanta Housewives, Reality TV shows, and other stupid shows the revel in the material and the selfish. There are few family shows, and the family shows highlight friction, denigration, and struggle. Other shows highlight or accentuate homosexuality or frivolity. Then there is Hollywood houses the most useless citizens on the planet. Hollywood produces nothing the world needs; with all the money the Hollywood grosses, they cannot get past being drunks, addicts, and prostitutes. One would think that in the land of make believe they could of a better job of pretending to be happy.

The purpose of pornography and porn related topics is to sell sex. Purveyors[139] of porn type material are not interested in selling porn they are greedy and would sell anything to make a buck. It just so happens that humans, especially human males like porn.

- 70% of men look at porn
- 30% of women look at porn
- 2/3 employers have found porn on employees' computer
- Average time on porn site 12 minute
- Average porn watcher, 7.5 visits per month
- Estimated #450 million visitors to porn sites monthly[14]

Society would have us believe that this is because men are low-lives. This is not the case; men are men. God created the human form and put in that form a heightened sexual awareness. As we study the book of Genesis, we find that porn started when the *sons of God saw the daughters of men were fair.* Once Satan realized he could out breed righteousness, the need to distort sexuality arose. Since then Satan has perverted our heightened sexuality for his own purposes. Homosexuality, rape, pedophilia, necrophilia, and bestially, all have one thing in common they do not produce Godly offspring. These attacks aid Satan in weakening marriage and therefore slow down the production of Godly seeds.

63.0
Fornication as a Weapon Against Marriage

"Behold, there a woman met him with the attire of a harlot, and subtle heart. She is loud and defiant. Her feet do not stay in her house. Now she is in the streets, now in the squares, and lurking at every corner. So, she caught him, and kissed him. With an impudent face she said to him: 'Sacrifices of peace offerings are with me. This day I have paid my vows. Therefore, I came out to meet you, to diligently seek your face, and I have found you. I have spread my couch with carpets of tapestry, with striped cloths of the yarn of Egypt. I have perfumed my bed with myrrh, aloes, and cinnamon. Come, let's take our fill of loving until the morning. Let's solace ourselves with loving. For my husband is not at home. He has gone on a long journey. He has taken a bag of money with him. He will come home at the full moon.' With persuasive words, she led him astray. With the flattering of her lips, she seduced him. He followed her immediately, as an ox goes to the slaughter, as a fool stepping into a noose. Until an arrow strikes through his liver, as a bird hurries to the snare, and does not know that it will cost his life. Now therefore, sons, listen to me. Pay attention to the words of my mouth. Do not let your heart turn to her ways. Do not go astray in her paths, for she has thrown down many wounded. Yes, all her slain are a mighty army. Her house is the way to Sheol, going down to the rooms of death," - (Proverbs 7:10-27).

63.1 Short reasons
63.1.1 Fornication is effective against the flesh
63.1.2 Fornication is easy to maintain secret
63.1.3 Fornication seems to be victimless
63.1.4 Fornication joins us to the outsider
63.1.5 Fornication allows a joining with foreign spirits
63.1.6 Fornication leaves the gate open
63.1.7 Adultery often a preexisting problem
63.1.8 Adultery is a breaking of covenant
63.1.9 Adultery violates trust
63.1.10 Adultery disrupts spiritual harmony

63.2 How fornication works against marriage

63.2.1 **Fornication is effective against the flesh** - Fornication is the most popular sin. It feels good, and rumor has it has little to no side effects. Fornication is the perfect temptation because it is appealing to all normal people. No matter the person, Satan has more than a 50% chance of success using fornication as an attack. Woman lie about their fornication appeasement, but fornication works with them as well; they just want it to be the '*right person.*' In the case of women, all Satan has to do is supply the '*right person*' and pay dirt. Is it not amazing how many 'right people' do the wrong things in the relationship? Humorously, we cannot take the fornication back once we find out we do not like the person. Since we use our flesh to make most of our decisions common sense dictates that this is probably the best route to attack a person's heart, marriage, and future.

63.2.2 **Fornication is easy to maintain in secret** - Unlike obesity, drugs, gambling and other temptations, keeping fornication (adultery) a secret from our spouses is easy. Sloppy people are caught easily, but the seasoned liar can maintain their secret indefinitely. Fornication (adultery) related secrets require a cadre of other related secrets to keep the lie alive. Adultery in most cases becomes apparent not because of physical clues but because of emotional changes. It appears that the heart is desperately wicked: and not only do we not know it, therefore, we cannot control when it reveals its true self.

63.2.3 **Fornication seems victimless** - One of the many reasons fornication and adultery are prevalent is that people believe it to be victimless. If a spouse does not know we cheated how can it hurt them? We get to visualize with extramarital children, STDs and HIV what simultaneously happens in the spirit (spiritually transmitted diseases). When we cheat, we also link our spouses to that person spiritually. Just because our wife does not know we cheated does not make it any less dangerous or injurious. <u>There can be no benefit to the marriage from adultery</u>. Even the selfish gain does not offset the lying and deception that must continue. Satan engenders opportunities' because he knows that fornication has accompanying lying and deception, moreover he also knows that adultery rarely is a onetime deal.

63.2.4 **Fornication leads to other sin** - Fornication leads to other sins. In most cases, fornication leads to more lust and more fornication. In the case where fornication does not lead to more fornication, it leads to an unfulfilled sex life. A spouse that cheats always finds a reason to cheat. Good or bad, the reason is always that they want to be a happy. The problem is that when the spouse that cheats return home whatever makes them unhappy still exists.

63.2.5 **Fornication dilutes spiritual purity** - No matter how many years of purity and study we undertake fornication never occurs by accident it is always an intentional act. This one action can over shadow a life of honorable deeds. Fornication never occurs by accident it is always an intentional act. When we fall prey to our flesh, people see us as hypocrites because we could not live the life we preach. The bible also says that when we lay with a whore we become whores. *Whore* is not a skill that looks good on a resume.

63.2.6 **Pre-marital sex makes marital sex difficult** - The key to enjoying wine is to open it when we are ready to enjoy the entire bottle. Otherwise, the bouquet wastes in the fridge from the slightly shorn cork stuck in the neck. Fornication is the same way. It is far easier to maintain or enhance sexuality than it is to get the *bouquet of innocence* back into the bottle. Since God does not ordain test-driving our mates, the next best thing is to wait until we are ready to own a car to drive.

63.2.7 **Adultery disrupts unity** - Most couples would agree that an affair would wedge a gap between them. Even with forgiveness, scars and the pain remain. When we pretend that the Blood of Jesus makes everything ok, we fall victim to deception. The most righteous of us can admit that while the Blood of Jesus makes forgiveness for adultery possible, it is our decision to love the person that makes living with them after the affair impossible. The unity between two people takes time to develop. The introduction of the third person ruptures harmony and the growth between the two occurred between only two. Adultery also makes the victim feel cheated out of the just treatment they deserve.

63.2.8 Adultery creates civil war - When the American south succeeded from the Union, the country plunged itself into civil war. When a spouse succeeds from the union, they plunge the marriage into civil war. How can two agree spiritually when one spouse is laid up in the bed with another person? How can we have peace in the home when the piece one spouse seeks is not within the bounds of the relationship. **"Having eyes full of adultery, and that cannot cease from sin; beguiling unstable souls: a heart they have exercised with covetous practices;"** - (2 Peter 2:14).

63.2.9 Adultery harms children - Adultery introduces children to new spirits, new diseases, and new people. When we sleep with a new person the reason we change is because we change to maintain the happiness. The change in the cheating spouse affects the family, because the *new you* is not the person the family knew or desired. When a spouse discovers adultery the potential for divorce exists, and in situations when the marriage survives, children learn a lesson, but they only see the negative application of forgiveness. What they learn is that we can take advantage of the people we love, and they will just take it if they want to keep what they have.

63.2.10 Adultery destroys effectiveness - When adultery enters marriage, communication breaks down, and the unified chain of command dissolves. The cheating husband losses the respect of his wife and children and cannot effectively head his household. The cheating wife loses the respect of the husband and angers the children for betraying their dad. The family now has to try to weather the storm, while their personal prayers, needs, and desires go unanswered and untended.

63.2.11 Adultery makes lying necessary - There is no way to maintain or have an affair without lying. Even the lie of omission is still a lie. Actually, that is not true. The only way to have an affair and not lie about the thing is to have poor communication with an uncaring spouse. Other than this case, the cheater has to lie about what they do. As we all know, one lie leads to another. To maintain the first lie requires a whole deck of lies to support the house that jack built.

63.2.12 Adultery often arises due to a preexisting problem - Adultery is usually the result of a preexisting condition. People marry with many secrets and lots of baggage. Many people cheat because they find themselves cut off from their normal means of easing their pain. Once inside a marriage people often feel trapped, thus exacerbating the already existent problem that they failed to resolve.

Once the old problem rears its ugly head Satan finds a new target to attack; an old, unhealed injury makes a palatable meal for maggots.

63.3 **Redefining the definition of cheating**

Adult movie stars sleep around for a profession, but they do not generally consider this cheating? An adult movie star interviewed on HBO by Howard Stern show, they define cheating as an *emotional attachment to another person*. On the other extreme, we have cults that marry many partners.

So, what is the definition of cheating? Let us now redefine the definition of adultery or cheating, in doing such let us do what we should have done from the beginning. Adultery in our relationships should be defined thusly--WHATEVER DISPLEASES OUR SPOUSE IS CHEATING FOR OUR MARRIAGE. If our spouse does not want us to text or email exes, then by agreement, extra-marital-interpersonal interactions are cheating. Remember, marriage is personnel; the law should not be the determinant factor on the internal workings of our marriage.

Since many enter marriage with a sexual history, defining cheating is not easy. Rather than let the world tell us what is acceptable let us look to the Bible to see what God says is acceptable sexual behavior.

63.3.1 To lie with another man's wife is adultery (Leviticus 20)
63.3.2 To lie with a mother-in law is adultery (Leviticus 20)
63.3.3 To lie with his daughter-in-law is adultery (Leviticus 20)
63.3.4 To lie with a male, as with a woman is adultery (Leviticus 20)
63.3.5 To lie with wife and her mother is adultery (Leviticus 20)
63.3.6 To lie with an animal is adultery (Leviticus 20)
63.3.7 If a woman approaches any animal, is adultery (Leviticus 20)
63.3.8 To lie with his sister, his father's daughter, or his mother's daughter is

adultery (Leviticus 20)
63.3.9 To lie with his uncle's wife is adultery (Leviticus 20)
63.3.10 To lie with his brother's wife is adultery (Leviticus 20)
63.3.11 For women to lie with other women is adultery (Leviticus 20)
63.3.12 To do those things which are not fitting (wife swapping, multiple partners, children, rape) is adultery (Romans 1)
63.3.13 Fornication, and whoredom (2 Peter 2:14, Romans 7:3) is adultery
63.3.14 Spiritual adultery [Idolatry, covetousness, apostasy] - (Jeremiah 3:6-9, Ezekiel 16: 32-33, Revelations 2:20, Isaiah 1:21, Ezekiel 23:7 & 37, Matthew 12:39, James 4:4, Romans 7:4) is adultery
63.3.15 Lust and or covetousness (Ezekiel 6:9, Jeremiah 3:9) is adultery

If you cannot find sexual satisfaction within these boundaries, please do not marry, for you will destroy our marriage and put multiple souls in harm's way.

63.4 Cheat sheets

Many students use cheat sheets during test to either supplement their knowledge, or because they are too lazy to study. For married people, I complied this *cheat sheet*; a compiled from medical professionals, counselors and audience polls, which give a varied list of reasons men, couples, and women, cheat. Despite these reasons, the man reason for cheating is a self-centered hardness of our hearts. The whole purpose of marriage is to partner with another human that completes, assists, believes in and forgives us; until death do us part.

This section is for both group and home discussions. Approaching the discussion is precarious. Especially at home, but the fact is that you will divulge these reasons during arguments eventually. By expressing the deficiencies openly, we start to patch the holes in marriages. Couples, who use this workbook as cannon fodder, were doomed before they start this process.

Every surgeon asked you what is wrong before cutting. Then they cut into you through the healthy areas to get to the bad. They excise the bad, they close; leaving only what is good inside. This is the purpose of the Adam and Eve edition, to cut away the laying darkness hiding in each marriage.

Pick three sets of boxes;
1. Two main reasons people cheat
2. Reason I would cheat
3. Reason I believe my wife would cheat

63.5 Adam's Cheat Sheet[140]
☐ Immaturity
☐ Inadequacy Issues
☐ Toxic sexual shame
☐ Intimacy issues
☐ Selfishness
☐ Under appreciated
☐ To gain love and attention
☐ Ego booster

- ☐ Disillusionment
- ☐ Hyper-sexuality
- ☐ Sense of adventure
- ☐ To avoid commitment
- ☐ Convenience
- ☐ Infidelity is crime of opportunity
- ☐ Unhappiness
- ☐ Self-esteem issues
- ☐ Dissatisfied emotionally
- ☐ Men cheat when they do not feel valued
- ☐ Men cheat when they're needs are not met
- ☐ Undesired
- ☐ Disrespected
- ☐ Boredom
- ☐ Lack of potency or vitality due to age or health
- ☐ Do not feel vital to partner

63.5 **Eden's Cheat Sheet**[141]

- ☐ Early marriage
- ☐ Married for the wrong reasons
- ☐ Disagreement on core values
- ☐ Emotional disconnectedness between partners
- ☐ Differing or unmet life priorities
- ☐ No common or competing interests
- ☐ Need for excitement
- ☐ Career advancement
- ☐ Personal finances
- ☐ Physical dissatisfaction
- ☐ Kids lack either of or because of (Sad but true)
- ☐ Inability to deal with changes

63.6 **Eve's Cheat Sheet**[142,143]

- ☐ Emotionally dissatisfied
- ☐ Attachment style
- ☐ Emotional abandonment
- ☐ Pre-menopause/Menopause
- ☐ Intimacy issues
- ☐ Internal power struggle
- ☐ Money
- ☐ Revenge
- ☐ Aging
- ☐ To spice things up

- ☐ Unresolved father issues
- ☐ Feel ignored or overlooked
- ☐ Inadequate sexual relationship
- ☐ Boredom
- ☐ Low self-esteem
- ☐ To find themselves
- ☐ Sexual incompatibility
- ☐ To escape their real lives
- ☐ Tired of each other's quirks
- ☐ Being together is no longer fun
- ☐ Your friends do not like him
- ☐ Taken for granted
- ☐ He no longer enhance your life
- ☐ No longer in love
- ☐ Marriage cold and empty

63.7 What we learn from unhappiness

"**Finally, brothers and sisters, whatever is true, whatever is noble, whatever is right, whatever is pure, whatever is lovely, whatever is admirable - if anything is excellent or praiseworthy - think about such things and the God of peace will be with you**" (Philippians 4:8).

Paul admonishes us to think on things, which benefit us, However, I believe, that we learn many bad things from life with a selfish spouse. The marriage partner forced to accept the unattractive, uninteresting spouse finds a world filled with low–level potential. Where the spouse was selective, the new level they have been forced to accept either drives them away from their spouse completely, or makes it easy for another to sneak through the hole in the fence.

63.7.1 When we let ourselves got (gain weight, poor hygiene) we force our spouse to either avoid us, or learn to accept this new condition. All the people that were no eligible for their interest prior now become part of the eligible pool.

63.7.2 The spouse that develops drug or liquor habits, sets up for the spouse to learn to accept eligible people and sets the kids up for this failure as well.

63.7.2.1 The abuser allows harsh, belittling persons into the sphere of acceptance as well.

63.7.2.2 The spouse that makes the other feel unappreciated, unloved, unattractive, unintelligent, opens even more holes in the walls of our marriage. This is why so many spouses are more surprised at the quality of the spouse consorts than the fact that they are cheating. What well-groomed spouse is not humiliated when they are replaced but a truly unseemly person?

64.0
Week 10 - Work Area

64.1 What is reverence?

_____
_____
_____
_____
_____
_____
_____

64.2 How does reverence affect the church?

_____
_____
_____
_____
_____
_____
_____

64.3 How does reverence affect marriage?

_____
_____
_____
_____
_____
_____
_____
_____

64.4 Sex - frequency, quantity, quality, and infidelity are all common sources of stress and disharmony. Explain your view of your marital sex life and compare to yours.

64.5 What is sexual purity?

64.6 How would you describe your sex life?

64.7 Why do people look at porn?

___

64. 8 How would you describe intimacy?

___

64.9 Is intimacy important to marriage and why?

___

Week 11

Spiritual Warfare Marriage Mysteries

65.0 - Lust as a weapon against marriage
66.0 - The thoughts as a weapon against marriage
67.0 - The heart as a weapon against marriage
68.0 - The tongue as a weapon against marriage
69.0 - Un-forgiveness as a weapon against marriage
70.0 - Anger as a weapon against marriage
71.0 - Jealousy as a weapon against marriage
72.0 - Week 11 - Work Area

65.0
Lust as a Weapon Against Marriage

"*Dearly beloved, I beseech [you] as strangers and pilgrims, abstain from fleshly lusts, which war against the soul;*" - (1 Peter 2:11).

65.1 Short reasons
- 65.1.1 **Lust fosters envy**
- 65.1.2 **Lust fosters greed**
- 65.1.3 **Lust fosters dishonesty**

65.2 How lust works against marriage

65.2.1 **Prosperity** - Greed is the antithesis of decency. In the history of humanity, selfishness has not yielded anything beneficial to the world. We pretend we cannot live without conveniences, but the fact is that conveniences cost more in the end. The more we see the more we seem to want; this appears to be an axiom of humanity. Greed for money brings with it other greedy people. Women for sale gravitate to money. Men who excel at making money naturally attract these lose women. Solicitors and hustlers always seek those who have, because they need the possessions to use as tools. Marriage seeks the blessings of peace and righteousness. The material things people seek after are an artificial attempt to create the same peace we found in righteousness.

65.2.2 **People** - Lust for friends and popularity is not pleasing to God. The book of James warns that those loved by the world are not loved in heaven. When we learn to cherish the things, God wants the path to righteousness grows easier. Keeping up with the Jones's is too costly for most. Sadly, many do not realize exactly how much the Jones sacrifice to live the way they do. The fantasy marriage appeals to everyone. The reason it is appealing is that everyone wants to be happy. The sad tale is that if more people focused on making their home and marriage happy they would have the fantasy marriage--instead we prefer to dream.

65.2.3 **Pleasure** - The lust for pleasure is the greatest of all folly. Solomon warns us not to chase after wealth for it will grows wings[144]. The opposite is true of lust, it will not grow wings lust grows roots[145]. Lust is an entity of its own; it does not require any assistance to grow. Lust is not a plant lust is a weed. Lust's growth does not depend on a stimulus, it grows as long as there is food, and its rate of growth is not controllable. When Paul writes about sexual immorality in Romans 1, he tries to explain the manner in which lust grows. The one thing Paul makes clear is that in a short time, lust becomes the master and people learn to worship the creature (lust) over the Creator. The problem with lust is that it is a cannibal; it seeks only to please itself. Pleasure only exists for more pleasure, it does not improve life, or marriage pleasure it pleases itself. Think of the most romantic evenings we spent with our spouses. What made the romantic evening great is not the fleshly pleasure; it was sharing with our lover. Now think of the foods, porn, drugs, sports, weight lifting, gambling, or other extra-activity that brings us pleasure. How much do we spend on cigarettes and creature comforts only to want more and more and more? How many of us grow fat on lusts, lusts that produce no benefits? This is not because we were born to be fat; it is because lust lives only to serve itself. Lust will even destroy us if it feels the adventure is pleasurable, this is the application Eve displays.

65.2.4 **Pornography** - Many ask about pornography and its effect. Pornography has no effect. Hard to believe; why, alcohol has no effect on what is in our hearts, it simply lowers our inhibitions causing us to act out what is in our hearts. Alcoholic beverages do not create behavior. In the same manner, pornography does not create behavior, cause abuse, or adultery. What pornography does is give expression to the existing wretchedness in our hearts. Of course, people have seen things in pornography they would not have normally done, but a far greater number have seen things they never did. A good friend of mines correctly maintains that despite glorification porn stars are whores. By default, then those of us who frequent whores are whoremongers.

In answer to the question of porn Paul says the following, **"Casting down imaginations, and every high thing that exalteth itself against the knowledge of God, and bringing into captivity every thought to the obedience of Christ;** - 2 Corinthians 10:5. If we can uplift God watching porn, or if we would not be embarrassed if He showed up during the movie, then--have at it.

65.3 Design Flaw - Incest and Molestation
Then when lust hath conceived, it bringeth forth sin and when sin is allowed to grow, it gives birth to death - (James 1:15).

I resist using harsh adjectives when possible, but when I hear people say that people should just get over molestation and incest, it is in the past I can think of nothing else to describe such attitudes but the term **stupid**. According to a report commissioned by the U.S. Conference of Catholic Bishops from the John Jay College of Criminal Justice in 2004, *"10,667 people in the US had made allegations of child sexual abuse between 1950 and 2002 against 4,392 priests*[146].*"* This information amassed from only reported cases levied against Catholic priest and Nuns in the United States. The Catholic Church formalized under Constantine in 312 A.D., in the more than 1600 years since its formalization there is absolutely no way to estimate how many lives have been *touched* by the Catholic Church. How anyone can stand up and in good faith still purport to be a Catholic s beyond understanding.

As a victim of the *touch*, I devised another understanding of the effects of the *touch*, versus the folly of telling victims to simply walk it off. The following two definitions define quite adequately the effects of the *touch*,

65.3.1 *A form of chronic psychological stress that follows exposure to a traumatic event such as an earthquake, a violent crime (rape, child abuse, murder), torture, an accident, or warfare*[147].

65.3.2 *An anxiety disorder associated with serious traumatic events and characterized by such symptoms as survivor guilt, reliving the trauma in dreams, numbness, and lack of involvement with reality, or recurrent thoughts and images*[148].

These characterizations are manifestations of Post-Traumatic Stress Disorder (PTSD). The reason we cannot simply walk it off is because it is not on us, it is in us. When we alter the fabrication of an item such as a foundation, we weaken it irreparably. Like the Leaning Tower of Pisa, the flaw in the design is not reparable by normal methods, and it will if untreated destroy the item.

People react differently to PTSD, and there is no way to accurately determine when and where it will manifest, but it will manifest. What better to way to destroy lives that to destroy them at a foundational level? What better foundation to destroy that the backbone of righteous flesh--marriage?

This design flaw is not of God nor is it a fault of Adam; this is sabotage, next to Espionage the greatest weapon of warfare ever devised. By destroying the innocence of children, it makes the job of repair more difficult. Many cannot make the journey to 'normal' because they have never experienced 'normal' and their PTSD subtlety intertwined into their heart that they cannot tell what is the truth.

PTSD is demonic, but it is NOT a demon. PTSD cannot be cast out though, God can remove it. The cost to remove PTSD is expensive, not to God He already paid the cost, but the victim of PTSD suffers a gut-wrenching upheaval in their psyche when the virus leaves. The keen sensitive parent can offset this event, but a person destroyed by PTSD also loses their discernment as well, how sinister a tool Satan devised in molestation.

James 1:15, reminds of why Satan uses this method so effectively. Remember he worked in heave, he understands seed planting. By planting the seed of lust into the lives if the children, it will grow. LUST CANNOT GROW INTO SOMETHING GOOD, much as the apple cannot become a pear. The victim then has to deal with this seed before they can be healthy. There is a problem however, since sexual desire is normal, how does the pubescent child differentiate. Why are so many children turning to the LGBT community, because the seed is growing, the seed of darkness and death, a seed planted by molester that untreated will lead to death.

The 'seeding' of children is not about love, it is about increasing Satan's kingdom. This is not a multigenerational curse, this is multigenerational discipleship into death, be ye not deceived.

66.0
The Thoughts as a Weapon Against Marriage

"But when his heart was lifted up, and his mind hardened in pride, he was deposed from his kingly throne, and they took his glory from him -
(Daniel 5:20).

66.1 Short Reasons
- 66.1.1 **Thoughts determine actions**
- 66.1.2 **Thoughts determine self-image**
- 66.1.3 **Thoughts influence dreams**

66.2 How thoughts work against marriage

66.2.1 **Our thoughts constantly contain garbage** - God said men's imaginations are constantly evil. If the pond already overflows with sewage, how difficult is it to put more garbage into it. The other problem with raw sewage is it fosters the growth of new germs and bacteria, some more toxic than surrounding sewage. The heart already contains things that defile the man; therefore, the filthy heart in marriage defiles the marriage. There is no way for a defiled man to marry a woman and not defile her. Ephesians tells us to present our wives without spot or blemish; MEN-WE MUST THEREFORE CHANGE. The content of men's heart must change, if for no other reason that we cannot be pure and true to our wives as long as our hearts are wild and un-submitted. The reason God requires men to submit to our women is that once God cleans men's hearts; submission to another clean heart is necessary for righteousness. In addition, submission to another pure hearts allows pure things to flow between the two hearts not garbage.

66.2.2 **Thoughts constantly dilute the word of God** - The way that seems right unto men is not always man's attempt to be evil, but the result is the same; lost is lost. The flesh will never serve God in truth because it was fashioned in sin. Therefore, the only semblance of truth the flesh can operate in is flesh under subjection (righteousness). The problem with spiritual things is that they are difficult to prove. The other way in which thoughts work against marriage is that thoughts provoke men to manipulate spiritual matters and fleshly matters into whatever fables serve personal desires, perversions, or insecurities. Thoughts exacerbate many things; spiritual things are the easiest to lie about. Our thoughts convince us that it is ok to fornicate if we love the person. Our thoughts convince us that it is ok to cheat because our husband abuses us. Our thoughts convince us that it is ok to lie to our spouse about our friends they do not approve of. Our thoughts convince us that lying about these things does not harm a strong marriage. A marriage full of lies is not a strong marriage.

66.2.3 **Thoughts create doubt** - Doubt does not begin in the heart, it begins in the mind. Doubting our spouse does not begin in weird feelings, they begin in the culminations of those feelings; things we call *suspicion*. Strange behavior by our spouse, in and of itself is not reason to doubt. Thinking about the strange behavior long enough allows our minds to create scenarios to explain the behavior--in these thoughts begin our doubts. In marriage, our doubts begin in behavior we believe to be strange. Our spouse misses a phone call or gets a strange email from a female - to us, this means they must be cheating. When God does not answer, He must not love us, or He must have another favorite, He is also cheating. Poor communication leads to distrust, but there is a mark of maturity called good faith. If we did not trust our spouse at all, we never should have married them.

Creative forces in humans God gave to exalt Him, but we use it to wax great in His sight[149]. Sadly, the policies set forth by the Bramble in Judges Chapter 9 deceive even the most brilliant. Believing themselves to be wise humanity opted to serve the darkness not realizing what God warned about in the garden. Once we chose to eat from that tree, we became its fruit. As a result, we destroy ourselves at every venture. Like cigarettes and alcohol bear warning that go unheeded, God warned us about the danger of our evil thought--yet the darkness still finds new allies in the hearts of men.

67.0
The Heart as a Weapon Against Marriage

"But a certain man named Ananias, with Sapphira his wife, sold a possession, and kept back [part] of the price, his wife also being privy [to it], and brought a certain part, and laid [it] at the apostles' feet. But Peter said, 'Ananias, why hath Satan filled thine heart to lie to the Holy Ghost, and to keep back [part] of the price of the land? - (Acts 5:1-3)."

67.1 Short reasons
- 67.1.1 **The heart's content defiles the man**
- 67.1.2 **The heart is filled with evil**
- 67.1.3 **The heart is rebellious**

67.2 How the heart works against

67.2.1 **The heart brings evil to life** - No matter what we believe about our temperament, what is contained in our heart WILL SURFACE[150]? God does not punish the action He deals with the heart. It is a simple concept--our flesh does not conceive of things to do; it follows the heart. God changes the heart thereby slowly changing the flesh. When He changes the flesh, He changes actions and if He changes actions, He changes the world. Ergo: God so loved the world that He gave us a heart that changed flesh: that changed actions, which changed the world.

67.2.2 **Satan buries himself deep in the heart and waits** - Playing 'possum is a masterful game of waiting[151]. The reason the heart is such a bastion of hiding places, is because the heart continually refills with evil. The evil we feel joins the methods we contrive, and Satan adds the opportunity to manifest wickedness--this process produces sin. This flesh does not produce sin the heart does. We know about this process because the process begins in Ezekiel 28:15 (where there is no flesh). God found that evil existed within Lucifer. When the Bible says the flesh was born in iniquity, what it refers to is the process that resulted in the current state of sin. David writes about this in Psalms 51:1-5, **"Listen to my prayer, God. Do not hide Yourself from my supplication. Attend to me and answer me. I am restless in my complaint, and moan, Because of the voice of the enemy, Because of the oppression of the wicked. For they bring suffering on me. In anger, they hold a grudge against me. My heart is severely pained within me. The terrors of death have fallen on me. Fearfulness and trembling have come on me. Horror has overwhelmed me."** What David refers to is that the results of sin are manifest in the human lineage. We know the flesh itself cannot be sinful because God created it. Then it is to the humanity that lives in the flesh David writes. Evil and selfishness manifest in all humans as a result of the wretched input into our mold. Adam had good input from God but allowed Satan to use his heart and imagination to ruin the model. Now the model is no longer Adamic; Cain is the basis for our model.

67.2.3 **The heart magnifies evil thoughts** - Our thoughts and the content of our wicked hearts interact constantly. The heart has a desire, and the imagination enables the desire to come to life. The process is simple as pottery. The lump of clay is the heart. The wheel and the kiln enable the clay to shape and become whatever the clay is material enough to become. The wheel and kiln act as the imagination. All flaws found in pottery occur in one of two phases, either in the way we mold the clay or the firing process.

The heart [is] deceitful above all [things], and desperately wicked Jeremiah 17 reminds us, and in all the evil the heart is capable there is little room for God. The world is not against the church it fights to survive only Satan's kingdom wars against ours. A strip joint has no need to fear the church until parishioners ask the town to close it. In most cases, the world needs the churches money. Satan only wants to destroy what God loves; he does not care about material gain.

68.0
The Tongue as a Weapon Against Marriage

"Then said his wife unto him, 'Dost thou still retain thine integrity? Curse God and die'" - (Job 2:9).

68.1 **Short reasons**
    68.1.1 The tongue is unruly
    68.1.2 The tongue moves the whole body
    68.1.3 The tongue damages the body the spirit

68.2 **How the tongue works against weapon**
    68.2.1 **The tongue produces angry words** - Understanding that the pure tongue is a result of the pure heart is another kingdom mystery[152]. James chapter 3 tells us that anyone that can control their tongue is perfect. The tongue makes shapes and controls airflow through the mouth, which in turn produces speech. It is impossible to speak without a tongue. The tongue does not actually produce angry words. Like the imagination, the tongue allows the heart to come alive. Angry words come from neither the imagination nor the flesh they come from the angry heart[153]. The person we offend knows what we say, and how we feel. Therefore, the injury to our spouse is not the words but the feelings behind the words.

    68.2.2 **The tongue lies** - The tongue again gets the bad reputation for what the heart does. Many people use lies and profanity during sex play, this usage causes no injury. Again, we see that it is the intent of the heart to deceive or injure our spouse that produces the problem. Even in the case of adultery, lying about it only makes it worse. Any fool can commit adultery, most women realize that; but lying about it blocks forgiveness and coping. One of the main reasons lying blocks healing is because built into the lie is the potential for reoccurrence.

    68.2.3 **The tongue spreads gossip** - Lust, strife, and envy come from the same treacherous heart as lies and offensive language. One of the easiest ways to engender friction is gossip. In marriage, there should be no secrets; there is no room in marriage for gossip. Believers should not allow their imagination to shape the clay pots we see every day. The same mentality that gossips creates distrust and jealousy in marriage.

Jude 1:10 makes a harsh statement against soiling the kindness and virtue of marriage, "**But these speak evil of those things which they know not: but what they know naturally, as brute beasts, in those things they corrupt themselves**." Jude reminds us that those who speak against virtue do so because they lack virtue. Like all without virtue, they seek to despoil decency and modesty. Those that speak against marriage speak against the one institution God gave to quell lust and teach righteousness simultaneously. Therefore, those who speak against Godly marriages have no desire for decency and cannot be friends of virtue.

69.0
Un-Forgiveness as a Weapon Against Marriage

"FOR IF YE FORGIVE MEN THEIR TRESPASSES, OUR HEAVENLY FATHER WILL ALSO FORGIVE YOU: BUT IF YE FORGIVE NOT MEN THEIR TRESPASSES, NEITHER WILL OUR FATHER FORGIVE OUR TRESPASSES," – (Matthew 6:14-15).

69.1 Short reasons
1. Un-forgiveness blocks blessing
2. Un-forgiveness is bad for health
3. Un-forgiveness hinders trust

69.2 How un-forgiveness works against marriage

69.2.1 Un-forgiveness causes us to think evil of people - To forgive person, is to release them from the obligation to repay. In other words, if we take out a bank loan and do not have to pay it back, the bank forgives the debt. The forgiveness of the debt means we do not have to repay that which we owe. The fastest way to cynicism is un-forgiveness. When we do not forgive a person or a spouse for an action, word, or activity, the tension mounts. The cumulative effect of un-forgiveness is that every infraction exponentially increases. For tiny problems, the situation becomes tenuous because we refuse to forgive other issues. When I council married couples regarding adultery, I give them the following advice concerning forgiveness. God requires forgiving, the forgetting He does not deal with, that is our job. When asked how we achieve this I explain that it eventually feels like all memories. Wrong only remains wrong as long as we categorize it thusly like God, if we cast the events into the abyss most of the effect goes with it.

69.2.2 Un-forgiveness creates hypersensitivity - When we harbor ill feelings against our spouse both parties become hypersensitive. Hypersensitivity results from guilt, and insecure arising from the current situation at home. Hypersensitivity leads to friction and elevated conflict because there is never a diminishment of issues or the problems.

69.2.3 **Un-forgiveness prevents love flourishing -** Like plants, love flourishes best in a warm and friendly environment. Some contend that adversity matures love, but this does not apply to internal strife. Women who stay in abusive relationships are not in love nor are they in a loving relationship. God instructs us that the key to love is self-love. God does not mean conceit, He means valuing self as someone worthy of consideration, respect, and loyalty. This cannot exist between abusive people, and it cannot grow between those that do not forgive. When not forgiven, we tend to lie and to avoid the issues, so we do not have to deal with the rejection of an unforgiving spouse. When a person realizes their mistakes go unforgiven, they often turn callous, because like the one that will not forgive, they too soon stop caring.

People do not consider forgiveness from God's perspective. Forgiveness is not about deed it is about the relationship. What Peter asked was shall we forgive deed completely? Jesus answered by saying no; forgive the person completely[154]. There is a difference and the difference is that one allows us to go on without bitterness and the latter allows us to stay in a loving relationship. The purpose of this lesson was God's foreshadowing the way He does things. In order to maintain a loving relationship with people as sin filled as we, God forgives the person completely. And just in case we refused to heed the lesson or become indifferent and cold Jesus brings it home as He always does with the bitter truth of His sovereignty In Matthew 6: 18, and in Matthew 5:46[155].

In the case of infidelity, we are free to leave but we still have to forgive the unfaithful spouse. Do not plan on showing up at judgment with unforgiving practices in our hearts, like Joseph and Mary we may find no room for us in the Inn.

70.0
Anger as a Weapon Against Marriage

"**An angry man stirreth up strife, and a furious man aboundeth in transgression**," - (Proverbs 29:22).

70.1 **Short reasons**
    70.1.1 **Anger causes separation**
    70.1.2 **Anger makes marriage uncomfortable**
    70.1.3 **Anger leads to violence**

70.2 **How anger works against marriage**

    70.2.1 **Anger breaks up relationships** - Most angry interactions result in one or both parties moving away from each other physically, mentally, and spiritually. Another hindrance caused by anger is that it is often unpredictable and usually unwarranted. Anger ties itself up in other unrelated issues, which then roll into the current issue, which finally 'break the camel's back.' The Bible says it is ok to get angry, but WE MUST NOT SIN. Proverbs also warns that an angry person dwells in transgression. This accounts for grudge sex, grudge affairs, burning of clothes and houses and depletion of financial accounts. When we destroy the inner framework of a relation howbeit that we think we do not weaken, or destroy the relationship?

    70.2.2 **Anger causes us to make horrible decisions** - How many stupid decisions come about during angry periods? Divorces, break ups, even murders occur during periods of anger. Often, the cause of the anger is not the event that preceded the anger. In normal people, anger is a process by which we try to handle problems. Without forgiving the issue eventually, the garbage can explode because it is full. The secret to anger management is DO NOT STORE COMBUSTIBLES. Deal with issues when they occur, hash it out even if we have to get loud; and then resolve the issue. Married people know that make up sex is always fun and an excuse to fit sex into people's busy schedules, so do not go to bed mad at each other. Find another room in the house to fight other than the bedroom.

    70.2.3 **Anger makes healing and feeling difficult** - Humans cannot breathe under water because we do not have gills. Just as God did not design us to breath underwater, He did not design us to heal and feel while angry. Growth is a harsh process, yet it is a process without violence. Moses took 120 years trying to change, but never controlled his anger.

When we lift weights or stretch, the soreness we feel is because we tear muscles. The healing of the muscles requires it to produce more muscle to fill in the tears; thus, we swell. The human heart grows through endurance we call this aerobic conditioning. The heart also grows as we use it, but the heart is not designed to tear. Walking and running long distances builds the heart, without breaking it. The problem is that all this growth, tearing, and stretching causes fatigue, pain, regret, and confusion -- from this mass of unresolved emotions grows anger.

70.3 How to deal with anger

70.2.4.1 We must change our priorities
70.2.4.2 We must change our hangouts
70.2.4.3 We must change our movies & music
70.2.4.4 We must change our words
70.2.4.5 We must change our friends
70.2.4.6 We must change our thoughts
70.2.4.7 We must learn to forgive and practice forgiveness
70.2.4.8 We must work on becoming slow to anger

Anger has its place; exclusively this place is outside the marriage. There are few if any good reasons to include anger in a marriage. If there are issues, which warrant anger, there are problems in our marriage. Any issue that arises in marriage that produces anger is not good and should be resolved immediately so it does not fester into resentment.

71.0
Jealousy as a Weapon Against Marriage

"**Wrath [is] cruel, and anger [is] outrageous; but who [is] able to stand before envy?**" - (Proverbs 27:4).

71.1 Short reasons
    71.1.1 **Jealousy prevents trust**
    71.1.2 **Jealousy increases paranoia**
    71.1.3 **Jealousy creates underhanded behavior**

71.2 How jealousy works against marriage

    71.2.1 **Jealousy breaks up relationships** - Most jealousy stems from insecurity. If we have just cause to suspect our spouse is straying that is not jealousy. Many guilty spouses label suspicion jealousy because it casts doubt in the person's mind. If I give my wife rise to question my behavior, I welcome the inquiry. This inquiry not only abates the issue it helps me avoid careless words or behavior, which though harmless may make her uncomfortable.

    71.2.2 **Jealousy causes us to see things not actually there** - Once my wife asked me about a credit, card receipt she received showing payments for two hotel rooms in Vegas. When she called and asked, I denied the payments. She reminded me she was holding the receipt. I denied it, at which point she was irritated, and pointed out that there were two rooms. I responded, "Well if I was cheating there would have only been one room." The truth was that a coworker went to a training seminar and they needed a credit card to reserve the rooms, they did not have one, so they used mine. I reminded her that I got her permission to allow the transaction before it occurred and she remembered--conflict resolved.

        I never got angry for her inquiry. I encourage open lines of communication. Instead of having to go through my emails and phone numbers, she simply asked me. Because I encourage her to ask what she wants, we have no problems in this arena. If an old girlfriend emails me, or I see them in the world, I tell her. This is not a short leash, it is covenant relationship, why allow room for Satan to move?

        If my wife were the jealous type, there would be many problems in our house I deal with lots of women at work. I always come home with business cards, email address, and phone numbers, but they are always catalogued correctly and never secreted--she does not have a problem with it. Before we got married, we established interpersonal parameters in our marriage. One such parameter is that I do not council females without her. If a young woman will not consent to her presence, then I do not council them.

    71.2.3 **Jealousy increases covetousness** - A jealous spouse is a covetous spouse. The jealous spouse learns to see happiness in other peoples, relationships, or lifestyles. This is how the imagination encourages us to cheat. When we look at our fat, bald, disabled, pregnant, unemployed spouse, and see what other people have or have access to covetousness creeps inside. Once covetousness creeps in, the odds increase greatly that we will fall. We already have the flesh wanting, now there is covetousness: imagination marries the two. Our imaginations point out that the extra marital activity is justifiable, we tie our happiness up in it. Sometimes it is true we would be happier fooling around; however, happiness for stability or righteousness is often the sacrifice we make to build lives together. We determine that the life we intend to build is a greater reward then the jaunt into folly. This determination is the beginning of maturation.

A good friend pointed out that *love is not a feeling it is a decision. Once we decide that we are going to love a thing, we decide how to make the love grow, balance it off, and enable it to survive.* He gave me the push I needed to jump off into marriage. Even with all the preparations I made for marriage, I had no idea what was in store. Early in marriage, I realized that I had ill prepared myself for all the changes that come along with a spouse. I never had a problem coming home; I actually practiced marital discipline before marriage to make the transitions easier. What no one told me what going to happen was that my flesh had to change as well? I do not mean the obvious things like causal dating, lying all the time, wasting money etc. I learned early in marriage what Adam soon learned about Eve, but in reverse. Once my wife became my wife, all of the peculiar things I wanted to share with her, all the deep dark places I wanted to go as a lustful single man with sordid fantasies, all changed. For a long time, I thought we were sexually incompatible, in actuality, I saw my wife in a position that required respect. I saw her clean and decent, and I did not want to be the cause of tarnish. I did not realize it at the time, but marriage elevates the way in which we look at our spouses.

Concomitant with this newfound bliss comes a puerile type of jealousy. I could not despoil my bride and I was insecure because I did not know how to please her while being 'clean.' Soon I became jealousy of any male interaction she had, but the problem was in me, not her. My wife has never given me cause to distrust her; I distrusted her because I did not understand marriage. I did not know it, but I was jealous of the dream I had for myself, I was jealous that she could be so happy without me, because the new me was not who I was. I almost destroyed my marriage because I did not know how to be clean and I did not want her to get dirty.

72.0
Week 11 - Work Area

72.1 Does God prefer intimacy or sex?

_____
_____
_____
_____
_____
_____
_____
_____

72.2 Why must both spouses send to each other?

_____
_____
_____
_____
_____
_____
_____
_____

72.3 Who has a greater task of subduing their flesh the husband or wife?

_____
_____
_____
_____
_____
_____
_____
_____

72.4 Why is the married couple important to evangelism?

72.5 Are children of non-believers saved?

72.6 Do children of believers face spiritual attacks?

72.7 How do we protect our children from demonic influence?

72.8 Which is worse divorce or adultery?

72.9 Why is marital sex often unsatisfactory?

72.10 Why is adultery common among Christians?

Week 12
Combat Tactics and Marriage

"Two [are] better than one; because they have a good reward for their labor. For if they fall, the one will lift up his fellow: but woe to him [that is] alone when he falleth; for [he hath] not another to help him up. Again, if two lie together, then they have heat: but how can one be warm [alone]" – (Ecclesiastes 4:9-120.

        73.0 - Tactical marriage
        74.0 - Evangelism, marriage, & demoniacs
        75.0 - Marriage: A life unto death
        76.0 - Tai Sabaki - Oneness of movement
        77.0 - Eden work Area
        78.0 - Glossary of Marriage Mysteries
        80.0 - Discipleship basics
        81.0 – Facilitator's guide

73.0
Tactical Marriage

Just like spiritual warrior, married warriors need training and tactics to survive. Training to survive makes us creative, resourceful, and resilient. The added benefit in marriage is a stronger understanding of each other's abilities. Married couples must also employ the five basic combat tactics.
- Defense
- Attack
- Counter attack
- Tactical withdrawal
- Surrender

Unlike the single warrior who has less to lose and less to care for, married warriors have the added burden of emotions. In war, attachment is a hindrance. This is what Paul labored to convey when he advised not to marry. It is incumbent upon us therefore to ascertain why God sent saints into battle with a handicap. As with all questions dealing with the Christ, we look to the Christ for the answer. Not until resurrection was Christ truly, free from the flesh. Jesus was born to die. God created warriors to serve. The emotional attachment to our spouse acts to remind us that we live in the flesh and will not find freedom until it finds its end.

73.1 Tactic one: Defense

The first basic combat tactic manifests itself as defense. Married couples must rely on this tactic above all others. Satan attacks spiritual warriors sparingly; whereas the married warrior is constantly at enmity with Satan's kingdom. As a result, there will be fewer opportunities for the couple to strike out in Satan's kingdom.

By way of permission, let me give another marital kingdom secret. UNDER NO CIRCUMSTANCES ARE MARRIED PEOPLE TO REMOVE THEIR ARMOR OUTSIDE OF ESTABLISHED ZONES OF SAFETY. These zones include the prayer closet, the undefiled bed, and the home of another safe Christian couple. The church is <u>not</u> a zone of safety. The church God designed to accept sinners, demon possessed, and the lost--their can be no safety for tired warriors among these.

_____
_____
_____
_____
_____
_____
_____
_____
_____
_____

73.2 Tactic two: Counter-attack

The second basic combat tactic manifests itself as the counter-attack. Unlike the single warrior, couples should not be aggressors. The level of training and discipline required to attack as a team necessitates a more defensive posture. The married counter attack must be a series of strategic moves, never a frontal attack. When churches have couples losing battles to their flesh, they need to rein them in and find out what mistakes they are making in the spirit. Most of life's problems manifest due to a lack of spiritual discipline. Study the failing couples training tactics to discover their weaknesses. Along this line of thinking we must understand, no matter how gifted a person seems the divorcee or the single warrior should never be in charge of training married forces. According to God, the divorcee deals treacherously with their spouse, how then can they instruct in unity and *Tai Sabaki*?

_____
_____
_____
_____
_____
_____
_____
_____

73.3 Tactic three: Attack

The most common defense is attack. Under normal circumstances, attacks work well against sloppy troops. Satan however, is never sloppy. When a couple does attack, they should use *bounding over watch*. In bounding over watch, the couples leap frogs its way to safety. The spouse closest to the attacker counter attacks (*prayer* and *fasting*), while the other spouse tactically moves to an area of spiritual cover. What this means spiritually is that despite the problems the other person encounters the other spouse (under the least amount of stress) does the bulk of the praying and fasting for the couple. In this manner, we cover each other and fill in the gap when one of the pairs is deficient. The purpose of this type of attack keeps the enemy off balance because they cannot tell which of the two attackers is the most dangerous. In this manner, the couple constantly plays off each other attacking the enemy sporadically until they can destroy him.

_____
_____
_____
_____
_____
_____

73.4 Types of attacks

73.4.1 Frontal - This is a direct frontal assault, which relies on superior numbers and force. Married couples, during frontal attacks there is no room for error. Those attacking frontally always incur the greatest loses.

73.4.2 Stealth - A stealth attack utilizes time to make it successful. The stealthy attack is the best utilization of married couples. They must wait on the flanks until deployed and then when they strike they must be ruthless and relentless.

73.4.3 Flanking - Married couples use a *feint* not a flanking maneuver, they are too valuable to guard flanks. The feint is a trick, a ploy. In other words, the married couple uses tactical fellowship to maneuver themselves into positions to strike into Satan's kingdom.

73.4.4 Sneak - The feint is not a sneak attack, although it encompasses high levels of deceptive deployment.

73.4.5 Ambush - Married couples have no reason to use this maneuver. The ambush is tricky and often costly. The ambush requires separate entities acting in concert, not a bifurcated unit. The defense for the near ambush underscores the severity of this attack. The only defense against the near ambush is counter attack. The only way to escape this type of attack is the break out of the area through a weak link in the trap. Married couples should use *bounding over watch* to escape the ambush. There is seldom time to retreat to safety, cover is all time affords in the ambush. Once covered, the spouse should lay down a barrage of fire (prayer) to create a window to escape. If the counter attacking spouse fails or falls, the covered spouse needs to withdraw to safety. Two corpses serve no purpose in kingdom wars. We serve our fallen spouse better by making it to safety. Like the spouse who sacrifices self, so their spouse can present themselves spotless: we must learn to honor our spouse's battle especially if it leads to death. The best way to honor their death is a righteous life pleasing to God.

73.4.6 **Enemy in the wire** - In marriage this is a traitor, or a spy. Sounding the alarm '*enemy in the wire*' means that the position has been overrun. There are few palatable methods to deal with this posture.
    73.4.6.1 Withdraw from the battle and try save the marriage
    73.4.6.2 Withdraw from the marriage and risk losing the battle as well
    73.4.6.3 Counter attack
    73.4.6.4 Surrender I cannot say which tactic to employ, let God be our guide.

74.5 <u>Tactic four: Withdrawal</u>

Withdrawal requires both partners to ascent. Never withdraw and leave our partner in the fray unless it is an ambush. When we withdraw from the battle, strike the enemy repeatedly, and then pull back to a safe distance. If the enemy pursues then we must engage them the entire route of withdrawal.

If one partner is too injured to withdraw under their own power, then the uninjured partner must create enough distance between the injured partner and the enemy to affect the withdrawal. During proper deployment of evangelists, the infantry provides cover for the withdrawing couple.

74.5 <u>Tactic five - Surrender</u>

Couples cannot surrender they have too much to lose, if the battle is lost, mercy abounds but there is no surrender. If either spouse surrenders they make captive the unconquered spouse. Remember, in marriage two people make one unit. If we surrender the unit, we also surrender for our spouse. If Satan cannot conquer our spouse let us not be Delilah's' and trade them for our own selfish reason.

The phrase *ride or die* is popular in a certain segment of American society. Nowhere is this type of dedication more important than spiritual warfare and marriage. Why do we really think we make vows? They are to inform and agree by covenant that both spouses are in the fight until death; we both ride either the Golden chariots or die trying.

74.0
Evangelism, Marriage, & Demoniacs

"After these things the Lord appointed other seventy also and sent them two and two before his face into every city and place, whither he himself would come," - (Luke 10:1).

As a quick reminder, the term *Demoniacs*[156] describes demonic activity in the earth realm. Before we proceed, let us clear something up. As discussed in <u>The Lights in Patmos</u>, demons are fallen angels; therefore, they too are included in the concept of spiritual activity. It therefore falls to believers to discern which spirits operate in and near their lives. In 2 Corinthians Paul reminds us; though there are different gifts they all come from the same Spirit. Paul reminds us of this because there are spiritual gifts or attributes that do not come from the Holy Spirit.

- Divination (Acts 16:16)
- Casting out demons (Matthew 7:22)
- Healing the sick (Matthew 7:22)
- Witchcraft (1 Samuel 15:23)
- Prophecy (2 Corinthians 11:13)

74.1 Demonic tactics and marriage

Demons are far more resourceful than they are strong. Demons rarely use strength to accomplish their goals demons use cunning. We see in the book of Genesis two examples if the most common demonic attack against marriage: divide and conquer. Genesis 3 and 6:4 show us how demons attack marriage from without and within.

74.2 **Satan's spiritual attack** (Genesis 3:1-7) - Herein we see that Satan understands *human nature* far better than humans. Having been privy to the design, Satan understands that Life started in the flesh when God gave men souls. Therefore, there is s inequity between the flesh and the soul, God placed the soul in charge. As we look at Satan's brilliant attack against marriage, we see that the first thing he did in verse 1 was to drive a wedge between Adam and Eve. This is why we must maintain spiritual equality in marriage, the wife and the husband must have the same level of understanding and obedience or at least commitment if they are to stand against the Satan. Had Eve unified with her husband, the response from her should have been to usher Satan away, not try to argue scripture. On the other hand, had Adam known Eve's spirit better he would have also known that she would respond in that manner.

74.3 **Satanic Chess** - What we clearly do not see is the evil mastery in Satan's attack. As in the game of chess, Eve was a pawn of Satan's plan. The attack; all of his attacks Satan directs towards the King. The garden is no different; Satan attacked the King, so he could steal the throne. Eve was flesh of flesh bone of bones, in other words Adam's heart. Look, see what James 1:14-15 describes. Did not the lust of Eve' eyes bring forth death?[157] Satan knew then what took the church years to understand the way to a man's kingdom is not through his stomach it is through his flesh. By attacking Eve (Adam's flesh) Satan achieved what he never could have achieved directly. He accessed Adam's soul.

74.4 **Satan's attack on the flesh** (Genesis 6:4) - As Eve's lust grew, it brought forth sin. We see in verse 6 that Eve's disobedience grew to the point that war lust overrode obedience to God. In her fleshly desire to bring her lust to full growth, she shared it with the only person on the planet with enough power to control her--*Satanic checkmate*. Satan never sought to share knowledge with the couple he sought to destroy the couple. Satan understood the power of lust, and he knew Eve could not and would not try to control the power of the evil growing within her. Eve saw in Satan potential that she could not enjoy without Satan, the power of the flesh coupled with the power of a god. In this thought, this scenario, this schema the Hellenistic view of the gods found a home. What Eve wanted was what Zeus and Hera possess in fables the power to be a god yet enjoy all of the lusts of human flesh.

Because of Eve's desire to *share* with her husband, she brought Adam's flesh under her control. In a fleshly desire to exalt themselves Adam and Eve destroyed themselves[158]. In attacking Eve, entering marriage through the fleshliest vessel Satan overtook Adam's entire kingdom. This is why the attack against marriage continues, because we are again stewards of God's property and Satan wants control again.

74.5 **Deploying married evangelists**

74.5.1 **War and marriage** - In war, there are resources that are more valuable to the struggle. When we deploy forces, we must do so based on mission not friendship. Proper deployment of forces should resemble a traditional Napoleonic attack. The lines should consist of infantry, artillery, and cavalry.
- The laity is the infantry
- Elders and the seniors in the church comprise the artillery
- The married saints comprise the cavalry

In warfare of this type, soldiers fear the cavalry most, because they were the most ferocious. The addition of the horse made the regular soldier more lethal and more difficult to attack, not to mention the fact that the horse was also a weapon. The reason soldiers fear cavalry was that cavalry enabled soldiers to attack by trampling the enemy. Soldiers not trampled find themselves at a disadvantage trying to use weapons against men sitting 2-3 feet high than they stand. In addition, the cavalry has the ability to maneuver quickly and divide armies in half rendering their reinforcements useless.

74.5.1.1 **"And He said unto them, 'THIS KIND CAN COME FORTH BY NOTHING, BUT BY PRAYER AND FASTING'**[159]**."** Jesus lays how we must attack Satan's kingdom. Certain types of spiritual weapons work against certain demons so deployment is crucial. We can pretend that one person can do it all, but

74.5.1.2   men like Paul, Silas, Apollos, Billy Graham, etc. do what they do because they have to as we hide in the background. The journey was not meant to be solo, but the rest of Christendom (as was the case against Goliath) simply stands by too scared to step all the way up to the mark.

75.4.1.2 The pastor is <u>not</u> the source of power in the church; God is the source of power in the church. In whom did God place trust, and power, the married elders and deacons? The power in the church lies with and in those most able to control their flesh.

75.5   **Encroachment and marriage** - Let the infantry go out into the darkness, but the true attack comes from the spiritual warriors that have the fewest chinks in their armor.

75.6   **Siege and marriage** - "**And they, continuing daily with one accord in the temple, and breaking bread from house to house, did eat their meat with gladness and singleness of heart**," - (Acts 2:46). What makes a marriage successful is singleness of heart. What made the disciples powerful was the singleness of His heart. What made Jesus powerful was singleness of heart[160]. Power does not lie in people, it comes from God and He told us where unity abounds He and His power abound there also.

75.7   **Strongholds and marriage** - "**And at midnight Paul and Silas prayed, and sang praises unto God: and the prisoners heard them**," – (Acts 16:25). If we need to break strongholds, for kingdom building or in our home, we find that the people we need and the unity we need already exist. Another benefit of the marriage bed is that we can fast and pray with singleness of heart and flesh.

75.8   **Overtaking territory and marriage** - Luke 10:1 reminds us that when God launches an army He does so in even numbers, so there can be unity. To conquer demons in Genesis God called forth everything with the breath of life to go forth in pairs. To wage spiritual warfare in the New Testament God sent forth 70 men in pairs. The bible makes a point of describing them in pairs, instead of as 140 men. This is to illustrate the importance of unity, in both flesh and spirit. Defending and overtaking (going out into) demonic territory is one set of battles with one set of demons. However, to annex territory requires a different level of commitment and power.

75.9   **Annexing territory and marriage** - "**And Noah went in, and his sons, and his wife, and his sons' wives with him, into the ark, because of the waters of the flood. And they went in unto Noah into the ark, two and two of all flesh, wherein [is] the breath of life**," - (Genesis 7:7, 7:15). Demons never relinquish territory we must always conquer. The problem we see in the bible is that demonic territory always contains demonic people and people under the influence of demons. To that end, God ordained that in areas of demonic strongholds we destroy every living thing. However, He tempered His judgment at the cross. Now evangelists are to cast the demons out of the area and bind as many as possible.

Because we do not work together as believers, we simply shift areas of demonic activity to other parts of the country or world. In the strategy of Mission Fields, the missionaries, and Catholics of old had the correct idea, but they used Old Testament tactics. The old legalistic method of *judge, condemn, retrain* though efficient was neither Godly nor merciful. The old system of missions (outposts) worked because humans are fleshly and initially those not killed flocked to the churches in fear of the new God. Eventually demons realized that as it was in the Old Testament the people were going to church but there was little change. As the demons watched the slowly realized that what was once *The Way* of God turned into religion. In the folds of religion, demons found an even more powerful tool against men. Instead of the old ways, we need to understand what God said then applies now. The old ways were never Gods way, He did not tell us to go around erecting temples.

In Christ, in the marriage of the Lamb, we see the purpose of missions and evangelism--the purpose of missions and evangelism is to change the hearts of the people. We cannot change kingdoms unless we change men. We cannot change men unless we change their hearts. To this end, in ancient teaching, we find that this is what God told us to do in the first place; change men's hearts not make laws to govern their ways[161]. This is the mandate in the *Great Commission*; this is why we must spread the gospel of change. Without the law of God, man has no chance of righteousness. Without righteousness law is just a way to punish bad behavior, it cannot stop or control bad behavior.

Why is marriage important to spiritual warfare? Marriage shows that hearts can change. In changing hearts, marriage shows that our ways can also change. The renewing of the mind and heart leads to righteousness. Righteousness leads to a pure heart. Who but God allows the circle of purity to begin in darkness, go through the deeds of the flesh, and terminate in a pure heart? **Christians will never achieve righteousness as a people without marriage because flesh will never submit.**

_____
_____
_____
_____
_____

74.5 Spiritual casualties and marriage

I saw the cutest thing in church one day. A young woman who had attended the church for a while went up to receive prayer. She was an attractive woman but her former life consisted of a lot of nighttime employment. For church clothes, she consistently wore Star Trek length dresses and high heels. On this day, she stood before the only single man on the podium to receive prayer. After he prayed, the woman was moved and hugged him in appreciation. The funny thing is that as she hugged him she ran her hands up and down his back and then onto his buttocks and thighs. When she turned around she walked away reveling I the forgiveness of the Cross-oblivious to what she did. To her, that type of 'fellowship' was normal. The guy; on the other hand, stood flabbergasted: but did nothing.

In my book From a Fortress in Patmos, we explained the concept of a spiritual casualty. When spiritual casualties occur, a person's souls gives in to the vileness in their heart. Like the groping woman in the story, vileness becomes second nature. This is why the woman did the thing unintentionally; she existed in a place where that was normal. As human history shows, more people seek vileness than lives at the foot of the cross.

When we see saints fall or walk away from the faith they quickly sink in to the lower life; the neither reaches, the shadow controlled by Satan. From the darkness, it is easier to reach the contents of the average human heart than from the cross. Therefore, fallen saints, new converts, and the lost all have one thing in common; the darkness in their hearts controls their lives. As such, people who council them are prone to the effect of their dark hearts. A despondent woman or lonely man is far more inclined to they bring us into their world than vice versa. This phenomenon is the impetus for the professional relationship in counseling, it diminishes counselors from abusing, or falling prey to those they council.

As we wade through shadow territory, it is not death married couples must fear, but a resurging in their flesh. In the *shadow land*, a man is just a mound of flesh married, saved, or clergy. Therefore, *shadow women* use their ploys against clergy as they would any other man. Par example, I took my pastor on a raid into a massage parlor. As he spread the gospel, the prostitutes spread their legs. It is not that God has no power in the shadows, what we fail to accept is that many of those in the darkness choose to be there. The prostitutes therefore, were prostituting because the opted to live that life. In the prostitute's world men equal money. In this lesson, we see why it is pivotal to deal with those in need of first aid as couples. Those women would never have behaved in that way in the presence of a woman because the female saint would have called them on this behavior. As a couple, saints are better suited to resist temptation than unmarried saints. Call me paranoid, but if the DEA, CIA, FBI, and prison guards lose people every day to the shadows, what makes the church believe that their weak, barely armored flesh stands a better chance?

_____
_____
_____
_____

74.6 Spiritual first aid and marriage

"**BUT A CERTAIN SAMARITAN, AS HE JOURNEYED, CAME WHERE HE WAS: AND WHEN HE SAW HIM, HE HAD COMPASSION [ON HIM], AND WENT TO [HIM], AND BOUND UP HIS WOUNDS,]**" - (Luke 10-33-35). As couples traverse the shadow lands, we invariably encounter souls in need of first aid. As we know from scripture, certain types of demons respond to prayer, others to fasting, and others to prayer and fasting. This also means that demons chose their targets in like manner. It makes sense, that select territories incur certain attacks. As we encounter demonic activity in people, the first thing we encounter is their flesh.

A beautiful woman under demonic influence is still beautiful and she has little to no restraint. What chance does a man have against this type of battle, especially if the church sent him? When God sends His people on missions, He has already churned the water to receive Him. When the church sends people out they do not have this power, and they cannot prepare the area to receive them.

As we attack Satan's kingdom, in areas not prepared to receive God, we encounter acceptance, only God finds resistance. Thusly, the deacon that encounters the beautiful woman finds a place of acceptance, and decadence. The church does not have and has never possessed the power to defend against the flesh. When my wife and I meet said beautiful woman, I find her beautiful like any other man, but her power over me my wife quenches. In this case, my wife leads the rescue (so she will not have to rescue me) and renders this temptation less powerful against my flesh. While my wife contends with the issues of the lost woman's beauty and my flesh, I contend with the demonic activity and influence--Christian checkmates.

74.7 Children and Evangelism

By way of permission, I say that I do not take my children on mission trips or outreach. I teach them the principles, but I do not involve them directly in the fray--not yet. At 12 years old, I unwittingly entered the war as a combatant. My mother and her women's group routinely fed the less fortunate. One such mission was at the Children's Emergency Hostel. Many of the children had mental problems ranging from mild to severe. On this day, we brought Coconut cookies to the kids, at the time I saw them as kids. Until that day, all the church and prayer meetings were routine. That day, the day that changed my spiritual life and view of God and warfare I met an old adversary: His name was Legion. As the children approached and mauled me to get the food, their appearance changed. I saw what I first saw as children in the spirit. This was the day I first discerned satanic spirits and began to diligently seek God. The demons I saw, the snarls, mangled bodies; the horrific feeling of death and dread I encountered frightened me. I threw the tray and never went back. I was unprepared for that level of warfare. Even though I did not realize I was in the fight, I learned that day that salvation and compliance to ANY of God's laws in Matthew 5 cast us into the fray. By doing unto the least of men, Satan saw the potential for change in the hearts of the children and the employees as well as my own. The war between Satan and me wages on to this day.

According to history, around 1212 A.D., due to the failures of the first four crusades 15-30 thousand children (mostly under the age of 12) decide to wage war against Islam. Before the ever made, it to Jerusalem they were captured and sold into slavery. If we do take children into warfare, seek God's guidance first lest we lead a crusade like the Children's Crusade ending up in our kids loosing spiritual footing.

75.0
Marriage: A Life Unto Death

"Husbands, love our wives, even as Christ also loved the church, and gave Himself up for it; that He might sanctify it, having cleansed it by the washing of water with the word, that He might present the church to Himself gloriously, not having spot or wrinkle or any such thing; but that it should be holy and without blemish," - (Ephesians 5:25-27).

Nowhere is the scripture *No greater love hath a man that he lay down his life for a friend* more important than in marriage. The changes, sacrifices, and comprise required to make marriage successful cause great strain. The order is simple, but the method quite complex; we are to love our wives as Christ loved the church.

Ephesians tells us that we CANNOT love our wives properly unless we first love ourselves. Narcissism is not precisely what the Bible refers to but more of a parental love where we want the best for ourselves. A man that does not want the best for himself indicates a lot about his choices. If we do not care what we have that will also reflect in our choice of wife. As we choose wives, accept the gifts God has for us. God designed the relationship for her to be a suitable help-meet and change us into what He wants. This construct requires discipline. As it was with Joseph and Mary, only Joseph's discipline allowed him to handle Mary's illegitimate child in the manner he did. A lesser man would have made a big deal of Mary's illegitimate kid and embarrassed Mary.

Joseph showed maturity and patience. While still honoring God (though unsure and displeased with the scenario), a miracle happened for his life, in his marriage, and for the world. This is an example of a marriage mystery, God works wonders through our marriages and in our marriages. God needed a man that could love enough to overlook pride and let the Light of the world shine. In allowing the Light to shine, Joseph ensured that he and his family were never again in the dark.

In loving self, and wanting to live pure before the Lord, we learn to want this for our family. We learn as we suffer consequences that the pure life is the simple, less expensive life. Rather than pay child support we learn to want our sons to put their kids in college, so we teach them responsibility. Rather than abortions, we teach our daughters to wait for marriage then she will not have to hide the child. Rather than anger, management classes we teach our children coping skills and forgiveness. This is what makes marriage difficult, the many years admitting faults and mentoring our families not to make the same mistakes, this we do for love.

One of the more difficult duties in marriage is sharing the gospel. It is easy to take our family to church, but our duty exceeds taxi service, we are required to MAKE them follow the rules. Amazingly enough, we make our kids pledge allegiance to the flag, learn the presidents and states, trigonometry and a host for other useless subjects yet leave them to fend for themselves spiritually. A kid who pledges allegiance everyday invariably knows the pledge, but the pledge has no lifesaving value. The same child will also repeat scripture and learn scripture regardless of whether they believe it or not. We cannot stop our kids from going to hell if they want to, but we have to answer for the ones that go to hell because we did not relay the good news of the choice. How can we love a child and not teach it to be successful, productive, and pure? How can we love a child yet stand by and watch it go to hell? It is lucky for those useless parents that I am not God, because they would not just watch their kids go to hell they would most certainly join them. The reward for wasting a family should be forfeiture of our own salvation -- in my opinion.

One thing however; God and I do agree upon, is that a man that does not take care of his family and his children does not love them nor does he love himself. That same man, the man that cares not about his family will soon be forgotten because children do not carry on the name of bastard parents. Good parents leave their marks on good children. Who remembers or even cares for that matter about the names of Charles Manson, Jeffrey Damer, Adolf Hitler, or Sirhan Sirhan's parents. If we are not the light in our children's life, then we leave them in the darkness to find whatever glimmer or spark they can. I love my children, but I will gladly tell you that they drain me sometimes. I wake every day to see that many of the things once thought good are not good enough for my children. How hypocritical of me to correct their behavior for things I used to do. I have no choice; I love them, and do not intend to allow my kids to make the same mistakes as I did. To make the same bad choice I did or to walk in the same darkness I did. Many people sue their rescuers for the damage they do during the rescue, but they are alive to sue.

My kids may resent the discipline of the temple, but God promises me that if I give them the discipline of the temple they will not depart from it, which also means that God will not depart from them. I would rather have my son mad at me yet still rest in the arms of God[162]. When I go to bed at night, I wonder about my kid's future, but I no longer worry.

No greater love hath a man, the Bible says than he lay down his life for a friend. Perhaps we misunderstood what power this application has in marriage. To love one another is to sacrifice for each other, and to each other. This does not mean that we must live in a one-sided relationship; it means that the two cannot become one until they submit to one another. By way of permission, I urge us to think of marriage as a cocoon. To submit to each other in Biblical terms is to give ourselves to the Chrysalis stage, to walk willingly to the cocoon God has laid for us and undergo whatever change He thinks best.

Like the ugly caterpillar that slithers through life leaving it slimy trails, we walk out of our darkness, and allow the sanctity of marriage to purge our filth. No matter how ugly the caterpillar, or how long the trail, they all go into a cocoon. A little-known fact cocoons our poisonous when eaten in quantity. Therefore, this helpless, ugly caterpillar hangs from a tree and its God given defenses start as soon as it submits to God's change.

The caterpillar does not know what it will look like when it emerges, it trusts God to make of it a new creature that no longer slithers along on its belly, but a color filled delicate creature that has new abilities can fly through the sky, so all the world can see the wonders of God. Romans 1:20 says, "**For the invisible things of Him from the creation of the world are clearly seen, being understood by the things that are made, [even] his eternal power and Godhead; so that they are without excuse:**" Although we cannot see the internal changes God bestows upon us, like the caterpillar men see what we become in God once He transforms us into the His butterflies.

Although the butterfly must chew its way out of the cocoon, it does not do this until it matures and can feed itself and fly. Once the butterfly emerges from the cocoon it loses the defenses God put around it and must defend itself. This is why our Chrysalis never really ends, it is no because God does not want us to mature, it is because we never stop maturing. In maturation, we find the protection and guidance of God. Not until perfection do we walk out our cocoon and have the ability to say it is finished. When he said these words, He gave up His cocoon and soared into the heavens. This the desired outcome for all saints, perfect, just as our Father in heaven is perfect.

76.0
Tai Sabaki - Oneness of Movement

"**And they, continuing daily with one accord in the temple, and breaking bread from house to house, did eat their meat with gladness and singleness of heart, Praising God, and having favour with all the people. And the Lord added to the church daily such as should be saved**," (Acts 2:46-47).

Tactical marriage consists of both spouses applying gifts equally and also to benefit each other. In providing for and safeguarding each other, we build a fortress of our marriage that minions of the enemy cannot over take. Pertaining to marriage and spiritual warfare, tactical marriage consists of the following items, all of which apply to both spouses,

- Marital moats
- Marital walls
- Marital fortress
- Marital moats
- Marital walls
- Marital food supplies and stores
- Marital barracks
- Maintaining marital discipline
- Marital sanitation
- The marital loin protector
- The marital breastplate
- The marital boots
- The marital shield
- The marital helmet
- Prayer in marriage
- Alertness in marriage
- Subjection to our own husband
- Subjection to the Lord
- Sanctification
- A husband's love
- A husband's sacrifice
- A Godly self-love
- Unity
- Forgiveness
- Maturity
- Revelation
- Reverence

With proper application and conjoining the components of tactical marriage with the strategies and weapons presented, any married Christian couple can become formidable defenders and fearsome adversaries of Satan. Let us rehash a few warfare concepts pertaining to Christ's tactics for spiritual warfare.

_____
_____
_____
_____
_____

76.1 **The Art of Christ** - One of the greatest mysteries of the Art of Christ is that it is impossible to please God without faith and it is impossible to have faith without God. The Art of Christ is the greatest paradigm in the universe: *The Art of Not Being.* The Art of Christ is not self-nullification, the art of Christ self-denial. There can be no faith without discipline because faith requires no proof[163]. Consequently, in order to please God through faith WE must learn the discipline to follow the God with no name. **The concept is simple; it does not matter what**

WE add to our flesh WE will NEVER please God. No matter what type of sacrifice we add to our flesh we still fall short because of the natures in our hearts. The Art of Christ enables us to become like Him and not like the wicked creature in our heart. The Art of Christ is the way to a pure heart.

76.2 The Art of Christ revealed

76.2.1 Teaches we should die completely to self
76.2.2 Teaches us to crave inner peace
76.2.3 Teaches us to see the essence of spiritual warfare-peace in our own hearts
76.2.4 Teaches us the four spiritual paradigms;
- Restlessness vs. peace
- Rebellion vs. submission
- Indulgence vs. restraint
- Unification vs. division

76.2.5 Teaches that perfection is not the absence of conflict but the balance of conflict
76.2.6 Teaches that He is, and has the victory, which He makes available to those in Him
76.2.7 Teaches that darkness endures only for a season
76.2.8 Teaches us to deny Satan his victory is by submitting to God
76.2.9 Teaches that waiting on God is not the same as doing nothing
76.2.10 Teaches that the righteous and the wise are quiet because only God's Spirit moves them
76.2.11 Teaches that in stillness we learn about harmony
76.2.12 Teaches that in stillness we learn peace
76.2.13 Teaches that in suffering we learn sacrifice
76.2.14 Teaches that in stillness we learn patience
76.2.15 Teaches that in suffering we learn obedience
76.2.16 Teaches that in suffering we learn love

76.3 The Art of Christ revealed in warfare

76.3.1 Teaches we live for a greater good
76.3.2 Teaches us to crave peace
76.3.3 Teaches us to conquer our own hearts

76.3.4 Teaches us the spiritual warfare paradigm; *Life unto death*
76.3.5 Teaches that we find perfection only in God's will
76.3.6 Teaches that the victory belongs to Christ
76.3.7 Teaches that darkness exists within
76.3.8 Teaches us to deny Satan victory by warring in the Spirit
76.3.9 Teaches that waiting on God is not the same as allowing others to suffer
76.3.10 Teaches the righteous defend the weak and the lost
76.3.11 Teaches that in stillness we find our weaknesses
76.3.12 Teaches that in stillness we learn to subdue fear
76.3.13 Teaches that in stillness we learn to flee darkness
76.3.14 Teaches that in suffering we cease to council our own hearts
76.3.15 Teaches that in suffering we learn to conquer doubt
76.3.16 Teaches that in suffering we learn love

76.4 **The Art of Christ revealed in marriage**

76.4.1 Teaches we should submit to each other
76.4.2 Teaches us to crave marital peace
76.4.3 Teaches us to see the trouble in our own hearts
76.4.4 Teaches us the marital paradigms; our trouble lies within us
76.4.5 Teaches that love grows as self-dies
76.4.6 Teaches submission and humility are victory
76.4.7 Teaches that bitterness leads to darkness
76.4.8 Teaches us to deny Satan our bride by sacrificing all
76.4.9 Teaches that waiting on God is not the same as indecision
76.4.10 Teaches that unity works best when moved by the Spirit
76.4.11 Teaches that in stillness we learn about intimacy
76.4.12 Teaches that in stillness we learn tolerance
76.4.13 Teaches that in stillness we learn gentleness

|.14 Teaches in suffering we learn unity
|.15 Teaches in suffering we learn humility
|.16 Teaches in suffering we learn forgiveness

    Previously, we discussed some famous tacticians who dealt with conflict resolution. Sun Tzu, and Morihei Ueshiba wrote great strategy, but neither spoke of husbandry. The Art of War was about skillful destruction. The Art of Peace was about maintaining or attaining peace through skillful destruction. If a husband is a warrior, then it follows that war must also be part of husbandry. If Jesus had a bride, He was a husband. If Jesus fought spiritual warfare, then He was a spiritual warrior. Satan wages spiritual war against marriage far more than the unmarried, so we must look at warfare as it attacks marriage not as part of the marriage. In other words, the fight is against the matrimonial state. God never meant for war to be part of marriage. Spouses must grow and change, but we do not to war against each other.

    Every Marine has the basic job of rifleman, only the most dedicated marines go on to Special Forces. Every Christian has the basic job of Kingdom defense. The basic defense affords and maintains purity as a lifestyle. Those that are committed and dedicated actually respond to the Great Commission. The elect few choose to become *Special Forces* and push out into Satan's kingdom. To those couples that engage in attacking the enemy I tip my hat and offer my prayers. It is cold and dark in the valley of the shadow of death. However, fear no evil, for the Lord of Host is with us and His rod and staff shall comfort us. To those same couples be encouraged, in the fight, the pure marriage is the way to –

Love to fight another day.

77.0
Work Area 12
Eden Area[164]

This part of the book is the most fun; it will also be the most controversial. Sadly, it (as it has always been) is the foolishness of the church that has created a stigma against what God has undefiled. How foolish is the heart of the man that tries, advocates, or admonishes to put asunder what God admonishes us to enjoy. How deceptively, disrespectful is the heart that says and speaks in reserve of what God admonishes us to enjoy. Ecclesiastes 9:9 reminds us specifically to enjoy the wife of our youth. Song of Songs advises us to the let her breasts satisfy the husband at all times. How then the open expression of marital love be wrong. Of course, we must be modest in public, but this is a book focused on making marriages better and giving Satan less places from which to attack.

Sex is the most common cause of marital dysfunction and or failure if you look at the data. How so? Simple, let us look at the ways sex affects marriage;

MALE COMPLAINTS	**FEMALE COMPLAINTS**
Not enough sex	I am not satisfied with our sex life
She will not look at porn	He looks at porn
I want to have sex with someone else	I do not like sex
I do not get enough sex	Too much sex
Unfulfilled sexual desires	No warmth just
	He wants to have sex with someone else
	No emotional connection
	Weird sexual desires

Looking at these reasons, and all the reason that stem from or lead to these reasons, I believe the overwhelming issues in marriage are sexual, thereby proving that any religion or church that encourages married Christians to diminish their Godly pleasure, it just plain wrong.

With that being said, I believe the most important portion of this book is the Eden Patch©. The Eden Patch is simply, **"They were naked and not ashamed."** Take the flesh weaknesses in our armor off the table, by being well Gardened. Spend the time working through this book, in the tub, with a massage, painting toes, reading naked and do not be ashamed, for this is one of the secrets to successful Spiritual warfare - satisfied flesh.

_____
_____
_____
_____
_____
_____
_____

77.1 Ways to revive your marriage and the love[165]

77.1.1 Learn to show gratitude for what the good things in the marriage
77.1.2 Spend more time cuddling and touching
77.1.3 Bring the dating, flirting and chase back to marriage
77.1.4 Plan a romantic getaway
77.1.5 Find a pastime that both of you agree on
77.1.6 Communicate openly about the ups and downs of the marriage
77.1.7 Get some me-time
77.1.8 Go back to showing affection through gifts

77.2 And then we look to yet another list for #20 ways to make your marriage stronger

77.2.1 Eat healthfully.
77.2.2 Make time for exercise.
77.2.3 Talk about your early days of dating.
77.2.4 Bond with each other's friends.
77.2.5 Give your spouse alone time with their pals.
77.2.6 Bond with each other's families.
77.2.7 Touch as often as possible.
77.2.8 Drop your old issues.
77.2.9 Fight fairly.
77.2.10 Cook together.
77.2.11 Have a sense of humor.
77.2.12 Know when to listen (without offering advice).
77.2.13 Carve out quiet time.
77.2.14 Be financially responsible.
77.2.15 Speak well of each other.
77.2.16 Be playful.
77.2.17 Do not stall on each other's requests.
77.2.18 Accept that you will both have bratty moments.
77.2.19 Divvy up chores.

_____
_____

77.2.20 Ask your spouse, "What do you need more of?[166]"

77.3 **About Adam**

77.3.1 Are you in love your wife? ☐ YES ☐ NO

77.3.2 Do you love your wife selflessly? ☐ YES ☐ NO

77.3.3 Do give your wife the same consideration you do yourself? ☐ YES ☐ NO

77.3.4 Do you want to unify with your wife in all areas? ☐ YES ☐ NO

77.3.5 Do you cater to your wife? ☐ YES ☐ NO

77.3.6 Do you give attention to your wife? ☐ YES ☐ NO

77.3.7 Do you ever suggest divorce? ☐ YES ☐ NO

77.3.8 Have you ever considered adultery? ☐ YES ☐ NO

77.3.9 Do you respect your wife's sexual needs? ☐YES ☐NO

77.3.10 Are you still sexually attracted to your wife? ☐YES ☐ NO

77.3.11 Do you lead in your home, spiritually or physically? ☐ YES ☐ NO

77.3.12 Is your behavior drawing your wife closer to you? ☐ YES ☐ NO

77.3.13 Do you say kind things to your wife daily? ☐YES ☐ NO

77.3.14 Do you help your wife with his fears? ☐YES ☐ NO

77.3.15 Do you pray over your wife? ☐ YES ☐ NO

77.3.16 How much do you trust your wife? ☐YES ☐ NO

77.3.17 Do you exhort your wife privately and publicly? ☐ YES ☐ NO

77.3.18 Do you allow your wife to be himself? ☐YES ☐ NO

77.3.19 Are you empathetic? ☐YES ☐NO

77.3.20 Do you show you wife honor? ☐ YES ☐ NO

77.3.22 Are you pleasant? ☐ YES ☐ NO

77.3.23 Are you vengeful? ☐ YES ☐NO

77.3.23 Do you practice forgiveness with your wife? ☐YES ☐ NO

77.3.24 Do you admit your faults to each other? ☐YES ☐NO

77.3. 25 Do you plan fun time with your wife? ☐ YES ☐ NO

77.3.26 Are you envious of your wife? ☐ YES ☐ NO

77.3.27 Do you speak harshly to or curse at your wife? ☐ YES ☐ NO

77.3.28 Are you physically abusive? ☐ YES ☐ NO

_____
_____
_____
_____
_____

77.4 **About Eve**

77.4.1 Do you love your husband? ☐YES ☐NO

77.4.2 Does your wife submit to you? ☐YES ☐NO

77.4.3 Is your wife respectful even when you disagree? ☐ YES ☐ NO

77.4.4 Are you submissive even when your husband behaves poorly? ☐YES ☐NO

77.4.5 Are you respectful to your husband in public? ☐YES ☐ NO

77.4.6 Do you honor your husband? ☐YES ☐NO

77.4.7 Do you consider yourself above your husband? ☐YES ☐ NO

77.4.8 Do you seek advice and counsel from your husband? ☐YES ☐NO

77.4.9 Do you obey your husband? ☐YES ☐ NO

77.4.10 Do you serve your husband? ☐YES ☐NO

77.4.11 Do you ever threaten divorce? ☐YES ☐NO

77.4.12 Have you considered adultery? ☐YES ☐NO

77.4.13 Are you a friend and companion to your husband? ☐YES ☐NO

77.4.14 Do you respect to your husband's sexual needs? ☐ YES ☐ NO

77.4.15 Are you jealous of your husband? ☐ YES ☐ NO

77.4.16 Do you your husband? ☐ YES ☐ NO

77.4.17 Are you verbally or physically abusive? YES ☐ NO

77.4.18 Are you vengeful? ☐ YES ☐NO

77.4.19 Do you practice forgiveness? ☐YES ☐NO

77.4.20 Do you confess your faults to your husband? ☐YES ☐NO

77.4.21 Do you exhort your husband? ☐ YES ☐ NO

77.4.22 Do you pray for your family? ☐ YES ☐ NO
77.4.23 Do you ask your husband to teach or explain things to you? ☐ YES ☐ NO
77.4.24 Do you argue with your husband? ☐ YES ☐ NO
77.4.25 Are you gentle and kind? ☐ YES ☐ NO
77.4.26 Do you handle you home responsibilities cheeringly? ☐ YES ☐ NO
77.4.27 Do you practice good judgment? ☐ YES ☐ NO
77.4.28 Can you be trusted? ☐ YES ☐ NO
77.4.29 Do you encourage and aid in your husband's success? ☐ YES ☐ NO
77.4.30 Do you complain? ☐ YES ☐ NO
77.4.31 Do you try to make your husband happy? ☐ YES ☐ NO
77.4.32 Do you create money problems? ☐ YES ☐ NO
77.4.33 Do you take care of your health? ☐ YES ☐ NO
77.4.34 Do you take care of your image and the way you look? ☐ YES ☐ NO
77.4.35 Are you ambitious? ☐ YES ☐ NO

_____
_____
_____

77.5 **About us**
77.5.1 List all the things you would change in your marriage and why?
_____
_____
_____
_____
_____
_____
_____
_____
_____

77.5.2 What do you think about the most often regarding your spouse?

___

77.5.3 List all the things in your marriage gives you the pleasure?

___

77.3.4 What are you most proud of in your marriage? And why?

___

77.3.5 What are you most ashamed of in your marriage? And why?

___

77.3.6 List the things is your marriage that make you happiest / eager / comfortable / sad/ unsure / angry/afraid?

___

77.3.7 What things do you look forward to each day?

77.3.8 What things do you least look forward to each day?

77.3.9 List regrets in your marriage?

77.3.10 List what caused these regrets

77.3.11 Does your behavior interfere with your spouse's ambitions or accomplishments?

77.3.12 List all the things you like about your spouse

_____
_____
_____
_____
_____

77.3.13 List all the things you dislike about your spouse

_____
_____
_____
_____
_____

77.3.14 List all the great things about your marriage

_____
_____
_____
_____
_____

77.3.15 List all the good things about your marriage

_____
_____
_____
_____
_____

77.3.16 List all the bad things about your marriage

_____
_____
_____
_____
_____

77.3.17 Explain how you and your spouse handle with monetary issues.
_____
_____
_____
_____
_____

77.3.18 Describe parenting conflicts.
_____
_____
_____
_____
_____

77.3.19 How has your opinion on parenting changed since you have been married?
_____
_____
_____
_____
_____

77.3.20 How often are you and your spouse sexually active?
_____
_____
_____
_____
_____

77.3.21 How often would he like to be sexually active?
_____
_____
_____
_____

77.3.22 How often would he like to be active?

77.3.23 Are you passionate of clinical when active?

77.3.24 Describe fun time for you and your spouse and the not so fun time together.

77.3.25 List all people your marriage would benefits not having a part of it?

77.3.26 Does your spouse respect your opinion of your friends?

77.3.27 Are your friends more important than your spouse?

77.3.28 Do you think it is fair to ignore you spouses' needs and or wishes?

77.3.29 List your habits that harm or do not help the marriage.

77.3.30 List your marital expectations.

77.3.31 What are your spousal expectations?

77.3.32 Can you compromise on a few if you cannot have them all met? If so which are more important?

78.0
Glossary of Marriage Mysteries

"This is a great mystery: but I speak concerning Christ and the church. (Ephesians 5:32)"

If you are anything like me, you have sit in the window, looking up at the sky trying to figure out what, exactly what we are supposed to learn from all the difficulties of marriage.
Marriage is an example of a commitment of faith in Christ[167]. People fall in love and marry. As such, they commit to put their trust and lives to each other in front of witnesses. This is also what we commit to Christ and are baptized. We commit to being Christs bride for the rest of our lives.

Sadly, many fall out of love with their spouses. They chase other men, women, or other idols. Often times, they eventually seek divorce. This also happens to Christ's marriage, it grows cold as we sink into idolatry and adultery and eventually we seek a divorce from our commitment to the faith.

However, those successfully married do not understand that they are the fruit of a successful marriage to Christ, wherein He helped them stay faithful as a testament to Himself. Other marriage mysteries metaphors:

Flesh	**Spirit**
The waning sex drive	The fading power of the flesh
The less physical attractiveness	The fading power of the flesh
Trust	Developing faith
Parenting	Discipleship, love
Conflict resolution	Enduring faith as the flesh learns the power of the spirit, patience, temperance, long suffering, love, better prayer life
Finance management	Stewardship
Health management	Sensitivity to spiritual needs of the flock
Anger management	Patience on God
Living together	How to care for the things of God
Marital woes	Maturity (We cannot always get everything we ask for)
Sex	Spiritual intimacy
Infidelity	Idolatry
Unforgiving	Hard heartedness
Being turned off physically	Loss of faith
Indifference	Lukewarmth

78.1 Learn to love with your soul (page 217).

78.2 Time spent working with God develops bonds and closeness (page 108).

78.3 God works wonders through our marriages and in our marriages. (page 303).

78.4 That the love for the temple and the love for the marriage are the same mystery…they are a love for the things of God. The same sanctification God requires of the temple He requires of the sanctified marriage (page 44).

78.5 Praying spouses are that the two parts that make a whole. In prayer, unity is key. The way the mystery works is that the wife and the husband pray for the same things and the time the other loses from their single life they make up jointly. In other words, the man may lose four hours, but his wife makes up the other two hours. If the two pray with singleness of heart, they can maintain the relationship with God (page 85).

78.6 DO NOT STOP PRAYING AND DO NOT STOP TOUCHING. This is the highest level of intimacy humans can achieve. How could there be any greater blessing than to never have to leave the bosom of our mate and still be able to enter the Holy of holies. We should cleave to our spouse and never stop touching and then we learn the true pleasures of the flesh do not stem from sin, they stem from intimacy and sharing. This mystery elevates our fleshly undefiled lives into spiritual intimacy with God. (page 104).

78.7 Happily married flesh is virtually immune to Satanic attacks (page 105).

78.8 Out of the abundance of the heart the mouth speaks. The words we share with our spouses tell them what is in heart and our mind (page 145).

78.9 Sex is integral to a balanced marriage because it allows the normally unrighteous nature of the flesh to stay controlled. This is part of the of marriage mystery; the lack of controls is actually God's method for controlling the flesh of married people (page 199).

78.10 Many marriages fail because of discontentment and creating our own wisdom (page 255).

78.11 Blessed indulgence is the way in which marriage works its mystery against Satan (page 74).

78.12 In every way, marriage's mystery mimics the faith walk. We start both adventures by losing our freedom. In marriage, we find peace and absolution. In marriage, we find the love of God (page 323).

78.13 We find another marriage mystery hidden in the Garden of Eden. We understand that God made celibacy undesirable for His people. In doing so He ensured Godly seeds in marriage (page 66).

79.0
Discipleship Basics

79.1 Target group

    79.1.1 Age - Prepare parables (explanations) and the understanding or maturity level of the group you are called to serve

    79.1.2 Disposition - What type of scales will you be dealing with. If you are tasked with only one type of scales (scars / issues) then stick to that which you have been tooled to repair

___
___
___
___

79.2 Make contact

    79.2.1 Do not try to preach to them just be kind
    79.2.2 Make small talk about unrelated issues affording them the opportunity to ask why
    79.2.3 Meet as equals no matter what or where they are
    79.2.4 Make casual conversation about anything interesting until you develop a report

___
___
___
___
___
___
___
___
___

79.3 Use contact as inroad

    79.3.1 Back off if needed repeat step two
    79.3.2 Go slowly
    79.3.3 Stay within boundaries of step two for a safe period

79.4 Direct conversation
- 79.4.1 Let your words/ actions/ attitude be the reason they respond to you, let them mention God first
- 79.4.2 Let them mention church or religion first
- 79.4.3 Be indirect but adamant, do not be forceful but be consistent

- 79.4.4 Direct conversation back to God, once you switch to God stay there

79.5 Why
- 79.5.1 Most have had bad experiences with church, Christians, or God
- 79.5.2 When they ask 'why' tell them you used to be just like them, but you had help changing

79.6 Do not argue scriptures
　　79.6.1 Do not argue
　　79.6.2 If they want to argue facts speak of love and vice versa

79.7 The old church invite
　　79.7.1 Don't invite them they will not come
　　79.7 .2 Get a number or give them the church number to call
　　79.7 .3 Invite them to a church picnic or fair

79.8 Questions and answers
- 79.8.1 Give them an opportunity to ask questions and HAVE ANSWERS TO THEIR QUESTIONS or be able to find it in the bible (concordances are ok)
- 79.8.2 Nothing more pathetic than an unlearned evangelist

79.9 Convert
- 79.9.1 **DO NOT ATTEMPT TO CONVERT THEM** there on the spot that is not our jobs let Holy Spirit do His job
- 79.9.2 Our task is to lead them to the Holy Spirit and help them not to fall
- 79.9.3 True expertise in Evangelism lies in our ability to open a person up to receive from the Holy Spirit

79.10 Demons
- 79.10.1 **Never engage demons alone biblical model is two against any number of demons**
- 79.10.2 Ascertain which demons you fight, remember the person is not the enemy
- 79.10.3 If you have the gift of discernment use it, if not ask the demon for its name REMEMBER THE DEMON DOES NOT HAVE TO RESPOND TO YOU BUT THEY MUST RESPOND TO THE HOLY SPIRIT. Therefore, the more of the spirit is in you the more power you have. If you are fueled enough with the Holy Spirit no matter who the demon is they will leave
- 79.10.7 Always pray and fast before going out into the territory of your enemy

79.11 Attitude
- **79.11.1** Leave your attitude home they owe you nothing
- **79.11.2** Do not expect them to be overjoyed
- **79.11.3** Do not expect them to be overly trusting
- **79.11.4** What you are saying is not new they will probably not act surprised

79.12 Do not let you guard down
- **79.12.1** Remember that you are in enemy territory
- **79.12.2** Do not be fooled by familiar spirits
- **79.12.3** Don't be over confident you are not as far from falling as you think

79.13 Control
- 79.13.1 Never give up control of yourself, or your lifestyle. Do not drink, smoke or use drugs just to make contact
- 79.13.2 Never give up control of the situation
- 79.13.4 Never give up control of the conversation

79.14 Demons are evil they are not dumb
- 79.14.1 Do not underestimate them, they do not have to submit to you and they never will
- 79.14.2 Do not count on their slipping up. They make few mistakes and they know the rules well
- 79.14.3 Do not think they will fight fair; they are trying to get more souls in hell THEY HAVE NO BOUNDARIES

80.0
Facilitator's Section

Preparing for a group study requires you to prepare for the study, foster feedback and feedforward, guide lessons and answers questions.

This is student lead study, and it involves the most personal aspects of people's lives; the secrets in their homes. The facilitator therefore needs to be mature, open minded and transparent.

80.1 Facilitator format
- 80.1.1 Greet members and try to memorize as many names as possible
- 80.1.2 Pray openly and encourage others to pray with and for the class
- 80.1.3 Overview the content for the session
- 80.1.4 Use three colors each session and as many stories as time allots
- 80.1.5 A lot time during class to cover the material as quickly as possible
- 80.1.6 The reading done throughout the week should generate discussion and questions. If not discuss questions of point on class that you have heard of fielded most frequently
- 80.1.7 Create daily assignments
- 80.1.8 Organize prayer partners and couples' groups even within the group
- 80.1.9 Use scriptures to verify ALL points of teaching, steer away from opinion
- 80.1.10 Encourages meditation verses
- 80.1.11 Develop and enlist leaders from with the group
- 80.1.12 Disciple class mates and encourage them to make friends
- 80.1.13 Establish NON-PAROCHIAL class rules

80.2 Facilitator Bible verses about marriage and love
- 80.2.1 (Genesis 1:27-28) "**So God created man in his own image, in the image of God he created him; male and female he created them. And God blessed them. And God said to them, 'Be fruitful and multiply and fill the earth and subdue it and have dominion over the**

fish of the sea and over the birds of the heavens and over every living thing that moves on the earth.'"

80.2.2 (Malachi 2:14-15) "**But you say, 'Why does he not?' Because the Lord was witness between you and the wife of your youth, to whom you have been faithless, though she is your companion and your wife by covenant.**"

80.2.3 (Isaiah 54:5) "**For your Maker is your husband, the Lord of hosts is his name; and the Holy One of Israel is your Redeemer, the God of the whole earth he is called.**"

80.2.4 (Song of Solomon 8:6-7) "**Set me as a seal upon your heart, as a seal upon your arm, for love is strong as death, jealousy is fierce as the grave. Its flashes are flashes of fire, the very flame of the Lord. Many waters cannot quench love; neither can floods drown it. If a man offered for love all the wealth of his house, he would be utterly despised.**"

80.2.5 (Ephesians 4:2-3) "**With all humility and gentleness, with patience, bearing with one another in love, eager to maintain the unity of the Spirit in the bond of peace.**"

80.2.6 (Colossians 3:14) "**And over all these virtues put on love, which binds them all together in perfect unity.**"

80.2.7 (Ecclesiastes 4:90 "**Two are better than one, because they have a good return for their labor: If either of them falls down, one can help the other up. But pity anyone who falls and has no one to help them up. Also, if two lie down together, they will keep warm. But how can one keep warm alone?**"

80.2.8 (Ephesians 5:25) "**For husbands, this means loves your wives, just as Christ loved the church. He gave up his life for her.**"

80.2.9 (Genesis 2:24) "**Therefore a man shall leave his father and his mother and hold fast to his wife, and they shall become one flesh.**"

80.2.10 (Ecclesiastes 4:12) "**Though one may be overpowered, two can defend themselves. A cord of three strands is not quickly broken.**"

80.2.11 (Mark 10:9) "**Therefore what God has joined together, let no one separate.**"

80.2.12 (Ephesians 5:25-33) "**Husbands, love your wives, as Christ loved the church and gave himself up for her, that he might sanctify her, having cleansed her by the washing of water with the word, so that he might present the church to himself in splendor, without spot or wrinkle or any such thing, that she might be holy and without blemish. In the same way husbands should love their** wives as their own bodies. He who loves his wife loves himself. For no one ever hated his own flesh, but nourishes and cherishes it, just as Christ does the church, ..."

80.2.13 (Romans 13:8) "**Owe no one anything, except to love each other, for the one who loves another has fulfilled the law.**"

80.2.14 (1 Corinthians 13:4-5) "**Love is patient, love is kind. It does not envy, it does not boast, it is not proud. It does not dishonor others, it is not self-seeking, it is not easily angered, it keeps no record of wrongs.**"

80.2.15 (1 Corinthians 13:2) "**If I have the gift of prophecy and can fathom all mysteries and all knowledge, and if I have a faith that can move mountains, but do not have love, I am nothing.**"

80.2.16 (1 Corinthians 16:14) "**Do everything in love.**"

80.2.17 (Song of Solomon 8:7) "**Many waters cannot quench love; rivers cannot wash it away. If one were to give all the wealth of his house for love, it would be utterly scorned.**"

80.2.18 (Psalm 143:8) "**Let the morning bring me word of your unfailing love, for I have put my trust in you. Show me the way I should go, for to you I entrust my life.**"

80.2.19 (Proverbs 3:3-4) "**Let love and faithfulness never leave you; bind them around your neck, write them on the tablet of your heart. Then you will win favor and a good name in the sight of God and man.**"

80.2.20 (1 John 4:16) "**And so we know and rely on the love God has for us. God is love. Whoever lives in love lives in God, and God in them.**"

80.2.21 (Ephesians 4:2) "**Be completely humble and gentle; be patient, bearing with one another in love.**"

80.2.22 (1 Peter 4:8) "**Above all, love each other deeply, because love covers over a multitude of sins.**"

80.2.23 (John 15:12) "**My command is this: Love each other as I have loved you.**"

80.2.24 (1 Corinthians 13:13) "**And now these three remain: faith, hope and love. But the greatest of these is love.**"

80.2.25 (Song of Solomon 4:9) "**You have captivated my heart, my sister, my bride; you have captivated my heart with one glance of your eyes, with one jewel of your necklace.**"

80.2.26 (Hebrews 10:24-25) "**And let us consider how we may spur one another on toward love and good deeds, not giving up meeting together, as some are** in the habit of doing, but encouraging one another - and all the more as you see the Day approaching."

80.2.27 (Proverbs 30:18-19) "**There are three things that amaze me - no, four things that I don't understand: how an eagle glides through the sky, how a snake slithers on a rock, how a ship navigates the ocean, how a man loves a woman.**"

80.2.28 (1 John 4:12) "**No one has ever seen God; but if we love one another, God lives in us and his love is made complete in us.**"

80.2.29 (Proverbs 31:10) "**Who can find a virtuous woman? For her price is far above rubies.**"

80.2.30 (Ruth 1:16-17) "**Entreat me not to leave you, Or to turn back from following after you; For wherever you go, I will go; And wherever you lodge, I will lodge; Your people shall be my people, And your God, my God. Where you die, I will die, And there will I be buried. The Lord do so to me, and more also, If anything but death parts you and me.**"

80.2.31 (Romans 12:10) "**Be devoted to one another in love. Honor one another above yourselves.**"

80.2.32 (1 Peter 4:8) "**Most important of all, continue to show deep love for each other, for love covers a multitude of sins.**"

80.2.33 (Ephesians 5:21) "**Submit to one another out of reverence for Christ**."

80.2.34 (Ephesians 4:32) "**Be kind to each other, tenderhearted, forgiving one another, just as God through Christ has forgiven you**."

80.2.35 (Genesis 2:18-25) "**Then the Lord God said, 'It is not good that the man should be alone; I will make him a helper fit for him.' ... So the Lord God caused a deep sleep to fall upon the man, and while he slept took one of his ribs and closed up its place with flesh. And the rib that the Lord God had taken from the man he made into a woman and brought her to the man**."

80.2.36 (1 Peter 3:7) "**In the same way, you husbands must give honor to your wives. Treat your wife with understanding as you live together. She may be weaker than you are, but she is your equal partner in God's gift of new life. Treat her as you should so your prayers will not be hindered**."

We would love to help you write your dreams down. Each story is precious let White Marlin Media make yours known. Allow us to serve your needs with your family or Christian work: Poetry, stories, textbooks, children's books, we live to serve you. To order other books by this author, send

All available at our gift shop on the web

michaeldonaldson@asharaministries.com

or shop the web at

https://www.asharaministries.com/ashara-bookstore/

ALMOST EVERYTHING YOU NEED TO KNOW ABOUT THE FAITH AND SPIRITUAL WARFARE

81.0 BIBLIOGRAPHY

I would like to thank every contributor to this work. I cited other works, compilations, and or sources to make the point that gut feelings are simply not enough to certify and verify Kingdom workers. Benevolence, has it place, but teaching in the kingdom is no longer has a place for it any
longer.

[1] Printed in the United States of America.
[2] For more information log onto www.asharaministries.com.
[3] From a fishing trip in Patmos, The lights in Patmos, and From a fortress in Patmos.
[4] Genesis 3:17.
[5] A menstrual rag is the actual Hebrew equivalent used.
[6] The Lights in Patmos.
[7] "The heart [is] deceitful above all [things], and desperately wicked: who can know it - Jeremiah 17:9."
[8] For more information on this topic read Bonhoffer's, The Cost of Discipleship.
[9] The American Heritage Dictionary, Houghton Mifflin Company, Boston, 1982.
[10] For more in-depth information on this topic, please read, The Lights in Patmos - Illuminating the Origin of Spiritual Warfare.
[11] The Biblical application of this word indicates *Judge* means to *wage war against*, or to *make war against something*.
[12] Exodus 20:3-4.
[13] 1 Corinthians 2:8 - Which none of the princes of this world knew: for had they known [it], they would not have crucified the Lord of Glory."
[14] Matthew 18:6
[15] Genesis 6:3.
[16] 1 Corinthians 7:9.
[17] In this segment use of metaphor regarding Jesus as the bride conforms to scripture and is therefore acceptable and not degrading, or homosexual in nature.
[18] Marriage Mystery - The Trinity has three equal parts. The Son is only 1/3 of the Trinity He is not the Father. However, both Father and Son are equally important to success. Therefore, the bride/wife is the weaker vessel by virtue of being fleshlier, not in the test of strength and endurance. Ergo, when the Bible refers to the wife as the *weaker vessel* the proper application of this would be *fleshlier*.
[19] 'ishshah - is the Hebrew word used in Genesis. The word means or at least is identical to Man, a peculiar usage of the noun considering the male oriented views of the Jews. However, it makes sense in God's plan that the two are similar, how else could they become one flesh again? It also makes sense, to show that equality built into the relationship by God between spouses.
[20] For more information, see The lights in Patmos regarding the issue.

[21] For more information, read The lights in Patmos regarding the issue.
[22] Average wedding cost in the united states is $26,645. www.costofwedding.com/ 08/01/2018.
[23] 6-reasons-why-marriage-is-so-important-to-women, http://lovequotes.tips/6-reasons-why-marriage-is-so-important-to-women/ 08/01/2018
[24] Photo by Salvatore Vuono from www.freedigitalphotos.net used by permission.
[25] https://www.huffingtonpost.com/2013/05/03/internet-porn-stats_n_3187682.html. 080518.
[26] Matthew 19:12.
[27] Genesis 6:5.
[28] A Godly marriage is one that falls and stays within His boundaries for sex, and gender.
[29] John 1:3.
[30] Revelations 12:13-17.
[31] "… [to avoid] fornication, let every man have his own wife, and let every woman have her own husband…let them marry: for it is better to marry than to burn - 1 Corinthians 7:1-9".
[32] Matthew 19:12,
[33] "And thou shalt love the Lord thy God with all thine heart, and with all thy soul, and with all thy might."
[34] Matthew 16:19.
[35] Ezekiel 28:15.
[36] 2 Peter, 2:14, Romans 7:3.
[37] Jeremiah 3:6-9, Ezekiel.16: 32-33, Hosea 1, 2, 3, Revelations 2:20.
[38] Ezekiel 6:9, Jeremiah 3:9.
[39] Use of the term *whore* is gender neutral and refers to the adulterous affair.
[40] 1 Corinthians 4:5.
[41] "**AND I WILL NOT HAVE MERCY UPON HER CHILDREN; FOR THEY BE THE CHILDREN OF WHOREDOMS**."
[42] See footnotes 5, 6, and 7.
[43] Refer to Roman 1:20-32 for detailed information on this principle.
[44] John 10:30.
[45] Are apple seeds poisonous? - Medical News Today https://www.medicalnewstoday.com/articles/318706.php. March 13, 2018.
[46] Matthew 12:26.
[47] "But I speak this by permission, [and] not of commandment - 1 Corinthians 7:6."
[48] Matthew 19:12.
[49] Luke 9:62.
[50] Pertaining to normal sexual activity, nothing in this book or any of the Patmos series applies to homosexual behavior. God's blessings and laws governing the undefiled bed DO NOT apply to homosexuality.
[51] 1 Corinthians 7:14.
[52] BEWARE! The Top 12 Issues That Threaten Even Happy Marriages, https://www.yourtango.com/experts/brad-browning/marriage-issues-12-big-ones. 080418.
[53] 25 Ways to fight fair, http://www.foryourmarriage.org/25-ways-to-fight-fair/
[54] Matthew 6:5.
[55] Matthew 28:18, John 14:26, 15:26, and 16:7.
[56] 1 John 5:7-8.

57. Revelations 14:12 -13, "And I heard a voice from heaven saying unto me, 'Write, Blessed [are] the dead which die in the Lord from henceforth: Yea, saith the Spirit that they may rest from their labours; and their works do follow them.'"
58. Leviticus 18:5-24.
59. Songs 8:7.
60. Songs 4:12-15.
61. "**BUT WOE UNTO YOU, SCRIBES AND PHARISEES, HYPOCRITES! FOR YE SHUT UP THE KINGDOM OF HEAVEN AGAINST MEN: FOR YE NEITHER GO IN [YOURSELVES], NEITHER SUFFER YE THEM THAT ARE ENTERING TO GO IN** - Matthew 23:13."
62. Genesis 2:24.
63. Proverbs 5:19
64. Exodus 17:8-12.
65. James 3.
66. "Confess [your] faults one to another, and pray one for another, that ye may be healed. The effectual fervent prayer of a righteous man availeth much - James 5:16."
67. *To roam about in a visible form.* American Heritage Dictionary, (p.1360 <6>), Used by permission.
68. Genesis 35:11, Proverbs 10:1, Jeremiah 13:11, John 14:6, 1 Peter 1:13.
69. Isaiah 59:21, Matthew 5:8, Matthew15:16-19, Romans 10:10-11, John 5:17, 1 Thessalonians 5:8, James 3:2.
70. The Holy Bible, New International Version, NIV Copyright 1973, 1977, 1984 by International Bible Society. Used by permission. All rights reserved worldwide.
71. Luke 11:21-22.
72. For the record, a healthy marital sex life is righteous.
73. "**O GENERATION OF VIPERS, HOW CAN YE, BEING EVIL, SPEAK GOOD THINGS? FOR OUT OF THE ABUNDANCE OF THE HEART THE MOUTH SPEAKETH** - Matthew 12:24."
74. John 21:25.
75. Luke 11:22.
76. This applies to multi-cultural and ethnic appellations and the unbelieving husbands. Remember the Bible admonishes us not to marry outside our faith, however if we do that is no reason to sin.
77. See Genesis 3 for elaboration.
78. 1 Samuel 15:22.
79. Isaiah 45:9
80. Job 38 & 39.
81. 1 Chronicles 13:10.
82. Proverbs 21:19, 26:21, 27:15.
83. God is the only One that can curse a thing, but the Cross-lifted all-preexisting curses--John 9:1-6. Few things have been cursed or accursed since Golgotha. Once cursed by God only He can remove the curse.
84. 1 Peter 3:7.
85. 1 Corinthians 7:5.

[86] In From a fishing trip in Patmos we discussed Revelation being a perpetual communication process. Re-veiled knowledge constantly needs guidance. Nowhere is constant guidance more necessary than marriage.
[87] Proverbs 29:18.
[88] 1 Corinthians 14:3-4.
[89] 1 Corinthians 12:8-10.
[90] Proverbs 1:7.
[91] Matthew 6:8.
[92] John 13:22-26.
[93] "Marriage [is] honorable in all, and the bed undefiled: but whoremongers and adulterers God will judge."
[94] Ezekiel 12:2.
[95] John 20-21.
[96] 1 Corinthians 12.
[97] As long as you do not put your spouse before God.
[98] 1 Timothy 4:1-3.
[99] Matthew 19:12.
[100] Matthew 19:23 remember waiting until you are married is not abstinence it is waiting to partake. The lives of priests and nuns as a life of abstinence, is what the Bible advises against. The evidence reveled in the thousands of allegations against ecumenical abstainers engaging in unmarried, unnatural, acts proves that once again the Bible is correct.
[101] Matthew 11:29, Matthew 16:24 Mark 8:34, Luke 10:2.
[102] Genesis 2:23.
[103] See; From a Fishing Trip in Patmos, in the chapter called, *The other white meat*.
[104] Genesis 6:1-2.
[105] Matthew 23:15.
[106] Leviticus 18:22, 23, Leviticus 20:13, 15, Romans 1:22-32.
[107] 1 Timothy 4:1-3.
[108] Philippians 4:8.
[109] Colossians 2:8.
[110] John 2:17.
[111] For the time [is come] that judgment must begin at the house of God: and if [it] first [begin] at us, what shall the end [be] of them that obey not the gospel of God? - 1 Peter 4:17.
[112] 'The husband should not deprive his wife of sexual intimacy, which is her right as a married woman, nor should the wife deprive her husband.' 1 Corinthians 7:6. *Holy Bible*, New Living Translation, copyright 1996 by Tyndale Charitable Trust. Used by permission of Tyndale House Publishers.
[113] 'Defraud ye not one the other, except [it be] with consent for a time, that ye may give yourselves to fasting and prayer; and come together again, that Satan tempt you not for your incontinency - 1 Corinthians 7:6.'
[114] "And Jonathan, Saul's son, had a son [that was] lame of [his] feet. He was five years old when the tidings came of Saul and Jonathan out of Jezreel, and his nurse took him up, and fled: and it came to pass, as she made haste to flee, that he fell, and became lame. And his name [was] Mephibosheth -2 Samuel 4:4."

[115] Psalms 27:35.
[116] Genesis 6:5.
[117] Genesis 1:12.
[118] Romans 8:38, Colossians 2:18, Revelation 12:7, 2 Peter 2:4, Jude 1:6, Revelation 9:14 Revelation 12:9, Matthew 25:41, 2 Corinthians 11:14, Revelation 9:11
[119] 1 Samuel 15:23.
[120] Exodus 15:6 - "**Thy right hand, O Lord, is become glorious in power: thy right hand, O Lord, hath dashed in pieces the enemy.**"

- Deuteronomy 33:2 - "**And he said, The Lord came from Sinai, and rose up from Seir unto them; He shined forth from mount Paran, and He came with ten thousand of saints: from His right hand [went] a fiery law for them.**"
- 1 Kings 2:29 - "**Bathsheba therefore went unto king Solomon, to speak unto him for Adonijah. And the king rose up to meet her, and bowed himself unto her, and sat down on his throne, and caused a seat to be set for the king's mother; and she sat on his right hand.**"
- Psalms 17:17 - "**Shew thy marvelous loving-kindness, O thou that savest by thy right hand them which put their trust [in thee] from those that rise up [against them].**"
- Psalms 48:10 - "**According to Thy name, O God, so [is] Thy praise unto the ends of the earth: Thy right hand is full of righteousness.**"
- Ecclesiastes 10:2 - "**A wise man's heart [is] at his right hand; but a fool's heart at his left.**"
- Matthew 26:64/Mark 14:62 - "**Jesus saith unto him, THOU HAST SAID: NEVERTHELESS, I SAY UNTO YOU, HEREAFTER SHALL YE SEE THE SON OF MAN SITTING ON THE RIGHT HAND OF POWER, AND COMING IN THE CLOUDS OF HEAVEN.**"
- Matthew 27:29 - "**And when they had platted a crown of thorns, they put [it] upon his head, and a reed in his right hand: and they bowed the knee before him, and mocked him, saying, Hail, King of the Jews.**"
- Mark 10:40 - "**BUT TO SIT ON MY RIGHT HAND AND ON MY LEFT HAND IS NOT MINE TO GIVE; BUT [IT SHALL BE GIVEN TO THEM] FOR WHOM IT IS PREPARED.**"
- Mark 16:19 - "**So then after the Lord had spoken unto them, he was received up into heaven, and sat on the right hand of God.**"
- Acts 7:55-6 - "**But he, being full of the Holy Ghost, looked up steadfastly into heaven, and saw the glory of God, and Jesus standing on the right hand of God, And said, 'Behold, I see the heavens opened, and the Son of man standing on the right hand of God,'.**"

[121] N.B. These people are full of these traits. They do not simply exhibit them. For example, one instance of sexual immorality does not qualify. The people Paul warns about constantly engage in sexual immorality.

[122] "And the devil said unto Him, All this power will I give Thee, and the glory of them: for that is delivered unto me; and to whomsoever I will I give it." Referring to Adam in the garden and ultimately to human *choice.*

[123] Genesis 18:20.

[124] A phase commonly called puberty, this is the phase in which we become fertile.

[125] Genesis 18:20.

[126126] Sexless marriage divorce rate - marriage wyz, WWW.marriagewyz.com/sexless-marriage-divorce-rate/

[127] Matthew 19:12.

[128] https://www.christianpost.com/news/christians-are-following-secular-trends-in-premarital-sex-cohabitation-outside-of-marriage-says-dating-site-survey-113373/

[129] 5 things couples get wrong bout sex, https://www.crosswalk.com/family/marriage/engagement-newlyweds/5-things-couples-get-wrong-about-sex.html

[130] Genesis 18:20.

[131] When sex leaves the marriage, https://well.blogs.nytimes.com/2009/06/03/when-sex-leaves-the-marriage/

[132] https://www.factslides.com/s-Marriage

[133] Matthew 5:31-32, Mark 10:2-12, Luke 16:18, 1 Corinthians 7:39, Ephesians 5:33, Matthew 19:6-7, Romans 7:2-3, Deuteronomy 22:19, Jeremiah 3:1, Malachi 2:16, Matthew 1:19, 1 Corinthians 7:11-13, Jeremiah 3:8, Isaiah 50:1, Deuteronomy 24:1-4, Matthew 19:8-9, Hebrews 13:4, Romans 7:3

[134] https://s3.wp.wsu.edu/uploads/sites/2071/2013/12/Common-Planting-Problems.pdf

[135] Matthew 19:8.

[136] Holy Bible, New Living Translation®, 1996 by Tyndale Charitable Trust. Used by permission of Tyndale House Publishers, Wheaton, Illinois 60189.

[137] Galatians 5:22, and Ephesians 5:9.

[138] (Galatians 5:19-21) **Now the works of the flesh are manifest, which are these; Adultery, fornication, uncleanness, lasciviousness, Idolatry, witchcraft, hatred, variance, emulations, wrath, strife, seditions, heresies, envyings, murders, drunkenness, revelings, and such like: of the which I tell you before, as I have also told you in time past, that they which do such things shall not inherit the kingdom of God.**, (1Corinthains 7:5) **Do not deprive each other of sexual relations, unless you both agree to refrain from sexual intimacy for a limited time, so you can give yourselves more completely to prayer. Afterward, you should come together again so that Satan will not be able to tempt you because of your lack of self-control.**

[139] *The pornography industry has larger revenues than Microsoft, Google, Amazon, eBay, Yahoo, Apple and Netflix combined. 2006 Worldwide Pornography Revenues ballooned to $97.06 billion. 2006 & 2005 U.S. Pornography Industry Revenue Statistics, 2006 Top Adult Search Requests, 2006 Search Engine Request Trends are some of the other statistics revealed here.* http://internet-filter-review.toptenreviews.com/internet-pornography-statistics.html

[140] 30 Expert Opinions on Why Men Cheat in Relationships, https://www.marriage.com/advice/relationship/30-experts-explain-reasons-why-men-indulge-in-cheating/

[141] 12 reasons why people have extramarital affairs, http://timesofindia.indiatimes.com/articleshow/47418028.cms?utm_source=contentofinterest&utm_medium=text&utm_campaign=cppst

[142] Signs he's definitely not "the one, https://www.thelist.com/24955/falling-love-someone-isnt-one/?utm_campaign=clip

[143] The real reasons why women cheat: https://www.thelist.com/24955/falling-love-someone-isnt-one/?utm_campaign=clip

[144] Proverbs 23:5.

[145] James 1:15-15.

[146] http://www.pbs.org/wnet/religionandethics/week726/perspectives.html. 11/03/10, used by permission.

[147] www.johnshopkinshealthalerts.com/reports/depression_anxiety/922-1.html. 11/03/10, used by permission.

[148] wordnetweb.princeton.edu/perl/webwn. 11/03/10, used by permission.

[149] Genesis 19:19:1-17.

[150] James 1:15.

[151] For more information on this read *Playing Possum* in The Lights in Patmos.

[152] James 3.

[153] Matthew 12:34.

[154] Matthew 18:21-22.

[155] **"FOR IF YE LOVE THEM WHICH LOVE YOU, WHAT REWARD HAVE YE? DO NOT EVEN THE PUBLICANS THE SAME**?"

[156] "Of, resembling, or suggestive of a devil; fiendish: *demoniac energy; a demoniacal fit."* http://dictionary.reference.com/browse/demoniacs, 2008.

[157] "But every man is tempted, when he is drawn away of his own lust, and enticed. Then when lust hath conceived, it bringeth forth sin: and sin, when it is finished, bringeth forth death - James 1:14-15."

[158] Matthew 23:13.

[159] Mark 9:29.

[160] John 10:30.

[161] "But this [shall be] the covenant that I will make with the house of Israel; After those days, saith the Lord , I WILL PUT MY LAW IN THEIR INWARD PARTS, AND WRITE IT IN THEIR HEARTS; AND WILL BE THEIR GOD, AND THEY SHALL BE MY PEOPLE - Jeremiah 31:33."

[162] Matthew 7:11.

[163] Actually, more than fact faith requires the highest level of proof. Faith requires the voice of God. Faith therefore is not in the deed but in the doer. If we trust God whatever He says He we do we must also trust in because proper faith lies in the Doer not in the deed.

[164] Some material complied from internet blogs.

[165] https://relationshipsadvice.com/ways-to-revive-your-marriage. 08/28/2018.

[166] 20 Little ways to make your marriage even stronger, https://www.huffingtonpost.com/2014/03/01/marriage-tips-advice-_n_4870389.html

[167] Marriage: *A Biblical Illustration of Our Faith Commitment to Jesus Christ for Salvation* Sandy Simpson. http://www.deceptioninthechurch.com/marriagesalvation.html. 01/26/03.

[167] The Marriage Metaphor. Richard K. Hart. https://www.lds.org/ensign/1995/01/the-marriage-metaphor?lang=eng